KT-562-646

Table of Contents

Foreword by Issac Kramnick

When the news of Japan's surrender on August 14, 1945 was announced from loudspeakers in front of Willard Straight Hall, the assembled students chanted, "we want liberty." They got it. Freedom and democracy had triumphed over fascism and dictatorship. The end of World War II, the "good war," ushered in good times—a postwar economic boom.

LIFE magazine dedicated ten picture-filled pages to Cornell's graduating class in June 1948; the article's subtitle was, "Its Members Are Going Into A World Eager To Give Them Jobs." Profiled were students, "most of them in their middle 20s, who have been kicked around by the Army and Navy." But *LIFE* announced that the Cornell graduates were not worried, because "even an average student can have his pick of three or four good jobs."

The good times were fueled by factories that converted from war production back to turning out consumer goods, and by consumers who eagerly gobbled up those goods after years of privation. Government policies also contributed to the boom. Federal mortgage support and road building projects produced suburbia as we know it. The GI Bill sent hundreds of thousands of veterans to college, placing them firmly on the ladder of social mobility with access to those good jobs.

When the first class after the War was admitted in the fall of 1946, Cornell enrolled about 9,000 students. Nearly two-thirds of them were veterans, in what President Edmund Ezra Day described as the "GI invasion of East Hill." Many of the vets were married, and most of them were serious students. Day, who had been President since

1937, noted in 1947 that "we have never had a more diligent, intelligent, and generally satisfactory body of students."

The veterans on campus were more worldly than their predecessors had been, with a greater sense of personal freedom and autonomy. They had little tolerance for the restrictive social codes on women that were demanded by a university that was still committed to being *in loco parentis,* and was soon presided over by a Puritanical President, Deane Waldo Malott.

Many of the veterans, who had fought a war against the racist ideology of the Nazis, brought a new sensitivity to discrimination at Cornell. They were especially opposed to the overt discrimination by fraternities against the many Jewish students on campus, as well as against Cornell's very few students of color.

Much would change in student life at the university in the immediate postwar years, and the catalyst was in large part "the GI invasion." This would coincide with a profound transformation of the very soul of the place, as Presidents Day and Malott changed Cornell from a collegiate "halls of ivy" training ground for educated gentlemen and ladies, schooled in "gracious living", to a world class "research university" driven by Big Science.

No one has captured the tone and feel of this crucial moment, this incredible turning point, in Cornell's 150-year history, better than Brad Edmondson, a truly talented historian-journalist. A graduate of Cornell who never really left Ithaca, Brad chronicles the years from 1944 to 1952 with a vivid and lively sense of who its

students were in these transformative years. With equally sensitive and wonderful insights, he understands campus group and institutional life in those years "far above Cayuga's waters". Edmondson takes the reader on a marvelous journey back in time, to the era when present-day Cornell was born.

Isaac Kramnick is the Richard J. Schwartz Professor of Government at Cornell, where he has taught since 1972, and the recipient of many awards, including fellowship in the American Academy of Arts and Sciences and election by students in 1996 as "favorite professor of the year." He has written or edited 20 books, including *Cornell: A History, 1940–2015,* co-authored with Glen Altschuler.

Kramnick with his wife, the author Miriam Brody.

Postwar Cornell

How the Greatest Generation Transformed a University 1944–1952

By Brad Edmondson

With contributions from more than one hundred alumni and friends

© 2015 By Brad Edmondson.
All rights reserved.

Published by Cayuga Lake Books,
Ithaca, NY
www.cayugalakebooks.com

Distributed by the The History
Center in Tompkins County
www.thehistorycenter.net

Author contact:
www.bradedmondson.com

ISBN 978-1-4951-6920-5

Designed by Mo Viele, Ithaca, NY.

Printed on demand by IngramSpark.
Another edition with color
illustrations is available from the
author.

FRONT COVER: Looking northward
along Central Avenue toward
the library bell tower, 1946.
Windows of Uris Library are
visible through the trees.

BACK COVER: The Cornell campus
in 1949.

Prologue by Brad Edmondson '81

"The Greatest Generation" is the cohort of Americans who pulled together to win World War II, then came home to drive a sustained economic boom in the 1950s and 1960s. Tom Brokaw (who coined the term) and many others have written movingly of their patriotism, ingenuity, and self-sacrifice in pursuit of greater goals. It's often said that these were ordinary people called upon to do extraordinary things. But they were not born knowing how to do those things.

Cornell University was one of many colleges, universities, and vocational schools that taught the Greatest Generation the skills they needed to win the war, then taught them how to continue innovating after the war ended. And in many ways, college students of 2015 are following a trail that was blazed by their predecessors in the years just after World War II.

The distance between 1945 from 2015 is vast, and when you compare the ways American higher education operated then and now, the first things that jump out at you are the differences. Cornell University has 21,600 students in 2015, roughly twice as many as it did in 1950. Half of 21st-century Cornellians are women, compared with about 20 percent back then. And more than one-third are black, Hispanic, or Asian. In 1950, all of the university's minority students probably could have fit into a single lecture hall.

Cornell is also a lot richer now. In the late 1940s, it was struggling to recover from four years of military occupation and a severe case of growing pains while it balanced the budget and completed its first professional fund-raising campaign. In the four months between the Class of 1945's graduation and the beginning of classes in 1946, enrollment increased 40 percent. Many postwar Cornellians lived in poorly insulated temporary dorms, ate in shifts, and attended classes in Quonset huts.

Other differences are just as striking. In 1946, nearly two-thirds of Cornell undergraduates were veterans of World War II, attending on federal scholarships that paid most of their tuition and expenses. In 2015, veterans are less than one half of one percent of the student body. Cornell now offers its students "gender-inclusive housing," but in the 1940s, the university locked women into their dorms at night. Co-eds who violated the curfew faced disciplinary measures that escalated all the way to expulsion.

Those numbers don't tell the whole story, however. Some important things about Cornell haven't changed all that much. Some of the same books and methods that were taught in the 1940s are still taught today. Students still work too hard and stay up around the clock to study for exams. They still fall in and out of love. Some of them still party too much, although the average college student's alcohol consumption today is probably much lower than it was in the 1940s. Back then, any 18-year-old could go into Willard Straight Hall and get a beer.

The most significant similarity is in values. Students of the 1940s were taught to use scientific methods to solve all kinds of problems, including social problems. They also tuned in to the advice of psychologists and other experts who urged them to seek self-fulfillment instead of blindly following tradition. College students today study the same methods and pursue the same personal goals. Back in the 1940s, these ways of thinking were new.

This book is based on interviews with 67 Cornell University alumni from the post-World War II era. I conducted the interviews between 2012 and 2015 and combined them with excerpts from another three dozen contemporary articles, letters, and diaries. Cornell's University Archives and other sources proved an inexhaustible source of photographs and memorabilia. Each chapter is organized by themes, and I have kept narration to a minimum. My goal is to immerse readers in a critical moment of American history, using the voices of those who lived through that time.

Shortly after the United States entered World War II in 1941, the military occupied Cornell and other campuses across the country. In just a few months, academic buildings became training facilities for soldiers, sailors, and aviators. Bob Purple (p. 12) enlisted as soon as he turned 18 because he wanted to become an engineer. The Army trained him, at Cornell, in exchange for his military service. Kirk Reid (p. 120) did the same thing, starting at Auburn University and continuing at Cornell; Like Bob Purple, Kirk also paid for his engineering degree in barter.

As the war was ending, President Franklin Roosevelt called on the nation to build "a just and honorable peace, a durable peace," and asked Congress to fund a massive expansion of university research and scholarships. Congress agreed, passing legislation that turned colleges and universities into national centers for upward social mobility, innovation, and economic development. Postwar Cornellians were among the first to benefit from a big new idea: that people who seek higher education should be granted it, with substantial public support.

Title II of The Servicemen's Readjustment Act of 1944, popularly known as the GI Bill, paid most of the college tuition, room, and board charges for any man or woman who had entered the US military after mid-September 1940, had served for at least ninety days, and had not received a dishonorable discharge. Disabled veterans got more. And in 1945, Congress made the educational benefits even more generous.

The GI Bill gave Daniel Roberts (p. 30) a free ticket to Cornell—and, because Roberts had been severely injured in Europe, the government also provided him with a specially equipped automobile. It was the first car his family had ever owned. The GI Bill also picked up the tab for Ken Dehm and Don Smith (p. 33), two farmboys from upstate New York who knew their alternative was a lifetime of manual labor. Shortly after the war, Don told Ken that he would do anything to go to Cornell. Both men were smart enough to see the opportunity and grab it.

The government's investment in ex-GIs was a spectacular success. It educated fourteen future Nobel Prize winners, three Supreme Court justices, three presidents, a dozen senators, two dozen Pulitzer Prize winners, and hundreds of thousands of teachers, scientists, doctors, engineers, accountants, journalists, dentists, lawyers, nurses, business leaders, artists, actors, writers, and pilots. The men and women of postwar Cornell went on to become members of Congress like Richard Ottinger (p. 88), CEOs of large corporations like Bruce Davis (p. 54), important inventors like Wilson Greatbach (p. 52), and strivers for social justice like Jacob Sheinkman (p. 89).

The critical role scientists played in winning the war convinced a lot of people that science could solve social problems, too. Prominent psychologists like Carl Rogers and Abraham Maslow advocated a "humanistic" approach to therapy and a scientific approach to evaluating its effectiveness. An economist, Gunnar Myrdal, analyzed race relations in the United States and issued detailed instructions on how to address inequality (p. 56). In the years after World War II, society's emphasis shifted away from religion and tradition and toward science and self-actualization.

World War II destroyed large parts of Europe and Japan, and it also tore at the social fabric of the United States. Families were traumatized by the 420,000 Americans who died, the 672,000 who were wounded, the 130,000 prisoners of war, and many thousands more who were scarred by "combat fatigue," the term used to describe post-traumatic stress disorder in those days. But even ex-GIs who held desk jobs at home had given up years of their lives. Almost everyone who returned from the war was eager to make up for lost time—to live a little.

The war and its aftermath obliterated millions of marriages and engagements. The divorce rate per 1,000 women doubled, from 9 in 1941 to 18 in 1946, before falling back below 10 in 1951. Many unions that survived were severely challenged by infidelity, alcoholism, or the simple inability to connect. When these problems were treated, they were identified as behavioral disorders instead of sins.

The 1950s are often described as a conservative era, with Republicans in control of Washington and church attendance on the rise. But there was a counterweight. "Rocket 88," the first rock 'n' roll record, was released in 1951. Many Cornell students of the late 1940s and early 1950s have vague memories of regular all-night drinking binges. They were passionate about black jazz and blues musicians, and they loved to engage in what they called "heavy petting." On television, married couples were portrayed sleeping in separate beds. In reality, the rate of premarital pregnancies per 1,000 white American women aged 15–24 doubled in the postwar years, from less than 12 in 1943–46 to more than 25 in 1955–58.[1]

Listening to the men and women who came of age at postwar Cornell makes it clear that the social revolutions of the 1960s didn't come out of nowhere. World War II was a break point in America's gradual shift toward a view of the good life that is humanistic and secular. Huge increases in college enrollment simply accelerated the trend.

The years just after World War II were the beginning of something new. Just 10 percent of 18- to 24-year-old Americans were enrolled in college in 1945; that share

---

[1] Alan Petigny, *The Permissive Society: America, 1941–1965* (Cambridge University Press, 2009), p. 114.

increased to 14 percent in 1950, 17 percent in 1955, 24 percent in 1961, 30 percent in 1966, and 40 percent in 1975. Far above Cayuga's waters, as the fog of war cleared, the world started to change.

Acknowledgments

This book is a revision of an edition that was funded by Cornell's Class of 1950 and given to Class members at their 65th Reunion. The entire

Stan Rodwin

project would not have been possible without the steadfast support of class president Patricia Carry Stewart and vice-president Stan Rodwin. Pat and Stan never wavered as the work went far beyond its initial scope.

I was extremely fortunate to have editorial supervision from Marion Steinmann and John Marcham, both of them master old-school journalists. Marion was the manager, with a relentless focus on details. Whenever the text lacked a telling detail or hung up on a fuzzy fact that needed sharpening, Marion would dive into the voluminous files she accumulated as the Class Correspondent. She usually emerged with the answer or a clue that led me to my goal. John was the idea man; he invited me to join the project, uncovered half-buried stories and photographs, read the text with pencil in hand, chose the cover image, and approved the overall design before he passed away on December 4, 2014.

Special thanks go to several friends who read and commented on an early draft: Class of 1950 members Paul Joslin and Donald Christiansen; Walter LaFeber, Cornell professor emeritus of history; Carol Kammen, Cornell lecturer and Tompkins County historian; and Elaine Engst, university archivist emeritus. Thanks are also due to Mo Viele, designer; Fred Conner, proofreader; Isaac Kramnick, for the foreword; Laura Linke, photo specialist at Cornell's department of rare books and university archives; John Sutton, for his color photograph of the J.O. Mahoney mural; John Schroeder, for providing the correct caption for the cover photograph; Jeremy Hardigan and Marlene Crockford of Cornell Athletics, for several illustrations; and everyone who donated stories and materials.

Dedication

This book is dedicated to John Marcham, editor in chief of *The Cornell Daily Sun* in 1949–1950, editor in chief of the *Cornell Alumni News* from 1961 to 1991, and a longtime director at The History Center in Tompkins County. John's 1950 Cornell classmates once wrote, "He has never shied away from calling a spade a spade; rarely missed his target when he tossed a well deserved editorial dart in the direction of Day Hall; and never missed a deadline." Although all of that is true, they forgot to mention his irreverent sense of humor.

I was privileged to have John as my editor on several projects and, like hundreds of Cornell alumni, to call him a mentor and friend. We both loved to find and tell stories, especially funny ones. I will always remember the way John looked at me intently through his thick glasses, like a curious owl, when I launched into a good anecdote. When I got to the punchline he would smile broadly, open his mouth, and emit a loud cackle to show that he understood precisely what I meant.

The day before he died, John chose the images for Chapter Three and told me he was proud of the book. I have never received a greater compliment.

Brad Edmondson attended Deep Springs College and received a bachelor's degree in history from Cornell. He worked for the *Ithaca Times,* a weekly newspaper (1981-1985), and *American Demographics,* an award-winning monthly magazine (1985-1998), and was editor in chief of both publications. He is the co-founder of ePodunk.com and author of several books, including *Ice Cream Social: The Struggle for the Soul of Ben & Jerry's* (2014). More information: www.bradedmondson.com.

John Marcham with Stephanie Lehman at the *Cornell Alumni News* in 1987.

An army-style commando course was erected on Lower Alumni Field for the duration.

CHAPTER 1

War College

When the US entered World War II in December 1941, Cornell went all out. Nearly 4,500 undergraduates, or about two-thirds of the student body, left the university for the armed forces before completing their studies. The university was saved from insolvency by an influx of army and navy officer candidates whose tuition was paid with federal funds, but only a few of them became Cornell graduates: most were seventeen-year-olds who stayed only briefly in the army and navy's training programs, and were barred from participating in most student activities. Smaller numbers were enrolled in specialized training programs in Russian, medicine, engineering, and other fields. Between June 1943 and September 1945, Cornell trained 3,758 men for the army and 13,577 for the navy. The military training programs were dismantled in 1945–46 and converted to ROTC (Reserve Officers' Training Corps) programs in the fall of 1946.

Many men who came to Cornell as civilian or military students in 1943 and 1944 left to go to war a few months later. They returned to graduate with the classes of 1948 through 1951. Their absence sent the proportion of women in the regular student body soaring, with a civilian enrollment of 2,407 women and 2,079 men in 1943–44. For the duration, everyone made the best of it. The faculty taught what the military required or left on top-secret errands. Obstacle courses and battlements were built on lawns and playing fields. And everyone waited for the boys to come home.

Cornell During World War II

Kurt Vonnegut Jr. '44
(1922–2007)

Vonnegut was night editor of *The Cornell Daily Sun* when the Japanese bombed Pearl Harbor on December 7, 1941.

I heard about the bombing while I was sitting in a bathtub. I tore down to the office, and we laid out a new first and last page, keeping the stale insides of the previous issue, as I recall. We took whatever was coming off the AP machine, slapped it in, and were, I still believe, the first paper in the state to hit the streets with an extra.

Then we stayed up all night, getting out a more responsible issue. Drew Pearson, to whose column we subscribed, sent us a telegram listing all the ships that had sunk. The telegram was followed almost immediately by one from the Department of War, saying that it had no power to prevent our publishing whatever we pleased. It asked us as patriots to suppress the Pearson information. We suppressed it. Were we wrong?

Kurt Vonnegut left Cornell to enlist in the army in 1943 and did not graduate. He became a prisoner of war and survived the firebombing of Dresden. His novel drawn from that experience, *Slaughterhouse-Five* (1969), ranks eighteenth on The Modern Library's list of the one hundred best English-language novels of the twentieth century.

Edmund Ezra Day
(1883–1951)

Edmund Ezra Day was President of Cornell University from 1937 to 1949.

The Cornell Daily Sun, July 1, 1943: As all can see, the life of the Cornell campus is now undergoing rapid and radical change . . . Clearly enough, the university is now in the war. It will become increasingly so in the course of this academic year.

With the campus population so different from that to which we are accustomed, the close associations of campus life will doubtless present new problems . . . I have no doubt that in the continuing close contacts of the various constituencies that are on the Cornell campus "for the duration," repeated adjustments will be in order, but I am convinced that there will be every readiness to give and take, and that all can live and work together in mutual respect and common endeavor. After all, every one of us is impelled by the same fundamental purpose—to make individually his or her utmost contribution to the winning of the war.

John Marcham '50
(1927–2014)

My family's house was on Oak Hill Road, which is just north of Fall Creek and the fraternity houses. When I was a kid in the 1930s, I didn't know much about Cornell except that my dad [history professor Frederick Marcham] worked there. Also, I was a sports nut, and believe it or not, Cornell had the country's top-ranked football team in 1940. I listened to the games on the radio and drew play-by-play diagrams of each game on sheets of paper. Later I gave the whole set to Cornell's Sports Information Department.

I have a strong memory of walking to basketball games in the winter. I would stop to get a hot dog from the food truck that Louis Zounakos had just opened on Thurston Avenue. I remember the clouds of hot dog-scented steam around my face in the cold. The basketball team was good, too. They had seventeen wins and six losses in 1940–41. The football and basketball teams are usually not that good now, but Louie's Lunch is still there.

Cornell and Ithaca were smaller, quieter places before the war. The city's population was less than 20,000 in 1940, plus 6,800 students on East Hill. Today there are 30,000 people in town, and the number of Cornell students has nearly tripled. More people got around on foot or took the bus in those days, so there were fewer cars, and car traffic dropped off even more after gas rationing began. Before the war, most men wore hats and carried umbrellas. After the war, more people drove around in cars and went outside bareheaded. All kinds of things changed during the war, and when the war was over, they changed again.

When Britain declared war on Germany in 1939, a colleague of my father's called us with the news. I think it was probably a great relief to him. He was a citizen of Britain and had served in their army during World War I. During the blitz, he and other Brits on the Cornell faculty asked their consulate what they could do. They offered to go back home. But the diplomats told them they would be more useful to England if they stayed in the United States, so my parents stayed. In 1945, they became American citizens.

I was a teenager during the war, and the sudden shortage of adult men in a small town opened up all kinds of opportunities. In the Boy Scouts, for example, I found myself working at their summer camp at the age of sixteen, in charge of boys who were only slightly younger than I was. When the campers would get together, I would get up and lead songs for hundreds of boys. I couldn't sing, but I knew all the words to tunes like "John Jacob Jingleheimer Schmidt."

I met all the requirements to graduate from Ithaca High School at the end of my junior year in

1944, except for one course. My parents decided to put me in college a year early so I could get some experience before I went into the service. I thought I wanted to be an engineer, so I entered Cornell's electrical engineering program in September 1944, even though I didn't get a high school diploma until 1945.

I remember walking to campus across the suspension bridge. I liked to read novels while I was walking, and that must have been quite a sight. Whenever I was killing time between classes, I would go to the marvelous stuffed couches in the Willard Straight Memorial Room and just sink down into them to read a book. I also remember going to an empty lecture room in Rockefeller Hall, where there was a clean blackboard, so I could draw out wiring diagrams for model railroad layouts. I was kind of a nerdy kid.

This was an unusual time for Cornell, because a lot of the students were soldiers in training programs. They went to class with Cornell students, but they did not socialize with us much. Many of the soldiers would march to and from class in uniform, and in formation. That was something to see. Also, the university stopped taking the summers off. Cornell went on a trimester system, so no one really ever got time off. The Christmas vacation in 1943 lasted one day.

The teachers were all shuffled around, too. The government paid Cornell to send some of the engineering faculty to train war workers in two dozen industrial extension centers all over New York State. A lot of faculty members also left to work for the military, so any teacher who stayed in Ithaca had a big workload. English and history professors were teaching courses in military tactics and foreign languages. I think the quality of the teaching was strained.

When I took freshman chemistry in Baker Hall, a block of seats in front was always reserved for the naval trainees. I quickly learned that the best place to sit was right behind them, because a lot of them would usually doze off. They had done guard duty the night before, or had stayed up late playing cards, or something. So if you sat right behind them, you got a clear view of the blackboard as soon as they all slumped over. It was like something out of a silent film. Like a bunch of robots had marched in, and then someone switched them all off.

John Marcham was an army sergeant in Manila, Philippines, in 1946-47, as news editor of *The Daily Pacifican*. He became editor in chief of *The Cornell Daily Sun* in 1949-50, got a BA, and married Jane Haskins '51. He spent two years working for the weekly *Life* magazine in New York City and held other journalism jobs before serving as editor in chief of the *Cornell Alumni News* for three decades. Marcham also held a seat on the Tompkins County Board of Representatives from 1968 to 1973, and again from 1978 to 1981.

Frederick Marcham '26 PhD
(1899–1992)

Frederick Marcham taught history at Cornell from 1924 until his death. He was also a boxing coach and the mayor of the Village of Cayuga Heights for thirty-two years. During World War II, he sent group letters to former students who were serving in the armed forces. From the February 1944 letter:

I would not dare to talk about the [unusually warm, sunny] weather if it were not so exceptional. For me the most remarkable thing about it has been the impression it has made on the thousands of army and navy boys who are studying here under the various programs. A great part of them have never seen Ithaca in the wintertime before. If they leave in the course of the present year they will go away with a notion that the place deserves to be a winter health resort—a second Sun Valley.

These army and navy boys, that is, of course, all who had not originally entered as Cornellians, are a remarkable bunch. They make the oddest group of students any of us have ever taught. They sleep. What they do at nights I don't know; indeed, I don't like to imagine. But in the daytime they sleep. They sleep in lectures. They sleep in recitations. They sleep in eight o'clock classes. They sleep immediately before lunch. And, of course, they sleep all the more soundly immediately after lunch.

My long experience in History 61 has, of course, made me well acquainted with the sleeping student. I always believed that no class was complete without a sleeping student and a sleeping dog. (That, by the way, reminds me that most of the campus dogs have gone and that one famous description of a lecture of mine, "laughs and a dog fight," could no longer apply.) I was always interested in the sleeping student and I got to know pretty well the sleeping habits of a great many. But this knowledge counts for little in the face of the scene I now see before me daily. Whole rows of students sleep.

Last Tuesday morning I taught a class at 9:00 and decided to begin it with a pep talk. In the space of ten minutes I spoke on the folly and scandal of this practice of sleeping. By the time I had finished, half the class was asleep. In the course of the rest of the hour, the best part of the remainder decided to follow suit.

But the best story on the subject has to do with the performance of another history teacher. He was shocked by the number of army boys sleeping in his classes. He warned them that he would take drastic action against offenders. When they took no notice of his warning, he sent in a report to local army headquarters and a lieutenant was detailed to attend the next class and take the names of all sleepers. The lieutenant came and, since the students spotted him and guessed what he was there for, he had a hard time during the first five minutes finding a name to write on his pad. But habit was too much for the students. First one and then another settled down to rest. He wrote their names out on his pad. At twenty minutes past the hour his pad and pencil slipped silently to the floor. The lieutenant himself was asleep.

Robert Purple '50

When Cornell accepted me I also enlisted in the military reserve, because I wanted to get into the army Specialized Training Program (ASTP). I arrived on campus on July 4, 1943, as a seventeen-year-old civilian student and joined the ASTP two months later. I wanted to be an engineer, and the army offered to train me.

I was issued a Reserve Officers Training Corps (ROTC) uniform and assigned to barracks in Cas-

cadilla Hall in Collegetown, the neighborhood just south of campus. There were two platoons with thirty men in each platoon. We wore our uniforms every day and marched in formation to and from class. We had roll call, calisthenics, and lights out. It was not college—it was the military. We got Saturday afternoons and Sundays off, but other than that, we kept our noses to the grindstone. If anyone did any partying, they did it on the sly. I don't think I ever heard of anyone in the ASTP ever having a date.

Eventually I did become an engineer and was trained at government expense, but it didn't happen quite as I had planned. In the fall of 1943, the army needed troops for the invasion of Europe, so I was inducted after just five months at Cornell. I spent a year in training and arrived in France on November 28, 1944. I was away from Cornell for three highly eventful years. When I came back, that seventeen-year-old was long gone.

Robert Purple spent one month as a mortar gunner for the 87th Infantry Division, participating in the Battle of the Saar. He returned to England because of frostbite and served there until the end of the war, then continued as a military policeman in France and Germany. After graduating with a degree in civil engineering, he worked for the New York State Department of Transportation.

Cynthia Craig

Cynthia Craig is the daughter of John Craig '50.

My parents, John and Mary Craig, went to school together in Montclair, New Jersey. They went on their first date when they were both fourteen. After they graduated from

high school in 1943, Mom went to a small college outside of Boston, and Dad went to Cornell to become an engineer, just like his father, John Craig, Sr., '19. He told me that everyone in his entering class that year started school knowing they were going to leave.

As soon as he left Montclair for Cornell, a week or so after his high school graduation, Dad started writing letters to my mother, and he said she wrote him back every day. He kept writing after he joined the army and went into combat in Europe. He kept writing after he got back to Ithaca, and he did not stop until they got married in June 1949. My mother kept all of his letters—over four hundred of them.

My dad did not enlist in the army before he arrived at Cornell, but he wrote to the War Department to waive his deferment, and he signed up for ROTC when he registered in Ithaca. He wasn't eager to fight, but he knew it was inevitable. He wanted to get it over with as soon as possible.

EMILY POST FOR A-12S

The Cornell Bulletin, April 7, 1944

LETTER TO THE EDITOR

Gentlemen:

Would it be possible to publish some simple rules of conduct for the group of high school youngsters who recently stormed the Cornell campus with no apparent background for life in a civilized community? I would suggest the following:

1. Holding hands during the passing of classes is not customary, especially if the co-ed is unknown and unwilling.

2. It is not polite to ask a Cornell Amazon if she plays football. Who knows what the Grey Fox[1] will do next?

3. Don't knock down co-eds when running to chow. How would you like a bunch of six-foot infants to trample on your mother?

4. The average Cornell co-ed is aged nineteen years, two months. She probably was aware that she was "cute," "beautiful," and "guhguss" while you were yet traveling on three wheels.

Nothing but strict enforcement of the above rules will protect the life and limbs of Cornell womanhood.

Very Truly Yours,

A Co-ed

---

[1] Carl "The Grey Fox" Snavely (1894–1975) was Cornell's head football coach from 1936 to 1944.

Waiter's Race Turned Over to "Waitresses"

Every spring, students at the Hotel School stage an annual "waiter's race." Contestants carry trays laden with pitchers and glasses of water, and the first to cross the finish line without spilling wins. During World War II, a shortage of male Hotelies temporarily turned the event over to "waitresses." The 1944 contestants were (l–r) Joan Blaikie [Horwath] '45 (winner), Amy Mann [Dixon] '47, Jacqueline Rogers [Mather] '46, Janice O'Donnell [Edelbut] '44, Patricia Will [Adams] '45, and Joyce Heath '47.

EDITORIAL: In a letter appearing on page four of this issue, a co-ed has vented her spleen on one of the most critical situations that stands today before the student body and army officials. The problem of the A-12 men —their position in campus life—has been left to wallow long enough in its own scattered debris. The attitude of mutual disdain that underlies the relationship of A-12s and Cornellians grows deeper as the seventeen-year-olds become more enmeshed in the shackles of the program and the students become more irritated by their behavior.

The A-12s just don't care any more. They aren't concerned about their dress, their manner, their speech. They have become psychologically depressed. They feel that the work offered to them is too vague. They have been told and now realize that being in the Army Specialized Training Reserve Program will not necessarily lead to a quick advancement in the ranks, nor to a position in any of the ASTP's specialized engineering or pre-med courses. That the army program, whether it be ASTP or ASTRP, doesn't allow any participation in Cornell activities, only adds to the A-12s' growing belief that

they are here to pipe their dreams on the pariah's lute ...

It is the responsibility of those in charge to embark on a campaign to rescue the A-12s from their current doldrums by means of a constructive program of social and extracurricular activities, or any other methods at their command. The A-12s must take hold of themselves to see that such a program is made effective. Finally, the other nine-tenths of Cornell must abandon its present intolerance, and actually cooperate in the effort to elevate the ASTRP to a position of respect on the Cornell campus.

The war had a huge effect on my father, although he never really talked about it. He would only say that for the entire time he was at war, he was cold, tired, hungry, and scared. And he missed my mother. Yet my father *loved* Cornell, and it made him extremely happy when he came back in the fall of 1946. Perhaps he loved Cornell so much because he had spent all that time in Europe hoping he would live to see it again.

John Craig '50
(1925–2012)

JUNE 18, 1943: Dear Mary, Last night Tommy and I went up to the agriculture school, which is up on the other end of campus, and we had a swell time. Tommy is interested in that stuff and I think he would be a better farmer than an economist. It probably is not the usual way to spend a Saturday night, but for us it was fun. I think we had more fun up there than Nort or Jim had downtown soaking up beer, which they don't really like, but just to be one of the frat boys they soak it up anyway.

It sure is hard to get to sleep in a room that has two guys that have been drinking beer, as they smell the place up something terrific even with the windows and doors wide open. Anyway, Tommy and I made some connections up there, and the fellows up there said to come back whenever we could.

Those farm boys up there are all nice fellows, but usually there are some people that think that engineering students and arts students are a bit better than the boys from the agricultural school. But there is as much, if not more, science in farming than in anything else.

We had all the milk we could drink, and that is plenty. It was right off the top and we even had it right out of the cow, which made it the first time I have milked a cow. They have several world's record cows and about one hundred Holsteins. They also make ice cream experiments up there, and if they want, they can try it on us, as the ice cream nowadays isn't like it used to be. Up there it is the real thing, so next time we go back we will go earlier while it is still open. We had so much milk that we could hardly walk, but on the way home we went over the commando course. That really fixed us up fine.

JULY 1, 1943: Dear Mary, Registration is very complicated . . . there are a lot of tables with very unhelpful signs such as 87G9, 3CS11, etc., and some very nice men behind them who turn out to be professors. The problem is to find the right table in about a million scattered over two acres, in a mob that makes Macy's basement look like [our old high school lecture hall] one minute after the bell for second lunch. It took about two hours and then we went downstairs where a typical sergeant measured us and gave us a gray uniform with a dark heavy blue topcoat . . .

The different thing about college is that they say *once* where something is going to be and that is where they stop, no more pushing and helping, although I must say they are glad to answer any questions. If you don't register or do it wrong, which is not inconceivable, that is OK. It is OK to sleep all day. In fact you can do any darn thing you want, but heaven help you if you do. This is such a good place that they don't care if you get by or not as they can get millions more. It seems to be entirely up to the individual.

JULY 15, 1943: Dear Mary, I am writing this in front of Goldwin Smith Hall, which is where they teach English in this institution. Today I had English 2 from eight to nine a.m., and now I have a vacant hour until Math 60A at ten a.m., which lasts until eleven. Math 60A is what they call calculus and what we call #$?^%---. Last night I was too tired to concentrate, so I left the math until just now and it was lots easier.

The best course up here is drill. It comes three hours a week and is very interesting. At first it was just rights and lefts, etc., but now they are teaching our class the 105mm howitzer, which would correspond to a four-inch cannon. It can throw a fifty pound shell eight miles and can be used as an antiaircraft gun, but is built primarily as an anti-tank weapon. It is supposed to be very simple, but it sure is not. But compared to other cannons, it is relatively easy to take apart.

So far we have learned about the equalizer, which is a new development that keeps the tube (barrel) level even though the wheels (carriage) are on uneven terrain (ground). In the old guns it was necessary to dig holes to make the tube level, but this gun was only developed two years ago. We have also studied the recoil system, which is very complicated, composed of two cylinders on the top and bottom of the barrel connected by a yoke and containing oil, nitrogen gas, and assorted pistons. The purpose of the recoil system is to absorb some of the tremendous (25,000 lbs/sq. in.) pressure that is developed at the time of firing. The gun jumps back three feet and then returns very slowly to its original position. It is based on the principle of the compressibility of air and nitrogen and the incompressibility of oil.

Thanks for the bracelet—it sure is wonderful and I even wear it and like it. Johnny

John Craig reported for duty in October 1943 and shipped out for France at the end of 1944. He was a rifleman for the 86th Infantry Division Blackhawks and saw thirty-four days of fierce combat as the war was ending. In April 1945, the Blackhawks advanced into the Ruhr region and liberated the Attendorn civilian forced-labor camp. They crossed the Danube River and entered Austria on April 27. When the Germans surrendered on V-E Day, May 8, the Blackhawks had suffered 84 deaths, 653 wounded, 21 missing, and 473 "noncombat casualties." After the war,

everyone in the division was awarded the Bronze Star. As he marched, John carried this note with him:

Dearest Johnny, With all the love and luck in the world to the sweetest soldier in the U.S. army. Wherever you go, whatever you do, remember I'll always be waiting for you. Be good, Johnny, and keep

your chin up. God bless you, honey. Lovingly yours, Mary

MAY 22, 1945 (two weeks after V-E Day, May 8, which celebrated the end of the war in Europe): Dear Mary, This afternoon I read an article in a magazine that was to tell the people back home how to act when the boys came home. It was all wrong. I saw some horrible things, was under a lot of fire, came close to death very often, lived for weeks without knowing when all hell would break loose, saw a lot of death, lost a lot of buddies, closed enough with the enemy to get after one with my bare hands, but I'll talk about it whether or not anyone asks me about it. I just want to be treated naturally. The period of combat I was in is a most vivid period of my life, and it is too much to expect me to forget about it.

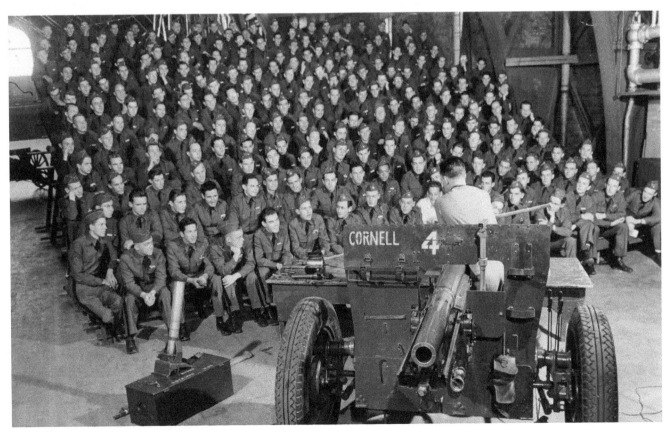

Military students in class.

After the war in Europe ended, John Craig was put on a troop ship to the Pacific and expected to participate in the invasion of Japan. He was on the ship when the Japanese surrendered. John and Mary were married in 1949. He graduated with a degree in industrial engineering and was employed by the Crane Company, which made products for the chemical, construction, aviation, power generation, and food industries. He left Crane in 1983 and continued to practice as a consultant in Livingston and Basking Ridge, New Jersey. When he was dying in 2012, John Craig told a hospice assistant that Mary "wrote to me every single day for three years, and that's what kept me alive."

Romeyn Berry 1904, Law 1906
(1881–1957)

"Rym" Berry's column, "Now, In *My Time!*," ran in the *Cornell Alumni News* from 1936 to 1950.

Cornell Alumni News, September 1945: Now that it's over and all self-imposed censorships have been lifted, we can tell you what really happened around here in wartime.

Cornell was a madhouse for a while. The place ran in three shifts, twenty-four hours a day, seven days a week. The campus highways echoed to the measured tread of marching men proceeding in formation from Ballistics 6 to Russian Conversation 58. Scores of prominent professors departed overnight on undisclosed missions, whispered to be of great importance. Those who stayed were worried, overworked, and unhappy.

The help had to be shifted around to perform unfamiliar tasks. Recognized authorities in the fields of philosophy or fine arts found themselves teaching Trigonometry to sailors. They were tired and perturbed at night, but the morning found them consoled by the realization they were still on Mr. Rogalsky's[1] payroll in some capacity, however fantastic.

Campus talk and concern centered too much on the problem of mere survival, on the sordid details of university housekeeping, on tangibles and petty questions of organization and procedure; too little on the vast, dim future and our own place in it. It's hard to see now how this could have been otherwise.

That was the first phase. The second dealt more with grotesque rumors of plans for post-war education: American universities were to be tuned to the practical, everyday needs of the American people; would be more closely geared to industry; a reconverted economy would demand an immediate supply of trained experts capable of beating swords into plowshares and jeeps into freezing boxes. Cornell would readjust its curriculum to meet this pressing need . . .

Oh, well, weeping may endure for a night, but joy cometh in the morning. It's all over now! You can get Luckies again, if they know you, and you don't have to smoke Spuds unless you want to. It looks as if you might be able shortly to subrent a locker at the freezing plant, too. Every day, more and more scholars are laying down their hoes for all eternity, to grasp again the more familiar niblick.[2]

It's now possible for an Old Timer, watching events from the cheap seats, to appraise the ravages of war and to plot, as through a glass darkly, the probable course of post-war education. You can say what you like about the Trustees and the Management—and at Ithaca everybody does—but you've got to admit that an astonishingly able job has been done in steering the University through the last four years and bringing it to port with its academic tone, its integrity and solvency intact.

I'd say that postwar education would turn out to be pretty much the same as prewar education. It's in the educators that the change is most marked. They seem to be resuming their old jobs with a new zest, a fresh vision, and a loftier ambition. All doubt and apathy appear to have been purged out of us. It has become the individual's chief concern to hold his job and make his accomplishments glisten, that he may not be shamed in the eyes of his fellows. The new spirit is competitive. You can't keep up at the old pace. It was a dramatic touch to have the bulldozers start excavating for new construction before the guns were silenced.

Perhaps you'd better stop worrying and get yourself a good night's rest. Cornell is a going concern!

Romeyn Berry grew up in Ithaca. In 1905, as an editor of the *Cornell Widow*, he wrote the lyrics for a fight song called "The Big Red Team," thereby dubbing Cornell athletics The Big Red. He was a lawyer, a sports administrator for Cornell and other institutions, and a contributor to *The New Yorker*, *The Ithaca Journal*, *American Agriculturist*, and other publications.

---

[1] Howard "The Count" Rogalsky was treasurer of Cornell from 1920 to 1953.

[2] Lucky Strike cigarettes had limited availability in the United States during the war because most of them were sold to the military. Spuds were a popular brand of menthol cigarettes. A niblick is a golf club.

TO SOME OTHER CORNELLIANS

The Cornell Bulletin, December 23, 1944

Elsewhere on this page, we have wished a lengthy Merry Christmas to Cornellians on campus. Now we want to speak to another group of Big Red undergraduates: the men and women who left school before the end of their freshman and sophomore years, who left when they were first-term juniors, or even just a few months before graduation.

Christmas will not be Christmas, the tinsel will be only shiny paper from the ten-cent store, the holly will be a bunch of red berries, until you are back again… The glamour of colored globes on the evergreen, the utter abandonment to the joy of just being young, will not be felt while you are remembering Cornell thousands of miles from the sound of the chimes. We will play at Christmas, but we cannot really celebrate until you men who lived in the little rooms down in Collegetown and the big fraternities lining the gorge, you men who starred in activities or waited on table and studied seriously, and you WAVEs and WACs who once lived in Risley and Balch, return from the war.

COLLEGES MUST TAKE VETERANS, DEWEY TELLS STATE EDUCATORS

The New York Times, March 8, 1945

Heads of the eighty-five New York colleges and universities met today with Governor Dewey in an emergency conference to determine how 100,000 more veterans could be admitted to already overcrowded institutions in the fall… Mr. Dewey insisted that it would be catastrophic to let 50,000 to 100,000 veterans walk the streets, unable to gain admittance and take advantage of the GI Bill. Standing before the two hundred educators who came to the meeting in response to his invitation, the governor warned that the colleges would have to change their attitudes and take in all qualified veterans, even though this meant lowering standards. A way must be found to provide the necessary room for the veterans, he said.

CROWD OF 30,000 CELEBRATES VICTORY

The Ithaca Journal, Wednesday, August 15, 1945

Deserted streets littered with straw, torn paper, broken glass, and a lost hat were the aftermath of Ithaca's most hilarious celebration as a crowd estimated at close to thirty thousand went wild over the news of Japan's surrender. Impromptu parades, snake dances, the tooting of automobile horns, the scream of the city hall siren, and the peal of church bells mingled with the happy shouting of a cheerful and orderly mob that jammed State Street to celebrate the news issued from the White House at seven p.m. Tuesday…

Little children in their pajamas, mothers in house coats, uniformed service men and women, screaming youths, the sedate and those who went "all out" made up the crowd that jammed the main street to watch automobiles—in some instances carrying as many as 20 persons—move bumper to bumper…

Service men and women at Cornell, given liberty shortly after President Truman's announcement, first congregated in front of Willard Straight Hall and on the slope between Sage Chapel and Barnes Hall. Here many officers were joined by their wives and children to thrill at the news and speculate about the future.

The radio loud speaker installed in front of Willard Straight Hall lost its appeal shortly after the announcement as the trek downtown began… Civilian students drove a horse-drawn hay wagon around the campus and some humorist left a sign, "For Rent," on the offices of the Tompkins County War Price and Rationing Board.

In front of Willard Straight Hall, August 14, 1945, students celebrate V-J Day when the Japanese surrendered, ending WW II.

CHAPTER 2

Born in Chaos 1945–46

The GI Bill funded a big, sudden increase in the size of colleges and universities across the country. At Cornell, total enrollment more than doubled in two years, from 4,783 in 1944–45 to 7,928 in 1945 and 10,560 in 1946. The Class of 1950 had 1,956 members, 64 percent of whom were veterans. It was the largest class in Cornell's history.

The result was a severe housing shortage, made worse because more than one-quarter of veterans arrived with their spouses. Many of these couples also had children, and lived in hastily erected housing complexes popularly known as "Vetsburg" and "Fertile Valley." When a large new men's dormitory complex on Kline Road burned to the ground six days before orientation was set to begin in October 1946, the conditions for male students went from bad to worse.

Fall-term classes finally started on October 11, 1946. As the weather grew colder, dozens of men slept in unfinished structures that had no running water. But living conditions for women were far better: *The Cornell Daily Sun* reported that some entering women were "disappointed to learn that individual telephones have not been installed" in their brand-new single rooms in Clara Dickson Hall.

SEVEREST HOUSING CRISIS IN CU HISTORY HITS VETS

The Cornell Bulletin, November 3, 1945

Hundreds of disgruntled veterans, their wives, and civilian men have been crowding the office of Dean Harold E. B. Speight, counselor of students, this past week in desperate attempts to secure housing accommodations for the coming term. Victims of the most acute housing shortage in the history of the university, many of these entering students still have neither permanent nor in some cases even temporary residences…

Eight hundred form letters were sent to members of the faculty and administrative workers of the university by Dean Speight urging them to rent out any vacant places in their homes to stranded students. Advertisements, radio appeals, and comments in the local press have been employed to persuade Ithaca residents to make available as many rooms as they can spare, even temporarily, for the emergency.

Evening Aims to Bring Back Pre-War Days

The Cornell Bulletin, December 7, 1945: Beginning with the presentation of Davy's Follies at 8:15 p.m. tomorrow, and followed by "Peacetime Pastime" with Vaughn Monroe's Orchestra at Barton Hall, the first big peacetime weekend in two years will officially open.[1]

Davy's Follies will have Julius Haberman '46 as master of ceremonies in the role of Theodore Zinck, taking us back to the old days with picturesque settings and songs. Following this, the Panhellenic Serenaders, comprising 26 girls, will sing Cornell songs. The Dance Club will present comedy acts. Other featured persons will be Vera Wagner [Hackman] '48 on the vibraharp, Laurel Fox [Vlock] '48 tap dancing, the Swing Trio, and Five Men and Two Tenors. Other highlights of the evening will be the football team performing as a daffodil kick chorus in crepe paper costumes...

Veterans Housing Survey Reveals Rent Profiteering

The Cornell Bulletin, January 4, 1946: The veterans' questionnaire, sent out in early December, asked returned servicemen for full particulars regarding their living arrangements... Out of 1,200 questionnaires mailed out by the Office of Veterans' Education, 955 replies were received; 27 percent of those replying were married, and 32 percent of these had children, in most cases one child, making a total of ninety-eight veterans' children.

[1] The annual tradition of "Fall Weekend," with a program of parties, sports events, and dances, was suspended during the war.

Of the 955 replying, 23 percent live in apartments, 40 percent in rooming houses, 15 percent in private homes where boarders are not usually taken, 10 percent in fraternity houses, 9 percent in houses rented by the university as men's dorms, 2 percent with relatives, and a miscellaneous few in rented houses, hotels, and firehouses.

Seventy-three veterans replied that it was difficult to secure rooms on account of children; fifty-one of these had been told they would not be considered because of children; and twelve have been unable to have their families with them... One veteran wrote that after three years in the service, and being used to communities where there was a housing shortage, "I can safely say that never before have I encountered a community in which every effort was bent to extract the last possible bit of profit."

Two apartment hunters sum it up: "My experience with those places I found vacant has been an eye-opener. Owners of only ordinary apartments asked from $50 to $80 a month for three or four rooms furnished. I turned down half a dozen places because the rent was too high. Owners' reasons for charging such prices were usually quite fanciful, never convincing. There appears to be a definite antipathy on the part of landlords to rent to people with or expecting children. Dogs appear to be preferred."

In the meanwhile, housing units for married veterans and their families are being built according to schedule in East Ithaca. Fifty two-family units will house one hundred veteran students. These units, moved from Massena, New York, where they housed war workers at the Aluminum Company of America's plant, consist of three rooms and are to be furnished. These new facilities will help accommodate more veterans who seek admission to Cornell.

"BETTER GRAB IT, MISTER—IT'S THE LAST ROOM FOR RENT IN TOWN!"–From *The Cornell Bulletin*, November 9, 1945

New Homes in Cornell's Temporary "Vetsburg"

The Cornell Bulletin, April 19, 1946: "You have to be efficient, for these houses were designed for efficiency," says Mrs. F. J. Swanson, wife of a veteran student in the College of Agriculture, describing her two-room house in Vetsburg, the temporary village erected to relieve the Ithaca housing shortage. "In a home as compact as this, if one thing gets out of place, you're sunk."

Veteran residents of the temporary community are literally starting life on the "wrong side of the tracks," for Vetsburg is located across the railroad tracks out Dryden Road. Most of them, however, are living there cheerfully and find a home of their own, no matter how small, far superior to leaving the wife and children at home.

Despite the fact that the houses were just opened for occupancy this term, gay curtains are already evident in nearly every window of the village. Cornellians' wives have created homey interiors, which make up for what the cottages lack architecturally outside.

Each house comes complete with an oil space heater and hot water boiler. For kitchen equipment there is a two-burner hot plate, an electric oven, and an icebox. The two-room homes have L-shaped living rooms with the kitchen in one wing. The rest can be used as a sitting room. Exteriorly the houses are square and gray. Landscaping is still in a gravel and mud stage.

Each building accommodates two families with entrances for each family on opposite sides of the house. "Right now the joke is that we know our neighbors across the street, but not the people in the same house," Mrs. Swanson continued. "As yet there's little community spirit, but a Veterans' Wives Club has formed which meets at Willard Straight, and that will probably help.

"We were very glad to get the house, for my husband and I spent two days a month for six months in Ithaca looking for accommodations. We were notified in the middle of February that we could live here. My husband had two years at Cornell before the war, and unless something happens that changes the Ithaca housing situation, we'll probably live here two years until he completes his course."

Peggy Godwin, another Vetsburg resident, arrived in Ithaca last month with her small baby son. "The house was much better than I expected," she said, "but as yet I've little to say about Cornell. With a new baby, I've been unable to get over on campus at all. During the warm weather we had no baby carriage and when the carriage came, the weather turned too cold for the baby.

"Our cottage seems warm so far, but there's a crack under the

Upper Vetsburg under construction.

door big enough to see through and the windows aren't tight. Weather-stripping is one thing they haven't got to yet in the building program, but it will be added during the summer. As for storage space—we've got two closets, but I can't help wishing there was an attic or a cellar," she laughed.

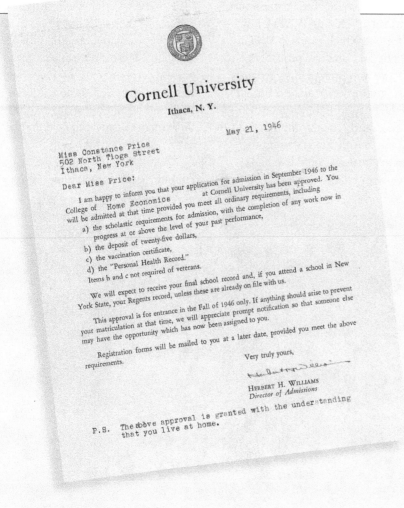

Constance Price Payne '50

The College of Home Economics accepted Connie Price on the condition that she continue to live at home with her parents. She joined Alpha Omicron Pi sorority so she could spend more time on campus. "I found myself socializing with married couples. I was a bridesmaid many times," she says. "I ended up having a big wedding on campus in December 1948 with a reception at Willard Straight." After her marriage to Lee Naegly '52, she moved to an apartment outside of town. She later married Robert Payne and helped him manage a ski resort in Vermont.

Suspended Fraternities

From the Report of the Counselor of Men Students, 1942–43: The fraternities, faced with decimation of their membership by the year's end, have been obliged to give thought not only to the question of what status to maintain for the war's duration, but also to such arrangements during the current year as might best provide for their dwindling membership...thirty-eight fraternities [of fifty total] remained open during the summer of 1942... For the duration of the war, and with most of the fraternity houses likely to be utilized by the armed forces, the fraternities as a normal phase of campus life face suspension.

Proceedings of Telluride Association Annual Convention

June 1946: During the years of uncertainty just prior to our entrance into the war and during the time the Marine Corps occupied Telluride house, only the more essential items in maintenance and repair were done in the house. To make up for these four or five years of deferred maintenance, we must undertake a major job of refurbishing in this coming year. It is recommended that convention appropriate $5,000 for the sanding and varnishing of floors, repainting of woodwork and ceilings, and papering or painting of wall surfaces throughout the house.

Opening Postponed

Cornell Alumni News, September 1946: Opening of most of the university for the fall term will be

RABBIT WARRENS

In 1945, Congress released funds to allow colleges and universities to build temporary housing for veterans and relocate military barracks to campus locations. Vets quickly christened the low-cost dorms with a variety of nicknames. "Rabbit warrens" was one of the printable ones.

Cornell's 1946 campus map shows five large new clusters of housing, much of which was incomplete as classes began:

1 Ten two-story barracks were moved from Sampson Naval Training Center to Kline Road, just north of Fall Creek, for 650 single men. These were nearing completion when five of them burned to the ground three days before classes began (see next page). The housing area did not open until February 1947.

2 Forty-six cottages relocated from Sampson Naval Training Center to the eastern end of Tower Road and named "East Vetsburg." About 136 single and married men lived in these structures before they were completed in February 1947, whereupon some residents were reunited with their wives and children, and another sixty-five families moved in.

3 About eighty duplex and triplex cottages constructed between Maple Avenue and Mitchell Street for one hundred veterans and their families, known as "Vetsburg" and also as "Fertility Valley." These were opened in 1947.

4 Seven military barracks relocated to the hillside just below Baker Tower and other West Campus dorms, along with a newly constructed "mess hall" for 540 single men.

5 Clara Dickson Hall, a luxurious women's dorm north of the Balch complex in North Campus (see chapter five).

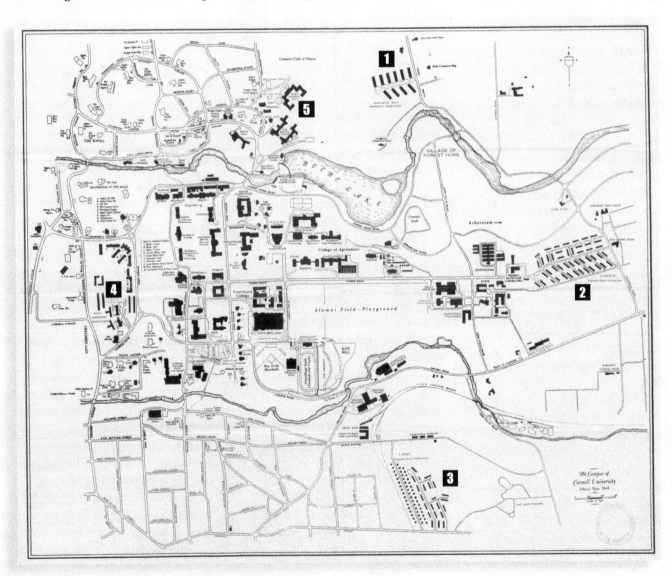

deferred to October 14, to permit more progress toward completion of housing and eating facilities for the unprecedented number of 9,300 undergraduate students expected in Ithaca than would have been possible at the original opening date of September 26. This decision was taken at a meeting called by President Edmund E. Day of deans and administrative officials, August 20. At this meeting and an earlier one called when it became apparent that Clara Dickson Hall for women and some of the emergency housing for veterans and additional faculty members could not be completed for occupancy by mid-September, all possibilities for meeting the situation were thoroughly canvassed.

With reports from the University Housing Committee, headed by Provost Arthur S. Adams, on the status of the various construction projects, it became apparent that three more weeks would allow for considerable progress toward housing and feeding approximately 450 women students who will occupy Clara Dickson Hall and toward completing housing for some 600 men students and additional instructors for whom quarters could not possibly be ready on the original date. It was unanimously agreed that postponement was the only feasible answer, and pointed out that even with later opening a considerable number, at least of men students and faculty, would probably have to go into temporary quarters until all the new housing can be ready. Time is also given for continued intensive canvass of fraternities and faculty and Ithaca families to find accommodations for several hundred single and married students who will have to be quartered outside the university facilities.

Dorm Fire on Kline Road

The Cornell Daily Sun, Friday, October 11, 1946: Fire that razed nearly completed barracks at the Kline Road housing site Tuesday morning prompted the university to renew their housing appeal. Residential Hall officials regard local response as excellent…

Of 650 students slated to live in the completed temporary dorms, 300 had previously arranged for rooms with townspeople until the barracks would become ready; the remaining group were to be quartered temporarily in the emergency facilities which are now being improved upon due to the delay which has been caused by the fire…

The spectacular flames were subdued less than an hour after Ithaca fire equipment arrived in response to alarms sent in at 4:07 and 4:20 a.m. Low water pressure, an inoperative fire hydrant, and a fresh northwest wind gave the fire a tremendous start before water could hit it. Four lengths of hose were lost as flames billowed over firemen working the line, connected to a low-pressure hydrant.

Glen Springs Hotel

Cornell Alumni News, September 1946: Glen Springs Hotel, at the top of the glen in Watkins Glen, has been leased by the university from its owner, Major William M. Leffingwell '18, and is being remodeled by the state into apartments for about 150 married student veterans, without children. Buses will make two trips a day each way to transport students the twenty-six miles to and from the campus.

The famous watering place of "Diamond Jim" Brady, John D.

Rockefeller, and the early stars of stage and screen was built in 1889 by the late William E. Leffingwell 1875, and has been closed since his son re-entered the army in 1942 and gave its registers and account books to the University Collection of Regional History. Now it is being refurbished into two-room-and-bath apartments, with meals to be served cafeteria style in the main dining room and evening bridge and dancing in the lounge and glassed-in terrace overlooking Seneca Lake.

The Glen Springs housing project closed in June 1948.

East Vetsburg Calls for Workers; Houses without Plumbing Facilities

The Cornell Daily Sun, October 31, 1946: Students are desperately needed at the East Vetsburg and Tower Road temporary housing projects. Men living in unfinished barracks, without plumbing or drinking water, are sending out a call for fellow students to help them complete their houses.

WORKERS WANTED!

Apply East Vetsburg at Watchman's Shack on Mitchell St. and at Tower Road Time Shack.

Offering ninety cents an hour and working hours any time suitable for the worker from 8 a.m. to 4:30 p.m., the project needs laborers, master carpenters, and plumbers. Most urgent problem facing the men is the plumbing.

The labor supply from downtown Ithaca has been exhausted so that the only possible workers to be obtained now must come from among the student body, or be imported from surrounding areas. Because the local unions cannot supply the labor and because they sympathize with the plight of the veterans, permission has been granted to allow men to work without paying the union fees.

Men lining up at 6:30 a.m. to shave with cold water tell the story. Water that has been piped into the central building serves all three units, which means men in the other units must go outside of the living quarters to get around to the only toilet facilities. All the water used for washing is cold because the water heating system has not been completed. "Roughing it" hardly describes the situation.

Running water is unfit to drink. Every morning milk cans filled with pure drinking water are delivered. Faucet water is too strongly chlorinated for drinking purposes.

In the completed units two men live in each room with twin beds and a combination desk and dresser allowing each man one drawer. A lamp without a bulb completes the furnishing. The central lighting fixture provides the only light for the room.

Under these conditions seventy married veterans are living in seven buildings with three apartments in each unit in East Vetsburg. None of the Tower Road houses are ready for occupancy. Awaiting completion of the project, the husbands hope to bring their wives and babies up to live with them in the sixty-four apartments that are planned for the completed housing project. Present estimates on final occupancy run from December to April.

With the co-operation of students living on campus in the dormitories and fraternity houses with every modern convenience and in the temporary housing units, all men may hope to move up to ordinary living facilities.

University Sets New Enrollment at 350 Women

The Cornell Daily Sun, October 11, 1946: "All around superiority, not scholarship alone, determined the selection of the approximately 350 entering women from among ten times as many fall term applicants," says Herbert H. Williams, director of admissions. Hardly more than half the size of the class admitted in 1944, the record year for women's enrollment, the entering class will combine with earlier classes to make a total of around 1,800 women in the various colleges of the university this fall. Since the College of Home Economics was not forced to restrict the registration of women students to make room for veterans, as were the other colleges, over 50 percent of the new class will be home economics students. A larger than usual percentage are agriculture students, while the fifty new women who will register in the College of Arts and Sciences have been chosen from among nearly 2,200 applicants. There are in addition approximately fifty female Cornell State Scholarship winners.

Only a few transfers from other universities have been admitted, for special reasons in every case. Therefore most of the available space was given to the new class in order that it may balance the other classes as nearly as possible.

The sudden reduction of new women registrants does not lower the total number of women to unprecedented levels, however. In the early 1930s, the usual enrollment was just above 1,100. A decade raised this to 1,300 and 1,400, and only during the war years from 1942 on did the figure climb to 1,600 and then over 1,800 on the Ithaca campus in 1944, with a total including graduates and students in the schools of nursing and medicine set at 2,843.

Though freshman women constitute about one-fifth of the expected class, they have been awarded a higher percentage of the new Cornell National Scholarships, eight out of the twenty-four winners being women. Of the twenty-nine Undergraduate LeFevre and Teagle Foundation Scholarships, eight will be held by freshman women.

Sonia Pressman Fuentes '50

I was the valedictorian of my high school class, and because of that, I was awarded two scholarships to Cornell. I moved into the top floor of Balch IV, a beautiful stone dorm. I had a solo room, too. I had no idea that other students were living in sheds and attics. I assumed that all Cornell students lived in luxury.

I was raised in a bungalow colony in the Catskill Mountains of New York, a mile and a quarter away from a small town, so I was totally inept when it came to social matters. I was good at going to school, but outside of classes, I knew nothing. I didn't know how to dress, I wore thick glasses, and the first year I wore braces on my teeth, so I never smiled. I never had a sister or someone else to tell me how to be charming or fix my hair. I was not very much in the world.

I also had never visited a college campus before arriving on East Hill. I was totally unprepared for the vastness of it. I had seen movies where a college was a single building, so I thought that's what it would be like. We got to Ithaca and stopped at a house, which turned out to be a fraternity house, and I asked a man on the steps where Cornell was. He spread his arms out wide and said, "This is all Cornell." I was completely taken aback. Suddenly I was in this place where everyone else seemed so sophisticated.

Sonia Pressman Fuentes earned a bachelor of arts degree and went on to earn an LLB from the University of Miami in 1957. As an attorney, she worked on sex discrimination cases for the federal Equal Employment Opportunity Commission in the 1960s. She was also a charter member of the National Organization for Women.

Elizabeth Severinghaus Warner '50

LETTER HOME, OCTOBER 13, 1946: Here it is Sunday and I am just getting around to writing. I've just been too distracted to sit down. We registered yesterday and they had given me the wrong registration blanks. They were for the College of Arts and Sciences instead of Architecture. I thought they were wrong to begin with but they wouldn't listen to me. Consequently I went back and forth between Barton and Goldwin Smith three times, which is not one of life's shortest strolls. We finally got that straightened out and just missed the kickoff. I don't know whether you read about the [Cornell-Colgate football] game or not, but it really poured rain. People left after the first half but I stayed 'til the bitter end. I was soaked to the skin, underwear and all, in spite of a raincoat, bandanna, and umbrella. Cornell barely won because its passing attack was ruined by the rain, naturally.

Friday night I went to the freshman rally at Bailey with that guy who yelled at me the night we got here. I can't stand him & last night I went to the Colgate Hop at the Straight with Carrow. We went down to Jane's first and played bridge. He's really very nice…

I am still horribly homesick and today is ghastly. This morning I missed church because of a two hour posture exam in which they silhouette you stark naked against a screen and take your picture. Then this afternoon we have the regular physical and really I think it's a little extreme. They poke you to find out if you have cancer of the breast and test you for venereal diseases. I think that's rather a difficult thing to go through. They also give the tetanus shots and I don't think I'd better have one so soon. I just had one last month…

Wednesday afternoon. It's a gorgeous day today although I thought it was going to snow this morning, and I am sitting here watching the many little passing Cornellians from my window. I can't understand why none of them have any work to do…

Separate freshman "camps" for men and women were held on October 7–10, 1946, continuing a tradition that was suspended in 1942.

Libby Warner is the daughter of Leslie Severinghaus '22, who was headmaster of the Haverford School, a private preparatory school on Philadelphia's Main Line, and a Cornell trustee. She was one of just three women in her class who earned a bachelor of fine arts degree from the College of Architecture.

Don Christiansen '50

I enlisted in the navy at the age of seventeen. I was trained as a radio technician, and assigned to the aircraft carrier USS *San Jacinto*. It was one of the group called "the nine sisters" that were deployed in the Pacific. Frank Clifford, a fellow Cornell '50 graduate, flew dive bombers from a sister ship, the USS *Belleau Wood*. Clifford later said, "War is a terrible thing. In Japan we saw people in bandages, people missing limbs. It's sad. The people who start the war usually don't fight it. I'd let the heads of state meet in the middle of some field with an axe, and fight it out."

I got my Cornell acceptance while in the navy, and after my discharge in 1946 I had just a few weeks to prepare for my arrival on campus. Knowing little about the university aside from its academic standards, my dad and I innocently drove to Ithaca College, which was in a single building, the Boardman House, downtown. We were promptly and politely redirected to East Hill.

During my freshman year I rented a room on Linn Street in downtown Ithaca and hiked up Gunshop Hill to my eight o'clock classes. After the Kline Road dormitories finally opened, I moved up there. These were wooden World War II-style barracks that housed two male students per room. As a veteran, I felt at home again!

Wilson Greatbatch, who later became well known as the inventor of the implantable cardiac pacemaker, was a fellow classmate in electrical engineering. He was also a navy veteran and, like me, he depended on monthly checks from the GI Bill. He had served on a sister ship, the aircraft carrier USS *Monterey*. He flew off that ship as the radioman on torpedo bombers, a role that required his doubling as the rear gunner during combat missions. While at Cornell he often spoke of the joy of wandering about our pleasant campus, a welcome change from the sound of "ack-ack" gunfire bursting all around him.

Don Christiansen earned a bachelor's degree in electrical engineering. He is a Fellow of the Institute of Electrical and Electronics Engineers (IEEE), the Radio Club of America, and the World Academy of Art and Science. During his 21-year tenure as editor in chief of *IEEE Spectrum*, he helped lead its staff to four National Magazine Awards. He writes "Backscatter," a column for *Today's Engineer Online*.

Moving into a "Vetsburg" cottage for married students, 1946.

CHAPTER 3

Marching Home

Veterans and the GI Bill

In the fall of 1946, three-quarters of male Cornell students and 64 percent of all undergraduates in Ithaca were veterans of World War II. The GI Bill had produced the largest freshman class in the history of the university, with 1,956 students. It also may have been the most socially and economically diverse, although only a few students were African-American and only 3.5 percent were from outside the United States. One-quarter of veterans were married, about fifty were Canadian, and several dozen veterans were women.

Many vets were the first in their families to go to college. Others were disabled or coping with the psychological effects of combat. But all of them had lost years to the war, and they were eager to make up for lost time. Non-veterans and faculty were impressed and intimidated as the veterans discarded old traditions and created new ones. They re-made Cornell.

Many veterans shared apartments in Collegetown, a neighborhood just south of campus.

Robert Purple '50

When I was discharged in May 1946, I had about six or eight credits from the time I had been at Cornell as a soldier (see chapter one). I spent the summer of 1946 enrolled in refresher courses in Ithaca, which I think were taught at the high school. It was not difficult for me to get back into Cornell, but finding a place to live was a problem. I was lucky. My dad had a friend in Ithaca who took me in.

I soon found another room in the home of Bristow Adams, who had just retired from the agriculture school faculty but was still active on campus and in town. I knew his wife, Luella, far better than I knew him. She was a really sweet lady.

I never did join a fraternity. After a year or so I found another room and moved there with my best friend, and we were quite comfortable. My social life revolved around music and church groups. I was invited to join "Rod and Bob," a social organization for civil engineering students that met in local drinking holes. So I did spend time in the Dutch Kitchen, Zinck's, and Joe's, but we only went out about once a month. I was trying to get an engineering degree. It was hard!

Daniel Roberts '50

On November 19, 1944, I stepped on a land mine while moving through Germany with the U.S. Army's 415th Infantry Regiment. If I had stepped squarely on the mine, I wouldn't be telling this story. I must have stepped on its edge, because a lot of the shrapnel missed me. It went through my right hand, cut the nerves in my right leg, and severed the muscle sheath in my left leg. Yet I did not lose my legs. So after a year of

---

Bristow Adams Praises Veterans as Determined, Unafraid, World-Wise

The Cornell Bulletin, January 18, 1946

"The veteran is excellent college material. He knows what he wants and isn't afraid of the professor," says Professor Emeritus Bristow Adams, counselor in the Veteran's Education Office at Cornell University. "Veterans were among my best students in my classes in the College of Agriculture after World War I," states Professor Adams, who retired from the teaching profession last June.

"Many ex-servicemen fear they will be at a disadvantage in college. Actually, they are in better shape for college than the boy just out of high school. They have been places and seen all kinds of people. They are able to grasp things.

"Most of these men are at least twenty-one years of age and so can enter college as special students. They do not have to work for a degree but can take the courses they need and leave. One veteran wants to learn to cut meat before he returns to his old position in a grocery store. He asked for and got a practical course in meat cutting in the Department of Animal Husbandry in the College of Agriculture," says Professor Adams, [who was] head of publications in the Colleges of Agriculture and Home Economics for thirty-one years…

"Most men have benefited from their stay in the service. They have gained maturity, poise, and forcefulness. Of the hundreds of veterans I have interviewed only one was adversely affected by the war," states Professor Adams. "His pale face, dull, lifeless hair, the cross-shaped scar on his forehead, and his gratefulness for decent treatment were results of his war experiences.

"Many veterans I interview never apply for entrance to Cornell. My job is to help the boys get the education they want at the place they can get it best. If Cornell cannot meet their educational needs I try to tell them which institution can."

surgery and rehab, and with the aid of a special pair of spring-loaded prosthetic shoes, I was able to walk with crutches.

I had always dreamed of going to Cornell. I grew up in Brooklyn in the 1930s as the son of Louis Krupnick, a typesetter, and his wife, Sadie, who were both Russian Jewish immigrants. I was a shy child, but my parents doted on my sister and me, and they encouraged our education. I graduated from Brooklyn Technical High School in 1943, enlisted, and applied for the Army Specialized Training Program (ASTP). I was studying engineering in the army program at Princeton University when I got my orders to go to Europe. I landed in Normandy three months after D-Day and had several close calls over the next two months, before the mine got me.

When I finally got back home to the states, I set about preparing for my new life. That's why I changed my name. Back in those days, anti-Semitism was strong and Jews were not able to get certain jobs. I decided that my last name, Krupnick, was not going to keep me from success. I opened a telephone directory and selected "Roberts," the most neutral-sounding name I could find. I wanted that name to be on my discharge papers. My father found a lawyer, and we made it legal.

I got a medical discharge in November 1945 and was accepted to Cornell under a special program for disabled veterans. I was treated well, with GI Bill benefits plus disability compensation. I even bought a new car, a black Oldsmobile with "hydramatic" transmission so I wouldn't have to shift gears. It was the first new car my family had ever owned.

Cornell was the tipping point of my life, and that car helped make me a popular guy. Betty Rosenberger especially liked it, and luckily she stuck with me after I left the car down in Brooklyn for the winter. We have been married sixty-three years now.

I lived on the second floor of Sage Hall and climbed up and down those stairs every day. I walked to my classes and to Willard Straight Hall, so I didn't have too much trouble getting around. I could even dance—Betty loved to dance. And people didn't treat me any different because I used crutches. A lot of veterans had stories about what had happened to us during the war, but we didn't go around telling people.

Daniel Roberts earned a degree in mechanical engineering and worked as an engineer and salesman, and then became the owner of fifteen Robert Half employment and accounting agencies.

Carman Hill '49

 One of the first things they made us do was stack up the dead bodies— Americans on the right, Germans on the left. I can still remember how stiff they were. And I remember their faces. There were so many of them, and they looked the same as me. Only their uniforms were different.

I was in the 242nd Regiment of the 42nd Infantry, and my job was to haul and set up anti-tank guns. I was nineteen, and I had never been that far away from home before, and I was terribly homesick. We were near the town of Haguenau, on the border of France and Germany, when I was captured in late January 1945. I remember that the day we were captured, Germans let us eat with the soldiers. We had some kind of stew that was mostly beans. That was the last time my stomach was full for five months.

The American artillery was shooting at German tanks. The Germans made us stand next to these tanks because they thought it would make the Americans stop shooting, but they didn't. I was blasted to the ground, and the man next to me was killed. Later, when I was taking off my clothes, I saw that my overcoat, field jacket, and undershirt had all been ripped open. But on my skin were just scratches. I was incredibly lucky.

We were put on trains and sent to Stalag IV-B, a huge camp about thirty miles north of Dresden, where we basically starved. They would give us a cup of watery soup and maybe some old potatoes, many of them rotten. It was cold, too. We were supposed to get Red Cross parcels. One of those was supposed to contain enough items to keep a man for a week, but the Germans always stole them. In all the time I was there, I only saw one Red Cross package. After a while it was difficult to stand up. I would get dizzy.

One night in February, the guards woke us and made us go stand outside in the cold. We could see flames in the distance. Dresden was being firebombed. We thought maybe they were going to execute us because they were so angry. But they just wanted us to see this horrible thing the Americans were doing.

Some prisoners did get shot, usually for trying to escape. But I never tried. I didn't know where the hell I was, and I was so weak I couldn't run very well.

I remember one day when the

guards thought they had some news that would upset us. They came in and said that President Roosevelt had died. That was April 12. But we didn't get upset. Instead, we got into an argument over who was vice president. Somebody thought it was Harry Truman, but he wasn't sure who it was. The guards were baffled. I mean, this was supposed to be our führer! I guess we all believed that the good old USA would keep going, no matter who was in charge.

The Russians started getting close to the camp, and the Germans knew it would be much better to be captured by Americans than by Russians. They marched us toward the Elbe River. Eventually the guards released us and surrendered, and we started wandering. After a while, we smelled food cooking and followed the smell. It was coming from an American field kitchen. That's how I found my way back to the army.

I did have some injuries to my back, but compared with a lot of guys, I came out of the war pretty whole. I was about 6′2″ and pretty strong. When I got to Cornell in the fall of 1945, I was in the registration line, and Harrison "Stork" Sanford, the crew coach, tapped me on the shoulder. He asked me if I had ever thought about rowing. I didn't even know what that was, but I ended up rowing for Cornell all four years.

After my freshman year I lived in Phi Kappa Psi, where a lot of the brothers were veterans. We never really talked about what had happened to us in the war. I tried to put it behind me and I did, except that I would have bad dreams. I would jerk awake, yelling and lashing out at people. The pledges used to poke me with a stick when they needed to wake me up because they didn't want to get hit.

The bad dreams went on for a long time. I married my present wife in 1976, and shortly after we were married she said I had been yelling and kicking in my sleep. I could never remember what the dreams were about, except that someone was always coming for me and I had to fight.

When I got to Phi Psi, they put me through a hazing exercise. They blindfolded me and took me out to an abandoned house early in the morning. They put me in an upstairs bedroom, nailed the door shut, and left. I took the blindfold off, did a chin-up on the rafter, and kicked the door down. Then I

Temporary men's housing next to Baker Tower in West Campus, 1946.

walked downhill until I got to the main road and hitched a ride back into town.

I got back around the same time the guys who had driven me up there did. They were so surprised to see me. They all wanted to know how I had escaped so fast. I didn't say anything but I thought, boys, you really have no idea.

Carman Hill earned two Purple Heart medals and a bachelor of science degree in agricultural economics. He sold Massachusetts Mutual life insurance in Ithaca, New York.

Kenneth Dehm '50 and Donald Smith '50

(1922–2014)

Kenneth Dehm   Donald Smith

Ken lives alone in a small house in Batavia, New York. He is visiting Don at his apartment in a nearby assisted-living facility.

Ken: We were both the first in our families to go to college. My mother asked me to come back home to the farm, but I was adamant about getting a higher education. I remember meeting Don at a Grange party after the war and comparing our plans.

Don: I told him I would do anything to go to Cornell.

Ken: We both grew up on subsistence farms east of Syracuse. The Depression came to us early when agricultural prices collapsed in the nineteen twenties. There was never any money. My parents insisted I stay in school, so I took vocational courses, graduated from East Syracuse High in 1936, and took any kind of job I could find.

Don: I am four years younger than Ken. He had a job in town when I was going to school, and we would ride our bikes into town together.

Ken: I worked for the Cooperative Grange League Federation Exchange (GLF), which was a purchasing and marketing cooperative for farmers. They owned the Agway stores and did a lot of other good things. Howard Babcock, their CEO, was on Cornell's Board of Trustees.[1] I did not know him, but I learned about Cornell through his influence at the GLF. I never thought I could ever go there.

I enlisted in the navy on December 8, 1941, and served on the USS *Barnegat*, a seaplane tender, for three years. We went to Scandinavia, North Africa, and Brazil. We saw combat at a distance but were never hit, which was lucky, because when we were loaded we carried 80,000 gallons of aviation fuel. For a farm boy to be able to see the world, all of a sudden, and wear that uniform—I mean, it was war, and I took it seriously, but I was also having a ball.

Don: I graduated from high school in 1940 and got a job as a screw-machine operator in Syracuse. We were making parts for guns, so I was deferred from military service until I was drafted in August 1943. Before I knew it, I was a tail gunner on a B-17 in the 305th Bomb Group. We flew thirty-five missions into Germany and never got shot down, thanks to the fighters that always escorted us, but we had several rough moments. Once the engines malfunctioned and we were forced to land in Belgium, at a base that had been liberated just the week before. We also flew in the Schweinfurt-Regensburg mission, when allied aircraft were being shot down all around us. I had a hard time getting over that one. My luck was amazing.

Ken: I was discharged in January 1946 but didn't have the course credits I needed to go to college, so I went back to my old high school with about sixteen other vets. I was nine years older than most of my classmates. We wore special patches on our shirts, which were usually our old uniforms, and we were allowed to use the stairways the teachers used.

Don: So anyway, I show up at Cornell in 1946, and lo and behold, who is my roommate? This guy right here!

Ken: We were really glad to see each other because we both felt out of place, and nobody made any attempt to welcome us. My first GI Bill check was stolen, and if there was an orientation, we missed it. We might have known that freshmen were supposed to follow certain rules, but we just disregarded them. They gave us a room in West Campus, Don took the top bunk, and we just moved in.

Don: I don't remember ever having one of those wool freshman beanies. If they had given me one, I would have just thrown it to the side.

---

[1] Howard Babcock (1889–1950) joined Cornell's board in 1930 and was its chairman from 1940 until 1947.

FROSH BEANIES

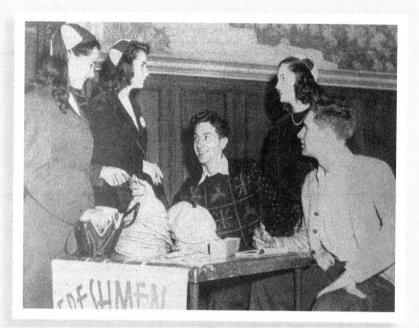

A Cornell tradition required male and female first-year students to wear wool beanie caps, or "dinks," for several months before tossing them into a bonfire. In the photo from the November 1946 *Cornell Alumni News*, Chris Larios '49 (seated) and Robert E. Smith '48 of the Spirits and Traditions Committee offer "dinks" to (l–r) new students Sali Carpenter, Jean Seguin [Edwards], and Joyce Wright [White], '50. Eve Weinshenker [Paul] '50 and other women were issued name tags to go on their red-and-white beanies. Men were less likely to put their names on their plain gray caps, and many veterans refused to wear them at all.

In 1949, following several episodes of sophomores forcibly shaving the heads of freshmen who were caught not wearing beanies, the Student Council ended all freshman rules and made the wearing of beanies strictly voluntary. By 1958, the beanies had been replaced by name tags.

We were fortunate that an old buddy of mine from the 305th, David Nagel '49, had been at Cornell since January. He was handsome and popular, a big man. He wore a bomber jacket with a patch sewn on it for every mission he had flown, and it worked like magic. Women crowded around guys like him, and teachers treated him with respect. Nagel was Jewish, but that didn't matter. The war had given us our own traditions.

Ken: After four years in the navy, I thought that Cornell was very relaxing. We usually ate at Willard Straight Hall or in Collegetown [the student neighborhood south of campus], using our GI Bill meal allowance. One of Don's friends had a brother who owned a restaurant right across the College Avenue Bridge, so we would go there. But we didn't do much in the way of sports, dating, or clubs. We went home whenever we could to help our families by doing farm work.

Freshmen to Hold "Cap Dance" Today

The Cornell Daily Sun, January 8, 1947

Possession of a freshman cap will be the only requisite for admittance to the Class of '50 night dance, which will be held in the Memorial Room of Willard Straight from 7:30 to 10 p.m. Following the dancing and entertainment part of the program, freshmen will burn their caps in a large fire in the field next to Myron Taylor at 9:45 p.m. The event is sponsored by the Spirits and Traditions Committee, under the chairmanship of Vivian Hoffman [Miller] '48. The cap-burning ceremony, which at one time occupied an important position in the Cornell calendar of events each year, will be the first to be held since the war.

Don: The vets were all kind of thrown together. We socialized, but we were there to work. We had to make up for a lot of lost time. And I am hugely grateful to Cornell and my professors at the agriculture school for helping me do that. If I hadn't gone to Cornell, I would have gone back to my old job as a screw-machine operator and stayed there.

Ken: It's the same for me. Also, without Cornell I never would have gotten to know Don. Years after we graduated, I moved to Batavia because it was my wife's hometown. And who should turn up living just five houses away from us? This guy right here!

Ken Dehm earned a BS from the College of Agriculture. He worked as a collector and controller for several agricultural supply firms in upstate New York, including Climax Harvesters.

Don Smith also received a BS from the College of Agriculture. He worked in the New York State prison system and became assistant warden at the Rochester Correctional Facility. He died shortly after giving this interview.

James Brandt '50

I was twenty when I arrived at Cornell in 1946. I had been on active duty in the navy for fourteen months but had never left the states. I was supposed to live in the Kline Road dorms that burned, so I rented a room downtown with a guy I had never met and rode the bus to school. After a couple of weeks, I found a new co-op that was starting on the hill, paid them seventy-five dollars, and moved in until I could get a bed

at a fraternity. That was my only requirement for fraternity life. They had to let me sleep there.

I was offered membership in several places, but only Chi Psi let me stay all four years, so that's where I lived. In 1946, twelve of the sixteen pledges to Chi Psi were veterans, and most of the older residents were vets, too. There were war stories, of course, but mostly I think we were there to get an education. Some of the freshmen who pledged with me were twenty-four years old!

I don't remember if I was ever given a freshman beanie. What I do remember is a big meeting—it might have been the Veterans Committee that met in Willard Straight Hall—where the vets all said, don't you dare tell us we have to wear beanies. We never did. They never pushed it on us. And

I don't know if the non-vets wore beanies. Maybe they did.

Jim Brandt earned a degree in mechanical engineering and married Nancy Hubbard '50, who earned a BA. He became vice president and general manager of the Marland Clutch division of Zurn Industries in LaGrange, Illinois.

Cynthia Craig

Cynthia Craig is the daughter of John Craig '50.

Food, lodging, and clothes were scarce after the war, and my father's monthly stipend from the GI Bill barely covered his expenses when he returned to Cornell. He and three friends decided to sign up for ROTC when they re-enrolled in the fall of 1946, because they would

Signing up for ROTC.

earn an extra twenty-five dollars per month. All of them were combat veterans.

When they went to the ROTC office on campus, they filled out applications and handed them to someone my dad described as a "young, wet-behind-the-ears kid." The kid mumbled something about "draft dodgers." My father and his friends took their applications back, threw them in the trash, and walked out of the recruiting office.

A supervisor saw what had happened. He chased after the four men and begged them to reconsider, because he needed skilled soldiers. Only one of them agreed to go back and sign up. That man ended up serving in Korea, an experience my father was glad to have missed.

Later, my dad and his veteran buddies pulled a prank on the ROTC students. They put brooms and mops over their shoulders and marched in perfect formation right through a parade drill.

John Craig '50

OCTOBER 24, 1946: Dearest Mary, Received your letter of the 22nd and a very nice letter it was, too. You should do more like that. As to your coming up here let me give you the dope on how things are set up. In the first place, I was up to the Straight (that's the campus hotel) yesterday to see the manager who is a classmate of my father's. Naturally I did not hit him for a room right off the bat or even mention it but it is still an in if you should pop up on the campus unexpectedly. And a

welcome sight that would be, too…

If you come over here [for a weekend visit from Wheaton College], we could have a wild time. Of course there wouldn't be much doing, and worse yet no place to do it. What I mean is that as yet I have found no little boudoirs such as you have at Wheaton. As you know, I have no inhibitions whatsoever, so there would always be your room at the Straight, although that would depend on how you feel about that. I'm not going to try to talk you into it although if you feel like your letter sounded, which is, incidentally, exactly how I feel, why it should be OK.

It's 1:15 a.m. now so I want to hit the sack, although I will probably go to sleep in my eight o'clock class tomorrow. Sweetheart, I miss you. Johnny.

APRIL 9, 1948: Dearest Mary, I went up to the Treasurer's Office today to see about how much time I had left under the GI Bill of Rights and it looks like there will be more than enough. In fact there will be close to a year left over. However I also walked into a nice big fat bill for 190 dollars for tuition not covered by the Bill, and that will have to be paid. So that leaves me feeling even more like a pauper…

John Craig married Mary King on June 25, 1949.

Walter Bruska '50

I played all four sports at Mohawk (New York) High School—football, baseball, basketball, and track.

I was named the outstanding boy in my class, and my wife was named outstanding girl. I still have the trophies. There was never any question I would go to college. My parents were immigrants from Russia, and my father worked in a factory, but when I entered school they started speaking English at home. They wanted me to succeed.

I enlisted in the Army Air Forces in the spring of 1943, but the army postponed my reporting date so I could graduate from high school. I wanted to be a navigator because I had seen the movie *Winged Victory*, where the navigator was the key man on the plane. He sent directions to the pilot so the plane could hit its target, and even more important, he knew when the plane had to turn around so it wouldn't run out of fuel. I didn't know it would take them almost two years to train me.

I finally arrived in Guam as a member of the 315th Bomb Wing at the end of June 1945. I flew on a couple of bombing missions before the war ended, and I was sent to Tinian Island as one of the back-up crew for the atomic-bomb runs to Japan, although I didn't go on either of them. I continued doing supply and delivery missions until I was discharged as a first lieutenant in May 1946.

I planned to use the GI Bill to go to Cortland State and study physical education so I could be a coach. But then I realized that I

The Vetsburg cottages under construction in 1946, looking south toward Mitchell Street.

could be a high school coach and also teach history, math, or science, which seemed more interesting. So I applied to Alfred University and was accepted, but they couldn't take me until the spring semester of 1947.

Around that time I ran into Edward Burns '18, a family friend who was an attorney and a loyal fan of Cornell football. He was on the lookout for promising young men, particularly if they were athletes. He asked me if I was going to college and I said yes, but I didn't think I could get into Cornell. So he made me an appointment and drove me to Ithaca for an interview, and about five days later I was accepted for the fall term.

I was twenty-one years old and married when I arrived at Cornell, and married students had to arrange for their own housing. So I bought a house trailer and an old Cord automobile—a big Mafia car, it would have carried a dozen people—and we towed the trailer from our home in Mohawk to a trailer park that had just opened in Varna. Our daughter Charlotte [who graduated from Cornell in 1969] was born on May 2, 1947. Her sister, Nancy, was born on February 12, 1950, a few days after I graduated.

Cornell, for me, was work, family, and football. After my wife got pregnant, we noticed that there was ice on the floor of the house trailer in the morning, and she said we couldn't bring a child into a place like that. So we went looking for another place, and we found a cottage in Harold Clough's backyard. He was a welding instructor in the Agricultural Engineering Department, and I helped in his class. We were there for eighteen months, and then we got a place in Vetsburg.

Vetsburg was great. Nobody who lived there had much money, so we co-operated with each other. We traded babysitting and did odd jobs. We used to have our parties once a month, when the veterans' payments arrived. My neighbor and I would each buy a pint of whiskey, and we'd go over to someone's house and have dinner and whoop it up.

I didn't party very much, though. With a wife and child, I had to work to make ends meet. I was a teaching assistant for two agricultural engineering courses during my junior and senior years. Between the end of classes and the beginning of football practice I worked on the university farm, driving a tractor, planting, cultivating, and cutting weeds. In the fall I'd work in the beef cattle barn. And I also worked at Long's grocery store on Eddy Street. Mr. Long was very good to me. We would close up the store at 10 or 11 p.m., and he would give me a bag or two of groceries to take home. A lot of Ithaca people were kind and helpful to us.

Mr. Burns urged me to join a fraternity, so I did. I got into Phi Kappa Psi, and he paid my initiation fee. But the main thing I did there was go with my wife to chaperon at fraternity parties. That was an eye-opener. Three times a year, there would be big weekend parties where the second floor of the fraternity would be reserved for girls who were visiting for the party, and the guys would be bunking on the third floor. It was hard to maintain the separation. These young guys would drink too much and try to sneak their dates upstairs. That was a different kind of Cornell than the one we lived in, for sure.

Walt Bruska earned a BS from the College of Agriculture and continued working for Cornell as an assistant football coach until 1953, and then as an administrator. He was director of development at Cornell from 1959 to 1963. Later he was vice president for administration at Kent State and Alaska Pacific Universities, and vice president of the Fetzer Institute.

Donald H. Moyer
(1905–1991)

Don Moyer, author of the excerpt below, was counselor of male students at Cornell from 1941 to 1943. After serving in the navy, he was appointed Cornell's assistant director of veteran's education in January 1946.

Cornell Alumni News, June 1947: Without a doubt, the greatest change to the student body is to be observed in the large proportion of benedicts[2] on campus; about 1,300 of them, with their wives and children. As these boys and girls eat together, you can spot them for their relaxed manner. As one student put it, "they aren't pressing!" Another, commenting on the married women, said, "Now you have to be careful whom you whistle at."

It is an interesting and significant experiment, this blending of family life and college life! It isn't going to be universally successful, and where it is, the triumph will often be at a sacrifice on both counts, because neither phase of this dual living is a normal or natural one.

Two veterans, man and wife, have an eight-month-old youngster. Both attend classes, but so staggered that one is always free to tend

ABOVE: Living area in a Vetsburg cottage.

LEFT: Gordon Nichols, a graduate student in chemistry, and his wife, Ophelia, celebrate their wedding anniversary by weeding their vegetable patch in the Vetsburg community garden. Gordon Jr. helps out.

the baby. This means rapid transportation by car and bike between classroom and "nursery." It means a valiant co-operative endeavor when one considers the diapers, the cooking, the study hours, and the privation. It is a trial by fire, and for Cornell to be a crucible in this socio-economic laboratory is both a responsibility and a challenge…

In December 1946, the Office of Veterans Education appointed Mrs. K. B. Bowen, the wife of a veteran enrolled in the Law School, as coordinator for family affairs. Mrs. Bowen went to work with the instruction that her function should be to grant the wives and children of our married veterans as much peace of mind and sense of security

---

[2] Slang for a newly married man.

as was possible under the unique circumstances of their existence.

Among the many activities which have claimed her attention are problems of medical care, nursery schools, employment, legal aid, social events, and the dissemination of information relating to services and opportunities for the distaff [maternal] side of veterans' families. Work on these problems is principally a co-operative function of the wives themselves.

After the Office of Veteran's Education was discontinued in 1948, Don Moyer continued working for Cornell as assistant to the provost until the early 1970s.

Paul Joslin '50

I grew up during the Great Depression on a 100-acre farm near Batavia, New York. Because most farms were self-sufficient, we were shielded from the worst of it. We ate well with our own meat, eggs, milk, and garden vegetables, plus wild strawberries, raspberries, cherries, and mushrooms. I owned one set of clothes for school, one for farm chores, another for church. I attended a one-room school with eleven other kids who were in six different grades.

My non-farm life revolved around school, church, and Saturday night shopping in Batavia. The annual highlights came in the summer: family reunions, the county fair, and the church school picnic. A lot of my classmates in the College of Agriculture had similar childhoods.

World War II began when I was thirteen. Our hired hand was drafted into the army, so as a young kid, I had to take over his adult duties. Three years later, my life changed dramatically when my father was injured in a farm accident and could not work for the better part of two years. Thus, from age sixteen to eighteen I was a full time farmer while I continued going to high school. For this, I was awarded the state farmer degree of the Future Farmers of America.

By spring 1946, my father had regained enough health to go back to work. He encouraged me to enlist so I could get GI Bill benefits and go to college. I tried to join the navy but, due to scarred eardrums, I failed the physical. A few weeks later, shortly after turning eighteen, I was drafted and quite strangely assigned to the navy. Another surprise came in August, when the navy decided they had too many sailors and I was given an honorable discharge with full veteran's benefits.

I arrived on campus a sort of hybrid. I was technically a veteran, but I was also a naïve country boy without the academic and social skills needed to thrive in college. I had been assigned to the temporary barracks on Kline Road that burned, so I started out sharing a single room in Sage Hall. In the middle of that first semester I was moved to one-story wooden barracks-type dorms that had been hastily erected just west of McGraw Tower.

In that first semester, my academic performance was a miserable failure. I earned a D average and went straight to probation. In the spring my average was still a D, but with an F in chemistry I was duly busted. I did not have the traditional farewell party, with songs and drinks at Zincks. I just went home, staring at the prospect of being a lifelong farmer.

I sincerely wanted a college education, however, so I made a personal appeal to the dean of the College of Agriculture, and it worked—he got me readmitted! Gradually I acquired functional study skills, learned the rules of test-taking, and improved my grade average to a B minus. I endured, but not without a bad case of envy toward well-attired classmates who had money, good grades, memberships in fraternities and special clubs, plus dates with attractive co-eds on weekends. Except for the campus chapter of the Future Farmers, the education fraternity Kappa Phi Kappa, and the Baptist Student Fellowship, I had no social life.

In the summer before my senior year I married Erma, my high school sweetheart. We lived forty-five miles off campus while I did student teaching that fall. In the spring, we lived in an apartment in Dryden, I commuted to campus, and we went home to Batavia on weekends.

Paul Joslin earned a BS from the College of Agriculture and went on to receive a doctorate in biology and science education from the University of Rochester. He became a professor of science education, chair of the Department of Curriculum and Teaching at Drake University in Des Moines, Iowa, and a distinguished science educator, author, lecturer, and university visiting scholar.

Elizabeth Campbell Booth '50

I joined the naval reserves for women at the end of 1944, after going to teacher's college in Montclair, New Jersey, for two years. They called us WAVES, which meant Women Accepted for Volunteer Emergency Service. The idea that women could be soldiers was supposed to be a temporary response to an emergency.

I went from base to base and finally ended up working in the meteorology department at the Norfolk Naval Station. After I was discharged with GI Bill benefits, I looked for a place to finish my degree. My family had always been in the hotel and restaurant business, and every year they went to the Hotel Show in New York City. One year at the Hotel Show my aunt ran into Howard B. Meek, who ran the Cornell hotel training program, and he suggested that I apply.

I didn't want to go back to the teacher's college. I had been accepted at Temple University, but they told me I couldn't start until the spring of 1947. So I went across the street to a pay phone, called Cornell, and asked Professor Meek if I could attend the hotel program starting in the fall term of 1946. He said yes, so I went home, packed up, and took the bus to Ithaca. All I had to do was pay a twenty-five dollar late fee.

I was at Cornell for three years, living in Risley and Balch Halls. I wasn't interested in joining a sorority. I didn't belong to any veteran's organizations, either, but I was allowed to join the Junior Hotelmen of America. I was about four years older than a typical freshman, the work was hard, and there were only four or five female students in the entire program.

Elizabeth Campbell Booth earned a BS degree and worked at a hotel in Chicago before returning to manage her family's resort on the New Jersey shore.

Barbara Cole Feiden '48

I had been in the Canadian Women's Army Corps during the war, and since Canadian and American soldiers served together, I was eligible for American GI Bill benefits. I was assigned to a pleasant two-room unit in Balch dormitory with Trude Kanaley [Yaxis] '50 and Phyllis Shaw '50. We were all veterans, and I often wondered whether or not Cornell, in its infinite wisdom, figured that our military service was a sufficient reason to make us roommates.

I was astonished by the house rules in Balch. They were so juvenile. I didn't need a dorm mother, because I had already had a top sergeant. I resented having to observe a curfew and getting penalized if I came in a few minutes late. So when I had a chance to leave in my second year, I jumped at it.

I moved into a small university-owned house that was mostly for graduate students. For some reason they let me share a room there with a classmate, Helvi Selkee [Edmondson] '48 MA '55, who had also worked before going to college. The curfew was not enforced in that house, although we did have to sign in and out. And there was nobody around to prevent your date from coming up to your room, although that was also forbidden.

Even with the GI Bill helping us, we didn't have much money. We bought used textbooks and we tended to eat in Willard Straight Hall. A dinner out in Ithaca was a real treat. We worked hard, because a lot of veterans felt like they had to make up for lost time. On the other hand, I don't think anyone graduated deeply in debt.

Barbara Cole Feiden received a Bachelor of Science degree from the School of Industrial and Labor Relations. She is a freelance writer in White Plains, New York.

Horst von Oppenfeld '50, MS '51, PhD '53
(1913–2010)

Horst von Oppenfeld was a German officer who served under General Erwin Rommel in North Africa, where he was captured. He spent two-and-a-half years as an American prisoner of war in Kansas. His introduction to Cornell came in a camp at Fort Getty, Rhode Island, in the summer of 1945, as he was being prepared for repatriation to Germany. But he actually detested Hitler, according to his unpublished memoir. He had been told that he could either join the German army, join the Nazi party, or be shot as a traitor, so he joined the army. Once he was captured and got to know a few Americans, he started to like the United States.

When the war was over, Horst was offered a job with the U.S. occupation government, helping fellow Germans reestablish a democracy. He was sent to Fort Getty for training. His favorite teacher there was William Moulton, a Cornell professor who was close to his own age. Moulton taught them English conversation by acting out all kinds of funny skits. A journalist reported that Horst loved to tell stories about that class and shout the punchline, "Max, have a cigarette!"

While working in Germany, Horst met Judith Pownall, an administrator with the occupation forces. He also gained experience with jobs that would later be called international development, although the field had not been invented yet. After they married, Judy brought Horst back home to Rochester, New York, as, he wrote, "a male war bride." He soon reconnected with William Moulton, who arranged for him to enroll at Cornell as the university's most unusual transfer student.

FROM VON OPPENFELD'S UNPUBLISHED MEMOIR: I enrolled in time for the winter semester in January 1949. Cornell gave me credit for studies before the war, for courses taken as a POW in Kansas, and for two semesters in Stuttgart. Still, I was required to study three more terms until I got my bachelor's degree. We found a primitive, though inexpensive, apartment with farmers ten miles outside Ithaca.

Frugal living was essential for us. Judy had found a job as a research assistant in Cornell's Department of Rural Sociology, earning about half of the federal government salary she had sacrificed to let me finish my studies. Most veterans received generous financial support for tuition, housing, and

living expenses, but I had been on the wrong side, so I was not entitled to that. We had to pay for everything. But not only did we manage to cover the expenses, we also had a good time, once we moved to an apartment in downtown Ithaca, and then into a university-owned apartment for foreign students.

Initially, I felt strange among students who were about half my age. Even the veterans were substantially younger than I was, at thirty-five. For them, the war had been shorter. In addition, the media, understandably, was full of crimes committed by the Nazis. Would they hold those against me, a former German soldier? Would I be a victim of discrimination? To my relief, I found that the opposite was true. The students and professors were fair and open-minded. It was easy to make friends.

I was studying agricultural technology, which emphasized constant renewal based upon research and experimentation. One of my

teachers, Frank Pearson, sparked my interest in economics. During the Great Depression, Professors George Warren and Pearson had been key advisers to President Roosevelt. The president had come to depend on Warren and Pearson to develop initiatives to solve rural problems when he was governor of New York State in the 1920s. They became his key advisers, and mine.

As my graduation approached, Judy wisely advised me to take a summer job in the Department of Agricultural Economics. She understood that because I was not yet a citizen, it would not be easy for me to find a good job. So we lived on her salary, and I was paid modestly to do the kind of work I liked. If I applied for admission to graduate school, I was told, I would also be eligible for a research assistantship. The benefits included reduced tuition fees and a modest salary, along with a small office and a secretary, who assisted me in completing two research projects for publication through the Department. One of them I could use for my master's thesis. At the same time, I was taking graduate courses and was able to prepare my PhD thesis, thanks to Cornell's incredibly generous logistical support.

Cornell gave me so much, but perhaps its most valuable contribution was a stimulating environment for becoming "Americanized." I learned about American institutions and made lifelong friendships with classmates and faculty. How fortunate for me, less than five years after that horrible war! I was still classified as an enemy alien immigrant, but I was being granted such opportunities!

I shared my first basement office in the Agricultural Economics Department with Clifton

Loomis '37, who had returned to get his master's degree.[3] He had been a lieutenant colonel of the American invasion forces in France and Germany, and I had been a captain in the German Africa Corps. Needless to say, we became the best of friends. Another graduate student, Risto Harma, PhD '54, had fought against the Russians in the same war. He would sometimes join us for late evening chats, where we exchanged our war experiences. Judy complained that I would have nightmares after those talks. But it was an extraordinary thing. I had been given the chance to become friends with my former enemies.

Horst von Oppenfeld received bachelor's, master's, and doctoral degrees from the College of Agriculture, with his terminal degree awarded in 1953. He became a Cornell visiting professor at the University of the Philippines at Los Baños, and a key

[3] Loomis (MA '51, PhD '53) went on to teach farm management at Cornell from 1955 to 1975.

contributor to Cornell's early programs in international agricultural development. He went on to a distinguished career with the World Bank.

John Symington Aldridge '50, MD '53

I arrived at Ithaca's Lehigh Valley railroad station early in the morning of October 9, 1946, with a trainload of fellow freshmen. It was a beautiful clear fall day. I was eighteen and not yet a veteran, although many others on that train were. We were informed that several temporary dorm buildings that were nearly finished, and had been meant for us, had burned to the ground the night before. They would not be ready until the spring. So I was assigned to Baker Dorm for the fall semester, and at first, things did not go well.

I had three roommates, all of them returning GIs. They were tough and loud, and I was not. They enjoyed running the radio full blast most of the day and night, playing poker, and smoking cigars well into the early morning hours. Studying in the dorm was hopeless. I wanted to be a doctor, but I couldn't concentrate on my classes. Several weeks into the term I visited a student adviser, Professor Perry Gilbert, a zoologist whose specialty was sharks. He coldly advised me that with my grades, I had no hope of getting into medical school. I explained that it was nearly impossible for me to study or even sleep, but it seemed to me that Professor Gilbert was far more interested in sharks than he was in students.

Shortly thereafter, my luck improved. A single room became available in Lyon Hall, the old Gothic-style dorm on West Campus. I grabbed it. By becoming a hermit, I helped my scholastic performance vastly. I also found

CONSCIENTIOUS OBJECTORS ON ICE

CORNELL ALUMNI NEWS, OCTOBER 15, 1946

In 1944–45, Cornell scientists experimented on a group of conscientious objectors who were confined for more than 200 days in a 30-by-26-foot temperature-controlled room behind Sibley Hall. Temperatures in the room fluctuated between sixty and zero degrees fahrenheit. The subjects (who were volunteers) wore government-issued arctic clothing, ate a high protein diet, and wore sensors to measure their physical responses. In this photo, the objectors are shown on a treadmill inside the room.

another student adviser, Lynn Barnes, who was far more helpful than Professor Gilbert had been. I went to the Ithaca campus for three years and two summer sessions and then was accepted by Cornell Medical School.

I did do other things besides study. I was on the 150-pound crew and football teams, and I joined the Reserve Officers Training Corps (ROTC). I was a good marksman, although I always had trouble moving smoothly through the sixteen points in the manual of arms drill. I also had trouble giving correct orders to a marching platoon.

One day I was leading a platoon that was marching in Barton Hall. I didn't give the order for column left or column right in time, so the cadets marched directly into the wall. This incident made it into *The Cornell Daily Sun*.

John Aldridge received a bachelor of arts degree in 1950 and an MD from Cornell Medical School in 1953. He practiced obstetrics and gynecology in New York City and Ithaca.

Richard W. Pogue '50

My choice of Cornell was almost a fluke. I went to Woodrow Wilson High School in Washington, DC, and did very well there. My parents and I assumed that I would go on to college, but I didn't give much thought to where. Then the father of one of my classmates, who was a Cornell alumnus, approached me about a new scholarship that Cornell had established called the National Scholarship. It offered full tuition plus a handsome

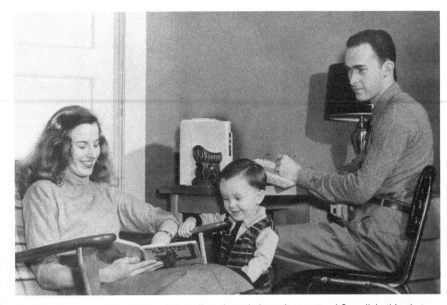

World War II veterans blazed the trail that allowed married couples to attend Cornell. In this photo, Suzanne Brigham MacLean '53 and Douglas MacLean '52, MBA '53 do "homework" with their 22-month-old son, Dougie. Douglas scheduled his classes on Tuesdays, Thursdays, and Saturdays; Suzanne on Mondays, Wednesdays, and Fridays.

cash stipend, which sounded good to me. So I applied and was successful.

That was literally the only thing I knew about Cornell until the night of October 10, 1946, when I boarded a train bound for Ithaca. I found myself standing on the Ithaca station platform at 2:30 in the morning, hoisting my steamer trunk, way down the hill from Cornell, with only the address of Baker Hall, to which I was assigned, to guide me. I did hail a cab, but at that point, Cornell did not seem so great.

At first I found Cornell intimidating. Young male freshmen right out of high school, like me, were a very small proportion of the class of 1950. It was traumatic for us, because the veterans were older, most were tough, and a few were battle-scarred. Many of them were married and had children. The veterans were anxious to get on with their careers; they were not there to party. We felt that many of them looked down on guys like me, who

were just barely too young to have faced the draft.

I now believe that non-veteran men in the Class of 1950 enjoyed what in the long run proved to be a unique advantage. We were subjected to unusually intense rivalry. The driving competition from veterans and extremely talented young women had a significant positive effect on us greenhorns. It propelled us to do well. If we didn't do our best, some hard-driving veteran or ambitious female would beat us. It was healthy and exhilarating, but at the same time strenuous and demanding. In high school, I was used to being at the head of the class. At Cornell, the competition was fierce.

After receiving his BA, Dick Pogue earned a law degree from the University of Michigan in 1953 and became managing partner of the Jones, Day, Reavis & Pogue law firm, based in Cleveland (now known as Jones Day). Under Dick's leadership, the firm grew from 334 to 1,225 lawyers and from five to twenty international offices. He continues as senior advisor to this firm.

Main library reading room in the 1940s.

CHAPTER 4

Classes & Mentors

Life-Changing Relationships

Vladimir Nabokov
(1899–1977)

Vladimir Nabokov was a professor of English at Cornell from 1948 to 1959, after a fellow English professor, Morris Bishop 1913, recruited him away from Wellesley College. These are notes for the concluding lecture of Nabokov's survey course on European literature:

To some of you it may seem that under the present highly irritating world conditions it rather is a waste of energy to study literature, and especially to study structure and style. I suggest that to a certain type of temperament—and we all have different temperaments—the study of style may always seem a waste of energy under any circumstances. But apart from this it seems to me that in every mind, be it inclined towards the artistic or the practical, there is always a receptive cell for things that transcend the awful troubles of everyday life.

The novels we have imbibed will not teach you anything that you can apply to any obvious problems of life. They will not help in the business office or in the army camp or in the kitchen or in the nursery. In fact, the knowledge I have been trying to share with you is pure luxury. It will not help you to understand the social economy of France or the secrets of a woman's heart or of a young man's heart. But it may help you, if you have followed my instructions, to feel the pure satisfaction which an inspired and precise work of art gives; and this sense of satisfaction in its turn goes to build up a sense of more genuine mental comfort, the kind of comfort one feels when one realizes that for all its blunders and boners the inner texture of life is also a matter of inspiration and precision.

In this course I have tried to reveal the mechanism of those wonderful toys—literary masterpieces. I have tried to make of you good readers who read books not for the infantile purpose of identifying oneself with the characters, and not for the adolescent purpose of learning to live, and not for the academic purpose of indulging in generalizations. I have tried to teach you to read books for the sake of their form, their visions, their art. I have tried to teach you to feel a shiver of artistic satisfaction, to share not the emotions of the people in the book but the emotions of its author—the joys and difficulties of creation. We did not talk around books, about books; we went to the center of this or that masterpiece, to the live heart of the matter.

Now the course comes to a close. The work with this group has been a particularly pleasant association between the fountain of my voice and a garden of ears—some open, others closed, many very receptive, a few merely ornamental, but all of them human and divine. Some of you will go on reading great books, others will stop reading great books after graduation; and if a person thinks he cannot evolve the capacity of pleasure in reading the great artists, then he should not read them at all. After all, there are other thrills in other domains: the thrill of pure science is just as pleasurable as the pleasure of pure art. The main thing is to experience that tingle in any department of thought or emotion. We are liable to miss the best of life if we do not know how to tingle, if we do not learn to hoist ourselves just a little higher than we generally are in order to sample the rarest and ripest fruit of art which human thought has to offer.

Nabokov's novel *Lolita* **(1955) ranks fourth on The Modern Library's list of the one hundred best English-language novels of the twentieth century;** *Pale Fire* **(1962) is fifty-third, and** *Speak, Memory* **(1951) is eighth on the nonfiction list.**

FACULTY AND THOROUGHBREDS

Cornell Alumni News, June 1946

It is interesting these days to sit back in the bleachers without personal responsibility and watch a university prepare itself for what lies ahead… Cornell, in common with kindred foundations across the land, is forced by circumstances not of its own creation to expand its academic horizons, its physical plant, and the number of its students. After the first two or three years, there may be expected a recession from the early peaks, but the chances are we will never go back to our former comfortable dimensions. Whether we like it or not, we're fated to grow. 1946 seems likely to become a year from which subsequent events are dated, like 1066, 1492, and 1776.

Everywhere one hears talk and sees signs of the extraordinary efforts that are being made to house the horde that is expected to descend upon us. But so far, we have picked up no mention in the Quadrangle of just how or where we are going to get the additional teaching staff to take care of them, although the matter is doubtless receiving prayerful consideration in high places.

And it is, of course, the crux of the whole business. You can dilute your student body with vast numbers of newcomers, lodge them hit or miss, but you can't, without grave danger, recruit a faculty from scrub stock to meet emergencies.

Building up and keeping a university faculty seems to have many points in common with creating a racing stable. If you have unlimited resources, it's possible to go into the competitive market and purchase horses of demonstrated speed and ability. But that method is expensive and seldom satisfactory. Continuing success in either venture is more apt to spring from the judicious breeding and handling of your own foals, from the intelligent selection and purchase of likely yearlings from competing stables. A youngster with good bloodlines, promising conformation, and a whispered reputation for speed in early morning time trials can often be picked up at a bargain. But once let him win a race or two, and the price becomes prohibitive.

Hold and train your own best colts; pick up the best of the young stock from other stables while they're cheap. That is commonly regarded as the secret of success in building up either a racing stable or a university faculty…

"Rym" Berry's column, "Now, In *My* **Time!," ran in the** *Cornell Alumni News* **from 1936 to 1950.**

Eve Weinschenker Paul '50

I spoke Russian fluently, but I wanted to improve my reading and writing of it. So in the fall of 1948, I signed up for Cornell's elementary Russian class. After that first class, the instructor took me aside and said that I could not continue, because my Russian was better than his. He said that I might want to try a new professor named Vladimir Nabokov who was teaching a seminar on Russian literature, and he sent me to Nabokov's office.

Nabokov had not written *Lolita* yet, and nobody was calling him a great author. He listened to my pitch without saying anything. Then he took a book down from his shelf and said, "read." So I did, and he said, "all right, you can take my course." That was it. There were about twelve of us, and we studied the great works of Russian literature in Russian. Gogol, Tolstoy, Pushkin, and Dostoevsky—although Nabokov didn't like Dostoevsky, he'd wave his hand and make a little dismissive noise whenever the name came up.

He kept to himself, mostly. He was very formal. It wasn't possible to make small talk with him. But his performances were indelible. He was madly in love with Tolstoy. He would go on and on about the luminosity of Tolstoy's writing. He would do all this wonderful, strange stuff. He would show us how Russians fought duels by getting up in front of the class and slashing away with an imaginary sword.

Mrs. Nabokov was another unusual thing about him. She was very lovely and she was always with him, and that was kind of mysterious. He would only refer to her as his

Nabokov wrote *Lolita* (1955) during summer breaks from Cornell. He wrote it in a moving car, while traveling on butterfly-collection trips in the western United States, Véra drove. When he attempted to burn unfinished drafts of the novel, it was Véra who stopped him. He called her the best-humored woman he had ever known.

Stacy Schiff

Stacy Schiff won the Pulitzer Prize in 2000 for her biography *Véra: Mrs. Vladimir Nabokov* (Random House, 1999).

What was Véra Nabokov doing in her husband's classroom, lecture after lecture? Nabokov had no graduate degree but was by inclination a master of specificity; the naturalist-professor instructed his students to dissect literature with a scientist's care. Which is precisely what they did in explicating the scene before them.

- Mrs. Nabokov was there to remind us that we were in the presence of greatness, and should not abuse that privilege with our inattention.
- Nabokov had a heart condition, and she was at hand with a phial of medicine to jump up at a moment's notice.
- That wasn't his wife. That was his mother.
- She was there because Nabokov was allergic to chalk dust, and because she didn't like his handwriting.
- To shoo away the co-eds.
- Because she was his encyclopedia, if he ever forgot anything.
- Because he had no idea what was going to come out of his mouth—and no memory of it after it did—so she had to write it all down so that he would remember what to ask on his exams.
- He was blind, and she was the seeing eye dog, which explained why they always arrived arm in arm.
- She was intended as living proof that he had a fan club.
- She graded his performance, in order to review it with him in the evenings.
- We all knew she was a ventriloquist.
- She had a gun in her purse, and was there to defend him.

assistant. We all wondered why she went to all of his classes.

I had a lot of remarkable professors during my years at Cornell. In English, I had Bill Sale; Morris Bishop, who was a great wit; and David Daiches, who was a world authority on Milton. I had Robert Cushman and Mario Einaudi in government. When I look back on it, I was just so lucky. And they weren't big classes, either. So many of these men were just starting their careers.

Eve Weinschenker Paul received a BA from the College of Arts and Sciences and a law degree from Columbia in 1952. She started working part-time for the Planned Parenthood Federation of America in 1971, joined it full-time in 1978, and was vice president and general counsel for the federation until 2003. She was also a Cornell trustee, serving from 1979 to 1984.

Meyer H. "Mike" Abrams
(1912–2015)

Professor M. H. Abrams began teaching English literature at Cornell in 1945.

Back in the early 1920s the *Saturday Evening Post* had just gone over to full color illustrations, which were quite new in those days. I was ten or eleven. They came out with an article about Cornell, and it began with a double-page spread of the terrace at Willard Straight Hall. On the terrace were tables and Cinzano umbrellas. Sitting at the tables were male and female students sipping long drinks. In the background was West Hill and Cayuga Lake. I looked at this and said, "What a magnificent place. Is this what college is like?"

In 1945, when I was asked to come to Cornell to be interviewed for the faculty, I had this image in my mind, so I asked to see the terrace. No umbrellas, no tables. Nothing but a gravel roof. But the lake and West Hill were still there, and that was enough to get me to Cornell. I found it to be a great and thriving university in an open environment that was a little less than rural. It was a combination I never dreamed I would see, and it exactly suited me. When I got to Cornell, I was able to relax and feel at home. I had been teaching at Harvard, which I found tense and competitive.

I was offered my Cornell job by George Holland Sabine 1903, who was not in the English department. He was a philosopher and administrator, and I thought he was making the offer because of some rule, but it wasn't that at all. He had been put in charge of the English Department because the professors there couldn't govern themselves. The department was in arrears.

Shortly after I got there, a friend of mine from Harvard visited me and we were standing in line for lunch. I saw Lane Cooper (1875–1959), the great Wordsworth scholar, in front of us and asked my friend if he would like to meet him. My friend turned white as a ghost and said he thought that Lane Cooper had been dead for twenty years.

So we hired like crazy after the war, and we brought in all sorts of people who wouldn't have been considered before. The department's size doubled in two or three years, all with younger people. The old-timers who couldn't get along were just outvoted. They persuaded an upstate New York native, Francis Mineka, to come home from the University of Texas. Within two years, Fran was chairman of the

English Department. He had incredible patience. When there was a contentious issue, Fran would talk to each teacher independently beforehand and work it out before the meeting. It became a very peaceful place, and Fran went on to be dean of the arts college.

Humanities at Cornell were deceptive in the 1940s. Everyone thought Cornell was strong in engineering and the sciences, and that was true, but the humanities faculty was full of diverse and innovative talent. One of the most memorable, to me, was Harold Thompson, who taught courses in folk literature. What he loved above all was ballads. He was passionate, almost fanatic about them.

Harold Thompson

Ballads were not a central concern of academia at that time, although they are now. Thompson was a pioneer. He was able to get all the great ballad writers and singers to come to Ithaca—people like Woody Guthrie, Pete Seeger, and many others—and he led the students in singing these songs, so the students nicknamed his course Romp and Stomp. I was crossing the Thurston Avenue bridge Saturday when a student pulled up in a car. He was from Syracuse, and he said he had come to visit Romp and Stomp, and where was it meeting?

Marshall Stearns was another. He was a professor of medieval literature, but he was also one of the first academics to be seriously interested in jazz. He used his personal resources to bring the great jazz musicians and orchestras to Cornell, and then he would invite them over to dinner at his house afterwards. They were glad to come, because very few universities were asking them at that time. I remember having dinner with Dizzy Gillespie and his orchestra, and also with the great Duke Ellington, who was the most urbane and courtly man I have ever met. Duke immediately became the host. He replaced Marshall. He met us at the door and said goodnight to us as we left with the utmost aplomb. I thought all universities did this sort of thing.

My office was in Goldwin Smith Hall. On one side of me was Morris Bishop, a major scholar of romance literature who wrote light verse perhaps as well as anyone in America ever did. He was a wonderful, portly, Edwardian person with a white moustache, and the master of the spontaneous limerick. On the other side of me was Vladimir Nabokov, writing what later turned out to be *Lolita*. The other English professors were just as impressive. At the end of the hall, clicking away on an old type-writer, was David Daiches, who with Morris Bishop was the best after-dinner speaker I have ever heard. He wrote learnedly about everything from Scotch whisky to the English translations of the Hebrew bible, with thirty volumes in between. At the other end of the hall, also clacking away, was Robert M. Adams, who wrote as fast as he could talk, and everything he wrote got printed. And here I was in the middle, silent and feeling guilty because I wasn't writing anything…

The son of an immigrant Jewish house painter, M. H. Abrams is best-known for writing *The Mirror and the Lamp: Romantic Theory and the Critical Tradition* (1953), which ranks twenty-fifth in The Modern Library's list of the one hundred best nonfiction English books of the twentieth century; for being general editor of the first seven editions of *The Norton Anthology of English Literature* (1962), which has sold more than eight million copies; and for teaching the literary critics Harold Bloom '51 and Eric D. Hirsch '50, the novelist Thomas Pynchon '59, and thousands more. He attended every Cornell football home game from 1945 through 2012, and received the National Humanities Medal in July 2014.

Eric D. Hirsch '50

After very confused freshman and sophomore years, when I lived in Sheldon Court surrounded by piles of dirty laundry, puzzling out who I was, and putting signs on the wall urging myself to "Study Russian!" (which absolved me from actually doing so), and having made very uneven grades, and having even been placed on "enforced leave" for a semester for not attending physical training and ROTC, I decided to reform. Henceforth, I would be a serious student. I would try to get into the English honors program.

M. H. Abrams was the program's director. He was already famous on campus for being really smart and interesting, and I thought he was just the sort of professor to guide my reformation. There was just one hitch. You had to be accepted into the elite program.

When I entered his office in Goldwin Smith Hall, he engaged me in quite a lively and genial chat, and this made me all the more intent on becoming serious. But I had to confess that my grades were not the best. In fact, the previous semester I had gotten into a big disagreement with my instructor over one of our assignments. I think it may have been *Henry IV, Part I*, but at this late date, I can't be sure. Anyway, I had to confess

(l–r) Professors Frederick Marcham (history), David Daiches (English), and Charles Jones (medieval studies) in 1948.

Cornell's main library was outdated and overcrowded in the 1940s, with 850,000 items jammed into a building designed for fewer than half that number. Crowding eased in 1961, when Olin Library opened on the former site of Boardman Hall.

the waiting room of an airport, and while we were chatting away I said, "Mike, have you read the latest porn sensation, *A Sea of Thighs*?"

"No," he shot back without a pause, "I haven't seen hide nor hair of that one."

E. D. Hirsch earned his PhD from Yale in 1956 and had a distinguished career as a professor of English at Yale and the University of Virginia. He is best known as the author of *Cultural Literacy: What Every American Needs To Know* (1987) and the founder of the Core Knowledge Foundation, which focuses on the content knowledge that should be taught at each elementary grade level. He is a member of the American Academy of Arts and Sciences.

Lydia Cushman Schurman '50

I didn't do well in school, and I was refused by every college I applied to except Cornell. I was also refused admission to the Junior Assembly dance, which is what really upset my mother. That put things into perspective for me. I could see what was important to her.

I went to the Chapin School in New York City. It was all girls, and not very challenging. Then, boom, I was at Cornell. All of a sudden I was competing with very bright people who were deadly serious about their work. They were grown men, and they weren't fooling around. The kinds of questions they asked were informed by their life experiences. I hadn't lived that fully and so I didn't know the questions to ask. Yet the men were not intimidating—they were challenging. They made you think.

to Professor Abrams that I had just gotten a C in the course.

"You got a C in English II?" he repeated.

"Yes," I replied, my heart sinking.

"It takes real talent to get a C in English II," he said. "Of course I'll accept you."

That was my first, indelible encounter with Mike Abrams. Over the years, as I built my career as a literary critic, we became friends.

In the midst of the jargon-infused wars constantly going on in English studies, he made a remark in his writing that was almost as memorable and important to me as that fateful one of 1948: "Good criticism requires a keen eye for the obvious."

And there was another Abramesque remark that I can't forget because it came so fast that only the quickest, most agile wit could have produced it. I encountered Mike in

I found freshman year very hard. Nothing in geology made any sense to me. Not only did you have to read maps, you had to draw them! Charles Love Durham PhD 1899, a professor who was a cousin of mine, was a classics teacher. Bless his heart, he gave me a C.

I remember one wonderful art professor. I had studied and studied how to identify paintings, and the exam was on Monday. I studied all weekend and on Sunday, I panicked. I called this teacher at home and told him I was a nervous wreck and couldn't take the pressure, and would have to fail. He said, "No, you're not going to fail. You're going home to Manhattan soon. Why don't you go to a museum when you're down there and write up your impressions of your visit. You can do that instead of taking the exam."

I have never forgotten that man. For the rest of my life, I have thought of him every time I went to a museum. I also turned in a good paper, because his kindness made me take the assignment very seriously.

Lydia Cushman Schurman is the granddaughter of Jacob Gould Schurman (1854-1942), who was president of Cornell from 1892 to 1920. Lydia worked for newspapers, taught school, and in 1968 became an English professor at Northern Virginia Community College. She earned a PhD in American Literature from the University of Maryland in 1984. She has published two critical anthologies of early dime novels and series books.

Bruce Ames '50

I attended the Bronx High School of Science, where I became immersed in biology and chemistry. I did my first scientific experiments there: I grew tomato root tips in

Bruce Ames

culture to determine the effect of plant hormones on their growth. The picture of those white roots growing on their own when stimulated by hormones stays in my mind. The pleasures of doing those experiments set me on the path to becoming a scientist.

I never was a top student, either in high school or in college. I had only a so-so memory and was easily distracted by some new enthusiasm, such as reading all of Tolstoy or mastering some new folk dance, when I should have been studying for an exam. Taking required courses was not a thing I could get very excited about—I am too undisciplined and driven by my own enthusiasms—though I did well in those few that sparked my interest.

Two such Cornell courses stay in my memory. One was a history class taught by Professor Frederick Marcham, in which we investigated historical incidents by reading all of the original documents, which, of course, were quite contradictory, and then tried to determine what was the most likely reality. The other was a course in biochemical genetics taught by professor Adrian Srb in the ag school. I had already taken several genetics courses, as I was interested in the subject, and Srb's course got me all excited because of my background in biochemistry. I applied to various graduate schools as I was finishing up, but was somewhat apprehensive because of my less than stellar grades. I was, in fact, turned down by Wisconsin. But luckily I was accepted by Cal Tech, perhaps because Srb, or one of my other references, saw potential in me.

Bruce Ames received a BA from Cornell and a PhD from the California Institute of Techology in 1953. He is professor of biochemistry and molecular biology at the University of California, Berkeley, and a senior scientist at Children's Hospital Oakland Research Institute. He is the inventor of the Ames test, a system for easily and cheaply testing the ability of compounds to induce genetic mutations and cancers. He is a fellow of the American Academy of Arts and Sciences and a member of the National Academy of Sciences.

Marion Steinmann '50

In biochemistry class, Professor Adrian Srb assigned us to raise fruit flies in glass jars back in our rooms. We had to keep the tiny flies fed, carefully keep the generations separated, and periodically dose them with chloroform so that we could inspect them with a magnifying glass and find out what unknown (to us) genetic anomaly they carried, such as different colored eyes or malformed wings.

Professor Srb and biochemistry professor James B. Sumner, who won the Nobel Prize in chemistry in 1946, taught us that the molecule that carries genetic information from generation to generation—of both fruit flies and humans—is deoxyribonucleic acid (DNA), although its structure was not then known. Molecular biology is all about structure, structure, structure. It was not until 1953 that scientists at Cambridge University worked out the now famous double-helix structure of DNA.

Professor Sumner was one of two Nobel Prize winners at Cornell in the late 1940s. The other was professor Peter Debye, chairman of the chemistry department.

Don Christiansen '50

In my sophomore year, Professor Everett Strong initiated the Cornell Engineering Cooperative Program, which sent electrical engineering students to work as engineering interns. I spent two off-campus terms at Philco Corporation, working in its component test laboratory and its radar systems development laboratory. The experience was invaluable in helping me choose my post-graduate employment. As graduation neared, recruiters from IBM, RCA, GE, and others descended on Ithaca with attractive employment offers.

When the general manager (himself!) of the Salem Division of the Hytron Electronics Corporation (soon thereafter to become the CBS Electronics Division) arrived, I was intrigued. I guessed that he had elected to travel to Cornell to interview students who had taken Professor Walter Jones's widely known vacuum-tube laboratory course. Jones, a 1925 electrical engineering (EE) graduate of Cornell, had risen to the position of chief engineer of the Sylvania radio tube division before returning to teach at Cornell. His industry contacts helped him obtain the equipment needed to make his Cornell laboratory a premium teaching facility. It may have been the only one of its kind.

During my interview, the Hytron executive seemed concerned that many newly minted EEs might not expect to get their hands dirty or even venture onto the factory floor. As the interview concluded he asked me whether I'd object to carrying a pair of gas pliers in my pocket, and I said I wouldn't. "You've got the job!" he responded.

My willingness to experiment, think flexibly, and get dirty was partly due to the example of my friend, classmate, and fellow navy veteran, Wilson Greatbatch. Wilson was always thinking, always ready for a discussion, never at a loss for words, and, oddly enough, seemingly never in a hurry or under stress, quite possibly good characteristics for a prolific inventor. He also possessed a good sense of humor.

Wilson was a ham radio operator, having acquired his license while still in high school. During World War II, he flew in torpedo bombers from the aircraft carrier USS *Monterey* as a radioman and gunner. At war's end, he married, worked a year as a telephone installer-repairman, and then entered Cornell. To supplement his income he ran the university radio transmitter on weekends, and built IF amplifiers for what became the Arecibo radio telescope in Puerto Rico.

Upon graduation, Wilson began aerospace work at the Cornell Aeronautical Laboratory in Buffalo. He also worked part time at the University of Buffalo's Chronic Disease Research Institute, where he built a Khz marker oscillator using a transistor and a UTC transformer. In a story he often repeated over the years, he accidentally inserted a much larger value resistor into the circuit instead of the intended 10K resistor. The result was a blocking oscillator that proved ideal for use as an implantable cardiac pacemaker. This discovery prolonged the lives of millions of people.

Wilson and I were both fascinated with the question of what skills an engineer needed to develop something worthy of being called an "invention." He died with three hundred and thirty patents to his credit, so I guess he had figured out the

Interns in the Cornell Engineering Cooperative Program, with electrical engineering Professor Everett Strong (front, center), the founder of the program. Beginning in their junior year, the "co-ops" spent three terms as engineering interns with a particular company. The first group, in 1945, consisted of twelve students with assignments at Philco Corporation. By 1975, seventy-five students participated with thirty-seven companies involved, including IBM, Hewlett-Packard, Xerox, and General Electric. Photo supplied by Don Christiansen (second row, fourth from left).

Wilson Greatbatch.

answer to our question during his long, productive life. After he died, I tried to summarize his philosophy of invention. Here is an excerpt:

On design and innovation, Wilson's paradigm was "to look for a place to use something I do very well," rather than to look for some intractable problem to solve.

In the initial design stage he preferred to work alone, so he would be aware of errors or opportunities for improvement.

On the subject of creativity, he warned the many young student classes he spoke to over the years that any set of rules for achieving creativity would be fruitless if not accompanied by hard work, long hours, and, at times, no monetary reward. In his memoir he wrote, "To ask for a successful experiment, for professional stature, for financial reward, or for peer approval is asking to be paid for what should be a labor of love."

His modest view of professional recognition notwithstanding, he em-phasized the importance of membership in organizations pertinent to an engineer's special interests.

His concern with ethics led to his warning that one should never allow his name to be listed as an author unless he participated in the work and fully supported its conclusions.

On the topic of persistence, Wilson accepted the inevitability of project failure, stating that while nine out of ten experiments may fail, the success of the tenth will pay for the others.

Wilson Greatbatch '50 (1919–2011) was named to the National Inventors Hall of Fame in 1986 and was awarded the National Medal of Technology in 1990. He was elected a fellow of the Institute of Electrical and Electronics Engineers (IEEE), the American Society of Mechanical Engineers (ASME), and the American College of Cardiology. He was the first winner of the Karapetoff Award for Outstanding Technical Accomplishment from Eta Kappa Nu, the honor society of the IEEE.

Marjorie Leigh Hart '50

I knew I wanted to go into engineering by the time I started high school, because I enjoyed analytical and mechanical things. My father was an engineer. He got me a tutor in higher math, and I did well enough that I got a math prize. I wanted to go to Cornell because its engineering program was renowned, and also because family friends recommended it to us.

I chose chemical engineering because I thought it would be easier for a woman to find a job in food processing, fiber, or some other industry where women already had a presence. The dean told me that so many veterans were applying to the engineering school that he couldn't take me that year. So I went into the College of Arts and Sciences, but with the understanding that if I did well in chemistry, I could apply again. My freshman chemistry grades were good enough that they let me in.

The director of the school was Fred "Dusty" Rhodes, PhD 1914. He was the founder of the chemical engineering school and was famous for being gruff and unapologetic

Dusty Rhodes

about how hard the courses were. Every year, he would start his classes by saying, "thirty percent of you won't be here next year." But underneath, I found him to be quite softhearted. When he interviewed me after I reapplied, he looked over his half-glasses at me and asked, "So you want to be an engineer. Do you drink beer?" I said, "No, sir, but I can learn!" He let me in.

Dusty turned out to be amazingly supportive. I found the courses hard, and there were several times when I could have dropped out, but each time he stepped in and said or did the right thing to get me past the rough spot. There were a couple of women in the class, but several dropped out. There were just three women engineers who graduated in our class: Eleanor "Mickey" Egan [Hartzell], Marion Francis, and me.

The big course in chemical engineering was operations research, which Dusty taught himself. You did a team experiment and wrote a report on it. He personally graded all forty or fifty reports, and he also rewrote how it should have been done, and he did all this in longhand. Then he gave you two grades—one for content, and one for writing—on a scale of one to ten. He had been an English instructor early in his academic career, and he believed that expressing your findings clearly was as important as getting the results. Lastly, he multiplied the two numbers to give you your final grade. So you had to get nines and tens to do well. Two eights would give you a grade of 64, and that's a D.

Dusty also got me my start at Exxon, which was called Standard Oil of New Jersey at the time. I was still thinking that I would apply to food and fiber companies, where women were more likely to find jobs, but he called up his contacts at Standard Oil and told them that they should take me, and they did.

And I must say, I never felt any sex discrimination at Cornell, and only once did I feel it at Exxon. My Cornell engineering professors knew how to listen and show you where you were going wrong. They knew how to get the best out of a person. Cornell and Exxon were both meritocracies. If you did good work, you would get the rewards.

Bruce Davis '50, MBA '52

A lot of people never made it through Dusty Rhodes's Unit Operations Lab. You had to get your report in by noon on Wednesday. That meant you had to hand it in before the chimes in the library bell tower stopped ringing. If you were late, you still had to do the report and turn it in, and also resubmit it with corrections, but you would get a zero.

I remember racing up the hill to make that deadline. I was on the football team in 1947 as a lineman. I would come back after practice on Tuesday and stay up all night to write the report. Sometimes I would even have to cut classes on Wednesday morning. I could not miss that deadline because I couldn't tolerate a zero in my average. So I would go to Wednesday football practice on no sleep.

Wednesday was scrimmage day. I remember several times when they called a trap play when I was on the offensive line. I was supposed to pull out and cut behind the line in order to block somebody on the other side, with the other lineman doing the same thing. There were many times when the two linemen would run into each other in the middle with the ball carrier between us, because of me.

But Dusty Rhodes ran a damn good ship. The discipline he insisted on was important. He taught us to set a timetable and live up to it, which is excellent training for business. I remember that he had a copper casting above his desk that read, "Enjoy yourself—it's later than you think."

Bruce Davis was an executive for several chemical companies. He was CEO of Hooker Chemical in the 1970s, during the clean-up of Love Canal, a toxic waste dump Hooker had created in Niagara Falls, New York, in the 1950s.

Eve Weinschenker Paul '50

I grew up in a Jewish household on the upper west side of Manhattan, and, although we were not a particularly religious family, our community was devastated by the Holocaust. My parents were good Roosevelt Democrats. I did have first-hand experience with anti-Semitism growing up, although I didn't recognize it for what it was at the time. I suppose I was ready to hear what Professor Cushman had to say.

Robert Cushman was not a lawyer, but he taught a course in constitutional law that had an enormous effect on me. The way he taught the law and constitutional principles was extremely inspiring. It unlocked my ambition. I took his survey course as a freshman, and went on to take seminars and independent study courses from him. His approach was to explain how certain principles of law were vindicated by Supreme Court decisions. He was a big defender of civil liberties, and he put the bug in me to follow the same path.

Many of us were fired with the desire to vindicate constitutional principles. It was a tense time, with loyalty oaths and witch hunts and so on, and the Holocaust kind of hung over everything. Cushman believed that these things violated the bedrock principles of the constitution, and that we had to defend those principles.

Robert Cushman

(1889–1969)

Professor Robert Cushman taught political science at Cornell from 1923 to 1957.

SEPTEMBER 19, 1951: I have been discussing some of the notable ways in which Cornell University broke new paths, some of the ingredients which went into the making of what we call the Cornell tradition.

I think if one stands off and looks at the composite achievement of these two pioneers, Ezra Cornell and Andrew Dickson White, one sees running through it all a dominating principle which governed all they did. They were driven by the conviction that American college and university education needed a new charter of freedom; and virtually every new idea that went into the founding of Cornell was a plank in that charter.

They were bent upon founding a university devoted to the ideal of a completely free intellectual life. The old restraints, taboos, prejudices, dogmas, and superstitions which had warped and suffocated American higher education were to find no place on the Cornell campus. The free life of a great university is a constant challenge to the teachers to broaden the vision and deepen the understanding of their students, a challenge to the scholar to extend the frontiers of human knowledge, and Cornell and White were determined that the life of Cornell University should be a free life.

It is unfortunately true that the tradition of a college or a university is not always noble or inspiring. It may be narrow; it may be bigoted;

it may even be shoddy. There are institutions in which tradition demands that the president be a devout and orthodox member of some religious sect or denomination. There are others in which he must be ruggedly conservative in his political and economic views. In many Southern institutions, he must sympathize with, and administer, rules of racial segregation. In still others, he may go his own way as long as his educational policies do not endanger the success of the football team! In all of these cases, tradition lies like the hand of the dead upon the university.

I have tried to make clear that the Cornell tradition is the tradition of freedom. That tradition does not dictate what [the president] must do, or what he must not do. It tells him merely that it is customary for Cornell presidents to lead and not to follow, to plot their own courses, to defend and cherish their own ideals. The only restriction or limitation which the Cornell tradition imposes upon him is that which is imposed by his own sense of responsibility to conserve scrupulously and to exploit generously the freedom which is the life-blood of a university.

A university is a community of scholars, teachers, and students in quest of the truth. Its life is the life of freedom, for "the truth shall make you free."

Robert Cushman was a major influence on campus life, serving as a Cornell faculty trustee. He was also a fellow of the American Academy of Arts and Sciences, and president of the American Political Science Association. After he retired from Cornell, he was editor in chief of the *Documentary History of the Ratification of the Constitution*. His book *Leading Constitutional Decisions* (1929) is still in print.

Wilbur Parker '50, MBA '50

I graduated from Southside High School in Newark, New Jersey, in 1944. My parents did not finish school and we only had one book at home, an encyclopedia, but I loved school. I ended up as the class valedictorian, and I was also a running back on the football team. It was a segregated environment. We had to sit in the balcony at the movie theater, we couldn't go into certain restaurants, and we could only use the public swimming pool on designated days. Back then, as a child, I accepted that this was how the world worked.

The principal of my grammar school, Mr. Snavely, happened to be the brother of Cornell's football coach. I was also good at mechanical drawing, so Cornell offered me a scholarship in electrical engineering with the assumption that I would also play football. I went to Ithaca within days of finishing high school. But I also enlisted in the army reserves, and two months after I got to Ithaca, I left and enrolled in the segregated pilot training program in Tuskegee, Alabama.

It was in the army that my attitudes started to change. On the troop train down to Alabama, for example, there were German prisoners of war, and they were treated better than the black U.S. soldiers were. During basic training, in a hot Alabama summer, they wouldn't let us use the drinking fountain. And I found that a lot of people thought African-Americans should not fly, so they stacked the deck against us. Most Tuskegee trainees never flew, even when the war was on, so when it ended I knew there would be no chance that I would ever get in an army plane. I started to think something wasn't right. I had volunteered to serve my country. I should be treated equally.

I could still play football. But the army had another rule saying that a person couldn't play football and be in the pilot program at the same time. So I quit the pilot program and joined the Tuskegee War Hawks, an all-black army football team. I was nineteen, and I got the chance to play with men who were much older and more experienced than I was. We traveled and played in big stadiums in Washington, D.C., and New York City. Then I was discharged, and I returned to Cornell in the fall of 1946.

Shortly after I got to Ithaca, two things happened that had a big effect on me. The first was a serious knee injury that ended my athletic career. The second thing was a book by a Swedish social economist named Gunnar Myrdal called *An American Dilemma: The Negro Problem and Modern Democracy*. Myrdal had been hired by a foundation to study segregation, and it had purposely chosen a non-American so the results would be free of bias.[1] When I was in the military, someone recommended that I read it. So as soon as I got to Cornell, I bought a copy. I still have it with me.

---

[1] The Carnegie Foundation for the Advancement of Teaching hired Gunnar Myrdal, a Nobel laureate, to study race relations in the United States. Myrdal's report, *An American Dilemma* (1944), gave an enormous boost to the movement for black civil rights. The book enumerates the obstacles that prevent African-Americans from full participation in American society and proposes solutions. Myrdal implores his readers to grow out of their prejudice, and he also recommends that Americans take steps to improve the circumstances of its African-American population, so that high-achieving blacks can disprove whites' preconceived notions.

Everything changed for me when I read that book. I suddenly realized that all the limitations I had been living under all my life were injustices, and I was being challenged to change them. I realized that if America was going to become a truly great nation, it needed to unite. We had to find a cure and overcome this moral, social, and politically senseless disease of racism. My whole life's effort was set in that direction.

I switched from engineering to economics because economics was more people-oriented. We were allowed to double-register in

William Shannon

the arts college and the business school at the same time, so I took undergraduate and graduate courses simultaneously. And I got some good advice from a professor, William H. Shannon, who had also been a captain in the army. He convinced me that I could have a great impact on society if I understood how to use accounting as a management tool. So I received a BA and an MBA from Cornell in 1950. I was the first African-American graduate of Cornell's business school.

I worked very hard as a student, so I didn't have much of a social life. I did go to parties at Watermargin house, and I went to meetings and dances sponsored by Alpha Phi Alpha, the black fraternity. There were not many black faces at Cornell then, but I never felt excluded or discriminated against. People took me for what I was.

Today, I give Cornell a lot of credit for the things I've done. When I got to Ithaca, it was a real challenge to adjust to such a small

town with so few black faces. But the acceptance and encouragement I received from my Cornell professors and classmates made the transition a lot easier. Cornell let me see larger possibilities.

Wilbur Parker became New Jersey's first African-American Certified Public Accountant in 1954. He was budget director for the City of Newark and the secretary of their school board. He also marched on Washington with Martin Luther King in 1963, and in 1969 he went to Fayette, Mississippi, to help train the administrative staff of the city's first black mayor, Charles Evers. In 2003, Cornell's business school gave him its first annual Wilbur Parker Distinguished Alumni Award, which recognizes "African-American alumni who demonstrate outstanding professional achievement and commitment to their community."

John Mellor '50 MS '51, PhD '54

I grew up on a farm in Vermont and when I was accepted by Cornell, my plan was to get an education, return home, return to raising chickens, and maybe run for political office. But I ended up going to Oxford University, getting a doctorate from Cornell, teaching there for twenty-four years, and then having a wonderfully rich and varied career in food policy and international development, which hasn't ended yet. I can trace every one of those twists and turns to the memorable experiences I had on East Hill.

I was just seventeen when I arrived in 1946, and there were veterans all over the place. I had to grow up in a hurry. After three months, my twenty-seven-year-old roommate, an ex-army captain, sat me down to sternly tell me that his name was Dave, not "sir" or "Mr. Spalding."

At the College of Agriculture I met professor Harry Love, chairman of the Department of Plant Breeding. He had built the plant breeding capacity at Nanking University in the 1920s, making a mighty contribution to China's agricultural output. Love taught me that if you want to develop agriculture, you should build capacity in higher education. I also learned from Professor Glenn Hedlund, who told me enthralling stories about traveling on the Trans-Siberian railway in the 1930s. He opened my eyes to travel. Hedlund also introduced me to John Lossing Buck's classic book *Chinese Farm Economy* (1930), which showed me the primary data resources I used for decades. And from Profes-

Harry Love

Glenn Hedlund

"Frosty" Hill

sor Stan Warren, I learned how to extract the wisdom of practicing farmers. I learned this while on a year's leave from Cornell in rural India, an experience that provided the core of my knowledge of development economics.

The most important influence I had at Cornell might have been Professor Forrest Hill, whom everyone called "Frosty." He had helped set up the Farm Credit Administration for

FDR during the Great Depression, refinancing millions of failing farm loans. We would talk over lunch, and I began to understand how poorer countries might get their economies on the right track. I got the benefit of first-hand experience from a man who had developed one of America's key economic institutions.

I lived at Telluride House, and one evening Richard Feynman, the brilliant young physicist who was also a faculty resident there, said that he would like to read some economics. So I dashed to the library and came back with a copy of Paul Samuelson's *Foundations of Economic Analysis* (1947), a book most normal people would consider highly mathematical. Dick had breakfast with me the next day to discuss it. He had read the whole thing the night before. He said it was interesting enough to keep him up late, and that the mathematics were simple enough that he could run through it at one sitting.

That interaction taught me that I did not have what it took to become an accomplished mathematical economist, so I moved on to applied economics and international affairs. It also impressed me to see a great mind at work on something new.

The next night, Feynman played the radiators of Telluride as if they were bongo drums. He loved to do this. He would go down in the basement and wail away on the pipes. The whole building would vibrate. From this I learned not to take myself too seriously!

John Mellor became a professor of agricultural economics at Cornell and was also director of Cornell's Center for International Studies. He left Cornell in 1977 and served as director of the International Food Policy Research Institute, and chief economist of

the United States Agency for International Development (USAID). He is a fellow of the American Academy of Arts and Sciences, the American Association for the Advancement of Science, and the American Agricultural Economics Association.

Richard Feynman
(1918–1988)

Richard Feynman was a professor of physics at Cornell from 1945 to 1950.

I had been invited to live at the Telluride House at Cornell, which is a group of boys that have been specially selected because of their scholarship, because of their cleverness or whatever it is, to be given free board and lodging and so on, because of their brains. They live at this house, and they like to have a faculty member live there too each year, and they select different ones, and I was living there. And this was very convenient. The meals were available and everything was available, and you didn't have to worry about all that. I could work in my room, or play with the

Richard Feynman

guys, or work on the place; so it was very good. It's there that I did the fundamental work…

I was seeing something in space and time. There were quantities associated with points in space and time, and I would see electrons going along, scattered at this point, then it goes over here, scatters at this point, so I'd make little pictures of it going… Instead of thinking so abstractly, then I would use the pictures more and more. And there was a time, definitely, when I was at this Telluride House at Cornell, and I was working on the self-energy of the electron, and I was making a lot of these pictures to visualize the various terms, and thinking about the various terms, that a moment occurred—I remember distinctly—when I looked at these [pictures], and they looked very funny to me. They were funny-looking pictures.

Feynman's "Penguin diagrams" refer to one-loop processes in which a quark temporarily changes its flavor and then engages in a tree interaction. John Ellis, a British physicist, named these diagrams in 1977 after he lost a bar bet in which he promised to put the word "penguin" in his next paper. Ellis says that he realized that Feynman's famous diagram looked like a penguin "and the rest, as they say, is history."

And I did think consciously: "Wouldn't it be funny if this really turns out to be useful, and the *Physical Review* would be all full of these funny-looking pictures? It would look very amusing…"

Professor Feynman shared the Nobel Prize in Physics in 1966 for "fundamental work in quantum electrodynamics, with deep-ploughing consequences for the physics of elementary particles."

Gerhard Loewenberg '49, MA '50, PhD '55

Two courses in my freshman year at Cornell turned out to have a decisive influence on my education. One was in comparative government, and the other was in American philosophy. The comparative government course was taught by an Italian émigré professor, Mario Einaudi, who fascinated me. The rumor was that his father was going to become the president of Italy. He had flashing eyes, a shock of dark hair, and a restless manner, pacing up and down as he lectured in a theater-like auditorium, and occasionally losing us because of allusions we did not understand or because of a pronunciation we could not decipher. The net effect was charismatic.

The second influential course was one in American philosophy that shaped my future at Cornell for an entirely different reason. The course had about forty students and I was among the minority who would raise questions and join in the discussion. That made me conspicuous to a fellow student who lived in an unusual self-governing

scholarship house on campus. He mentioned me to his fellow residents in that house, who invited me down for an interview.

Telluride House was a program of Telluride Association, which comprised senior members and recent alumni of the House. The association had the responsibility for running and maintaining things, adopting an annual budget, and inviting students to live at the house. Students were invited if they demonstrated "intellectual curiosity, democratic self-governance, and social responsibility." The house had been closed during the war and was getting started again, with just a dozen students in the spring semester of 1946, but looking forward to a full complement of thirty students by fall. I ended up living in Telluride House for four years.

The principle that Telluride followed for roommate assignments was to match people with others least like themselves. My first roommate was Roy Pierce '47, PhD '50, a tall, lanky, seemingly severe person… [Roy] encouraged me to take more courses with Mario Einaudi, who eventually became my PhD advisor.

I moved out of Telluride House for the 1950–51 academic year after I married Ina Perlstein '52. During those last two years at Cornell, our relationship with Einaudi deepened significantly. The European tradition of teaching includes caring for a student personally, and also expecting the student to do things for you in a personal way. Eventually we became house-sitters for Mario and his family, and we took care of their two teenage sons. Ina became his secretary, and he dictated his book manuscript to her.

Einaudi taught me high scholarly standards. He expected that

I would do extensive reading and research in Europe. He and his wife were highly sophisticated, and that was how I wanted to be, too.

Jerry Loewenberg, who escaped from Nazi Germany with his parents as a child, is an emeritus professor of political science at the University of Iowa, the former dean of its College of Liberal Arts, a fellow of the American Academy of Arts and Sciences, and co-founder of the *Legislative Sciences Quarterly*.

Mario Einaudi
(1904–1994)

Mario Einaudi was a professor of government at Cornell from 1945 to 1972. He wrote this in 1959.

One should first be clear as to what America has undertaken. This is nothing less, in principle, than the education, up to the age of about 20, of all American youth.

This was not quite true, notwithstanding Jefferson's dream, in the past. Education for most was limited to younger age groups. College education was reserved to the few who could afford it or who wanted it, or who satisfied the stiffer admission requirements then prevailing.

But within the last generation we have seen not only a tremendous expansion in the number of boys and girls going to secondary schools, but a universal craving to enter the magic world of college life. New conditions of life, the experience of war, a sense of freedom, the higher security and welfare of the American people, the coming of age of recent immigrant groups, a fresh realization of what college education contributes to help meet the new opportunities of a smoothly working economic

Mario Einaudi.

system, all of these factors are at the origin of the revolution in American higher education. As the older private universities could no longer satisfy the multitudes clamoring at their doors, state colleges and universities, throughout the land, undertook to bear most of the burden of higher education. Even in the East, state universities—until not so long ago the typical culture fruit of the prairies and the Western mountains—were called upon to face the incredibly large numbers of students. A new university world has sprung up, run by the people and for the people, ready to admit anybody with a minimum show of good will and literacy and offering new concepts of education to the startled consideration of those who remember the waning traditions of the past.

Nearly four million students will soon be crowding America's universities and colleges, most of them doing so at public expense. The United States is the first country to have given such wide practical translation to the theoretical conclusion that universal education is necessary in a democratic state.

One can visualize the day when no one who wants and deserves to go to college will be unable to

do so. Already the frustrations and class antagonisms showing up when one child goes to school while his neighbor does not, have tended to disappear. Scholarship assistance has diminished the waste of talents fostered by poverty. The broad sweep of liberal arts colleges—of education for education's sake, without regard to diplomas, degrees, or professional interest—has given a fresh lift and sense of purpose to the young men and women busy all over the country in the daily routines of their lives.

There is impressive moral intensity in a policy that sets out to treat everybody on equal educational terms and which, with unprecedented speed, attempts to extend to all the privileges of school up to adulthood. This is a binding and universal experience giving a unique democratic flair to American society and makes life in America one of relationships among equals, easy-going and cheerful, free from patronizing attitudes, the result of years of growing up shared in common.

It is only when one tries to measure the scope of the commitment and the high conceptions it is based upon, that one can evaluate the difficulties the experiment has faced, its shortcomings, and the troubled issues to which it has led.

Mario Einaudi was the eldest son of Luigi Einaudi, who was exiled from Italy in the 1930s when he refused to sign a Fascist oath. Luigi Einaudi returned and became the first president of Italy, serving from 1948 to 1955. When Mario began teaching government at Cornell, the department had five members; when he retired, it had twelve. After his retirement, Mario Einaudi endowed and spent decades building the Luigi Einaudi Foundation in Turin and the Mario Einaudi Center for International Studies at Cornell.

Richard Feynman

Professor Feynman left Cornell for the California Institute of Technology in 1950 for several reasons.

The worst thing [about Ithaca] is the weather... It was a day on which it was cold and raining and slushy. My car was beginning to skid, and I had to put chains on in the cold. I was trying to tighten those little clamps on the inside of the tire, and my hands were cold and the pressure hurt when I tried to push them. And I said to myself, "This is crazy!" So I decided—that was kind of a deciding moment—to get out of that part of the world. But altogether, other things always add to it.

You see, I'm a one-sided fellow. I understand and love the sciences. But there are many fields of intellectual things that I don't really go for, like literature, psychology, philosophy, and so on, unless it's done in a very sort of scientific way. I'm not a wide guy, only very wide in the sciences, but very much in the sciences and limited. So I found [Cornell] quite dilute...

It isn't exactly that the subjects weren't interesting, because I can find the history of the Aztecs and the Incas, and so on, fascinating. But somehow or other, these guys weren't—I don't know how to explain it. In addition to which, the student body is diluted to such a pitch by all kinds of things. Like they have home economics. They have lots of girls studying home economics, and it's supposed to be a university! If I compared the work and the care and the thought that goes into what I ask of my physics students to get a degree, to the nonsense which is all some little silly girl has to do to get a degree in home economics—and I knew precisely what it was, because I had girlfriends and they would ask me questions and I knew what they were doing—I began to get disgusted with the dilution.

Jane Wigsten McGonigal Crispell '50, PhD '84

I knew that some people thought we were not serious, but I didn't have much direct contact with those people. The College of Home Economics was a small state school surrounded by the College of Agriculture, which was a bigger state school. A lot of us were working our way through college. There was no tuition. I waited tables and that paid for my meals. So my only cost was the room, and that wasn't much. I think one reason people looked down on us was because we weren't well-to-do.

The college required us to study all kinds of different things. We did not specialize, and that was fine with me, because I have always believed that anything is connected to everything. And the courses were not easy. We took the same freshman chemistry course everyone else did. In one course, they said go find the oldest tombstone in the oldest cemetery you can and write an essay about that person. That was challenging, but also fun. I also took advantage of the rule allowing you to take courses at the other colleges, which was great. I took a history course from Clinton Rossiter.

My social life was all at the agricultural school. All the men I dated were aggies, and the parties I went to were at Alpha Zeta, the fraternity for ag students. I lived with four other women in a suite in Risley, all from the Class of 1950. There was Ellen Forbes [Andrews], whose father knew my father. She and I roomed together as freshmen because her father set that up in advance. We moved to Risley and roomed with Bev Collins [Adams], Kitty Rusack [Adams], and Frances Duncan [Stowe]. We were all from upstate New York—Syracuse, Homer, Horseheads—and Kitty was the only one who wasn't in home economics.

So we did come from these small towns, but I don't think we were provincial or small-minded. Cornell is a mix. One day, I went over to the livestock pavilion and braided the tail of a cow for my cousin, Warren Wigsten '50, whose cow was in a livestock show. His family owned Highline Farms in Pleasant Valley, New York, and their cattle were sold internationally. At the same time, as a freshman in Balch, I was on the same hall with two foreign students whose parents worked at the United Nations. We taught them how to walk in shoes with heels, because they had never done that before.

The College of Home Economics had an apartment where you would live and work as part of your training. I remember that the apartment had one telephone, which was out in the hall, and we signed up in shifts to decide who would answer the phone. You take care of the most important stuff first. And yes, there was a live baby in the apartment. It was a baby boy, which came in handy because my first child was a boy.

Jane Wigsten worked as an agent for Cornell Cooperative Extension in Ithaca and elsewhere in upstate New York, moved to California, and returned to Ithaca and the Cooperative Extension in 1978. She worked on statewide recruitment and staff development and was married to Carl Crispell '60 in 1986. She served on the Cooperative Extension faculty and was an adjunct professor in the education department of the Ag College until 1998.

Elizabeth (Betty Ann) Jacques Browne '52

I remember Denny Domecon as an ideal baby. He was very docile and sweet and comfortable and he slept through the night, even at five months of age. If every woman had one like him, twice as many would have been born.

We didn't know the baby's real name, because he was an orphan. And he would only stay a few months before a new one replaced him. Thinking back on it, I am appalled that Cornell got away with putting an infant in a lab for undergraduates to practice on. At the same time, he did get superb care. The apartment supervisor was right there if anything went wrong, and they even sent in a pediatrician to check on him every couple of days.

I met my husband at Cornell and we were married in 1954, while he was still studying for his master's degree in agricultural economics.

He ended up with a job that made us move a lot. Our first baby was born in Ithaca, and then we had another in Buffalo, a third in Pittsburgh, and the next six were born in Youngstown. We had two more after we moved to Cleveland. Who would ever thought that I would end up raising eleven babies?

I got interested in Cornell Home Economics when I was in high school in the tiny little town of Lowville, New York. I became fast friends with Margaret Redmond '52. We both worked our way through school as waitresses at the girl's dorms. She and I kept notebooks and every week we made a point of going to something new and different that we hadn't ever seen before. That was one of the best things about Cornell for me. I had never even seen a black person before I got to Cornell. It was a beautiful, unfolding part of my life.

Elizabeth Browne lives in Cleveland. She has eleven grandchildren.

MOTHERING DENNY DOMECON

LIFE MAGAZINE, APRIL 7, 1952

Each of Cornell's two practice apartments is equipped with a real baby. The five-month-old boy was lent to the college by a welfare agency, and since his name was not given out, the girls christened him Denny Domecon (for domestic economy). To most of the girls, who had never been held responsible for a child, the job of mother is the most bewildering of any in the apartment… Betty Ann Jacques, who took care of Denny for one week, found she had no trouble getting sitters because the other girls loved to play with him. Her only worry was that he was getting too much feminine attention.

"Sheila Domecon," seven months, was baby-in-residence in the home economics practice apartment in 1948. Her temporary foster mothers are Ruth Davidson '49 and Grace Hubbell '49 (at right).

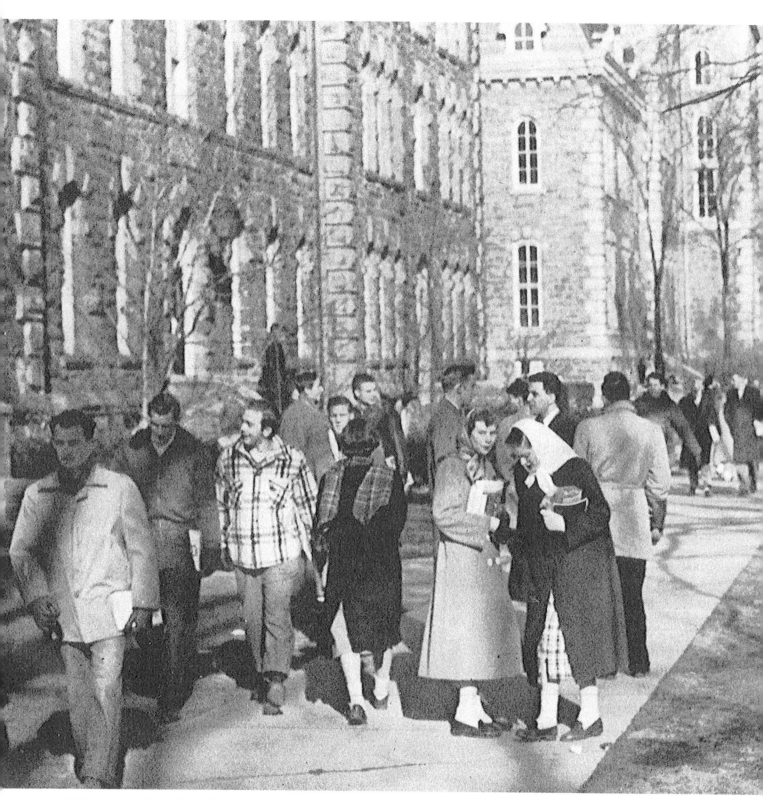

Main quadrangle of the College of Arts and Sciences, 1948.

CHAPTER 5

Containing Women

Three hundred and fifty women enrolled as Cornell freshman in 1946, making up 18 percent of an entering class of 1,956, or one woman for every 4.6 men. They were not spread around the campus equally. About one-third of students in the College of Arts and Sciences were female, along with nearly every student in the College of Home Economics. Yet only a few women were enrolled in the Colleges of Agriculture, Engineering, and Architecture.

Rules for the Fairer Sex

Unlike men, almost all undergraduate women were required to live in a university dormitory or a sorority house, all of which were supervised by live-in housemothers. A finite number of so-called "female beds" limited the number of women who could be admitted to the university. The women's dorms were clustered in a group just north of Fall Creek, across the Thurston Avenue Bridge.

Cornell women of the 1940s enjoyed officially unrestricted access to academics, but they were also subject to the detailed regulations of an organization called the Women's Self-Government Association (WSGA). Women had to obey a strict nightly curfew, follow a mandatory dress code, and observe restrictions on where they could go, both on and off campus. Many former co-eds have happy memories of luxurious dorms and what they called "gracious living." Some say that the curfew allowed them to develop intellectually and socially in environments free of social pressure. Nearly all women quietly accepted the rules as the way things were—even though the president of the WSGA in 1949–50 says she wanted the curfew abolished.

Marion Steinmann '50

We women were literally locked in at night. On weeknights in 1946, freshman women had to be back in their dorms by 9:30 p.m., sophomores by 10:30 p.m., juniors by 11 p.m., and seniors by midnight. On Friday and Saturday nights we could stay out until 12:30 p.m. On Saturday date nights, just before the chimes of the library bell tower struck the half-hour, we would all scurry back to our dorms or sorority houses, just like Cinderella.

When we returned to our dorm or sorority house in the evening, we had to present ourselves to a classmate who had been assigned monitor duty and sign in. The monitor was supposed to penalize us one "minute" for each minute we were late. If we accumulated more than a certain number of minutes, we had to go before a committee to explain ourselves and face the music. The penalties escalated all the way to expulsion. But there were exceptions. When I worked as night editor on *The Cornell Daily Sun,* I could stay out later.

In the fall of 1946, a proposal circulated to extend the Saturday night curfew to 1:30 a.m. A number of us actually opposed this. Asking your date to go home before the

Cornell's first group of National Scholars shows off student fashion choices in 1946. Among those standing are Ralph C. "Cooly" Williams Jr. (second from left) and Richard Pogue (third from right). Seated are Jonathan K. Woods (second from left) and then Audrey Rossman [married name: Sharman], Nancy Hubbard [Brandt], Marion Steinmann [Joiner], Ruth Williams [Drechsel], Jane Applebaum [Jacobs], Jean Thomas [Herrington], Alta Ann Turner [Morris], Lawrence Woodworth, and John Rose.

curfew was considered a great insult, and not all of us wanted to stay out that late, no matter how great the guy was. However, eventually, the Saturday night curfew did get extended, and somehow we all survived.

We women were not allowed to walk through, or even be in, the living rooms of our living unit if we were wearing pants. This meant that we always wore skirts to classes, social events, and extracurricular activities. If you were really going to play tennis, you had to wear a raincoat over your white tennis shorts. If you were really going to ride a horse, you could walk across campus wearing your jodhpurs and hacking jacket.

Some men also followed a dress code, but it was voluntary. A number of fraternities required their members to wear gentlemanly coats and ties to classes.

We couldn't just walk into the men's residences, either. We were only allowed in their dorms or fraternities if accompanied by a chaperone, or if we were attending a party that had been preregistered with the university's dean of students. We were also forbidden to leave campus for any overnight trips, even just to visit a classmate's home, without written permission from our parents.

Although the legal drinking age in New York was eighteen in those days, neither alcohol nor men were allowed in our residences. Gentleman callers could visit us in the first-floor living rooms, but they absolutely were never allowed upstairs.

Every few corridors in the women's dorms were organized into a unit overseen by a vice president of the Women's Self-Government Association, who was called a veep. She held regular meetings that we were all expected to attend and where we heard various instructions and announcements from on high.

Not only did men and women live in separate dorms—we also attended separate men's and women's freshman camps just before the semester started (see page 26). There were separate deans for women (Lucile Allen) and for men (Frank Baldwin). We had separate class officers. We women were systematically excluded from intercollegiate athletics, cheerleading, and the Big Red Band. This separation of men and women persisted even after we graduated. Alumni of the Class of 1950 had separate class officers until 1969, separate alumni reunions until 1970, and separate class columns in the *Cornell Alumni News* until 1985.

I haven't heard any reports of women being discriminated against in classes. But in all my four years at Cornell, I never laid eyes on a female faculty member. I did have a woman lab assistant in one physics course, but that was it.

The wonder is that it didn't occur to most of us to rebel or even protest about all these restrictions. It was just the way things were at the time, and we simply accepted them. Our minds were on other things: how to survive the chemistry exam tomorrow and what we were going to do on Saturday night. Not necessarily in that order.

And most of us women, who were fresh out of high school, probably had more freedom than we had had at home. We no longer had to tell our mothers where we were going and who we were seeing every time we went out.

In many ways, I think Cornell was easier for women than it was for men. Men had to scramble to find any place to live in the fall of 1946, while freshman women were automatically assigned to attractive, usually single rooms. In the dorms,

we had built-in companionship. We ate at common tables, and the regular meetings with the WSGA veep meant that we got to know the women who lived around us. And of course, the glorious Ratio—five men for every woman on campus—meant that it was easier for us to find dates.

Cornell was actually far ahead of other Ivy League schools in its treatment of women. Cornell was the only Ivy that was fully co-ed. Yale, Princeton, and Dartmouth were all male. Harvard, Columbia, and Brown did have affiliations with separate women's colleges—Harvard with Radcliffe, Columbia

Excerpts from the By-Laws of the Women's Self-Government Association

FEBRUARY 1944: A student is expected to show, both within and without the university, unfailing respect for order, morality, personal honor, and the rights of others. This rule is construed as applicable at all times, in all places, to all students of the university.

2. Class Hours.

(a) A girl must be in her living unit by her class hours, which are: Freshmen, 9:30 p.m.; Sophomores, 10:30 p.m.; Juniors, 11:00 p.m.; Seniors, 12:00 p.m.

(b) A student is permitted to sign out for any two of the following each week. These late nights are called Social Nights Out. A girl may sign out of her living unit until: Sunday through Thursday nights, 12:00 M; Friday night, 12:30 a.m.; Saturday night, 1:30 a.m.[1] A girl may register a caller in her living unit until: Sunday through Thursday nights, 11:30 p.m.; Friday night, 12:00 M; Saturday night, 1 a.m.

3. Chaperone Rules. NO WOMAN SHALL AT ANY TIME GO TO A MAN'S ROOM OR ROOMS OR TO A FRATERNITY HOUSE EXCEPT WHEN

(1) she has specifically signed out to a party which has been registered at the

Counselor of Student's office (a list of registered parties appears in the Bulletin each Friday), or

(2) she is accompanied by a chaperone registered with the Counselor of Students, in which case she shall sign out in her living unit.

8. Special Permissions.

(a) Each girl may have two extra Social Nights Out a term. These are called "Specials." In addition, each Freshman may have three 10:30 p.m. Specials a term, starting three weeks after Registration Day, to encourage her to attend concerts, lectures, and other university functions.

(b) Girls wishing to take their "Special" nights must note them on both slips in the upper left-hand corner. If not noted on slips, they shall count as a third night out and be penalized as such.

(c) Freshman 10:30 "Specials" will be cancelled if the girl takes no other or only one other social night out.

SEPTEMBER 1952:

11. Penalizations. Range of penalizations:

1) Reprimand.

2) Loss of Friday or Saturday late nights (meaning a girl must be in her living unit by 10:30 p.m. on the night or nights of her penalization).

3) Freshman rules: a girl must be in her living unit by 10:30 p.m. every night of the week or weeks in which she is penalized. The penalization of signing in at the desk between 10:20 and 10:30 p.m. every night may also be added.

4) Suspension may be recommended by the WSGA Judiciary Committee, subject to review by the Faculty Committee on Student Conduct.

5) Expulsion may be recommended by the WSGA Judiciary Committee, subject to review by the Faculty Committee on Student Conduct.

"I expect to return at…"

---

[1] Sometime between 1944 and 1946, the Saturday curfew time was changed back to 12:30 a.m.

with Barnard, and Brown with Pembroke. The University of Pennsylvania admitted women as undergraduates, but confined them in a women's college within the university, and it did not allow them access to all courses. And even though women were rare in large sections of Cornell, those who did venture into the masculine zones say they were treated equally.

Marion Steinmann was on the staff of *The Cornell Daily Sun* from 1947 to 1950 and received a BS from the College of Agriculture. She became an associate editor and science writer at the weekly *Life* magazine. She is the author of *Women At Work: Demolishing a Myth of the 1950's* (Xlibris 2005), for which she surveyed the women of the Class of 1950.

Sonia Pressman Fuentes '50

My parents were refugees who had fled from Hitler. They made great sacrifices for me, but they were also European and very proper. This caused a problem when my parents visited me one weekend during my freshman year. They left my room on Saturday night, and they were going to return the next morning. When Sunday morning came I heard all kinds of shrieking. Then my father barged in and told me to pack up, because we were going home. The shrieking was because men weren't allowed upstairs in the dorms.

The problem occurred because the night before, my parents went out the back door. The Balch dorms had a big area in the back where boys and girls kissed each other goodnight after their dates. So my parents walked outside on Saturday night and saw all of these young couples kissing and hugging. My father concluded that Balch was a whorehouse, and I could not remain there. I didn't know what to do. I didn't want to leave, but I had never said no to my father before.

At that moment the housemother, Helen Armor, did me a wonderful service. She had heard all the screaming, so she came into the room. She was a very strong woman, a strong moral presence. She invited my mother and father to tea in her apartment, right then and there. She turned my father around, and I was allowed to remain.

It's funny that I never questioned the position of women at Cornell, because I have always been inclined to act when I perceive an injustice. After all, my parents were chased out of Europe because they were Jews. And from the age of ten on, my parents and I would drive from the Catskills to Miami Beach every winter. We were powerfully affected by the racial discrimination we saw when we were driving through the south. In the 1960s, I became a leader of the women's movement. But when I was a student at Cornell, it never occurred to me that women were being discriminated against. I was interested in getting an education and fitting in, so I accepted things.

I mean, why don't dogs wear clothes? You could come to me all upset because dogs are running around naked, but in my world, dogs don't wear clothes and it isn't a big deal. That's what it was like. It was just the way things were. I didn't see it as sex discrimination until the 1960s.

We also had freedoms that young women today don't have. In my second or third year I was very homesick, and my parents were in Miami Beach for the winter. I suggested to my roommate, Eleanor Stevens, that we hitchhike down and back to Monticello to see my friends. Stevie said yes, so we went out to the side of the road in our blazers and skirts on Saturday morning and stuck out our thumbs. I had hitchhiked a lot to get around in high school. In the world where I grew up, hitchhiking wasn't considered outrageous behavior for girls.

I had a wonderful time at Cornell. My idea of fun was sitting around talking about philosophy and other big issues in bull sessions with my friends. I became very close to a half-dozen other women who lived on my floor at Balch. It was a little sanctuary. We called it Seventh Heaven.

Ruth Downey Crone '50

I lived in Balch Four during my first year, then Clara Dickson Hall after that. I also lived in Comstock Hall. It certainly was gracious living.

In Balch, we had private rooms with a connecting door, and we called the people on the other side of the door our roommates. We had to go down the hall for a bath, but each set of roommates shared a sink. We all had telephones in our rooms, although they only worked for local calls. And the rooms were beautiful. They were large, and each room had a comfortable bed, a desk and bookcase with a comfortable chair, and good closet space. We would go down to the dining room for our meals, and waitresses—students who were earning their board—would serve us. And there were even maids who changed the beds for us. It was very much like

GRACIOUS LIVING

Music room in Clara Dickson Hall.

There were about 1,800 undergraduate women at Cornell in 1946–47. Nearly all of them (87 percent) lived in these buildings:

RISLEY COLLEGE (built in 1911), with about 200 beds, a Gothic castle with fireplaces in the rooms, balconies, secret stairways, and a Great Hall that looked just like the one at Christchurch College in Oxford;

ANNA COMSTOCK HALL (1925), eighty beds, named for a professor and alumna who was a pioneering conservationist;

BALCH HALL (1929), 340 beds, four buildings with exteriors in the English Renaissance style, each with a different interior decoration scheme;

CLARA DICKSON HALL (1946), 420 beds, the largest dormitory in the Ivy League and so brand-spanking new that the paint had not dried yet;

CIRCLE COTTAGES, 80 beds, five remodeled homes adjacent to Balch;

CASCADILLA HALL (1866), 150 beds, Cornell's first dorm and, unlike the others, located south of campus in the Collegetown neighborhood; and

THIRTEEN SORORITY HOUSES with 290 beds, some of which were privately owned, all of them under the WSGA's jurisdiction.

About 235 undergraduate women lived in other circumstances, including eighty-three at home and sixty-two with their husbands. And about 360 women who were enrolled in graduate programs could live wherever they wanted.

a hotel. People today probably find this unbelievable, but it's true.

Ruth "Midge" Downey received a BS degree in home economics and became a reading specialist in the Fairfax, Virginia, schools.

Marjorie Leigh Hart '50

Clara Dickson Hall was not finished when I moved in as a freshman. I remember the smell of paint and the noise of construction. The grounds were all mud. But everything was brand new.

We were always supposed to look like ladies. We never wore pants—it was nothing but skirts. If it was really cold, you just put a heavy coat over your blouse and galoshes over your saddle shoes. It took a while to get your things on and off, and in the winter, the backs of the lecture halls were a steaming mess.

When it was time to eat, you would gather in a beautifully decorated living room and chat until you got six or eight people together, and then you would all go into the dining room and sit. No one would eat until everyone was seated, of course. Waitresses served your food and took away the dirty dishes. The silverware was shiny, and none of the dishes were chipped.

The housemothers kept us polite. I don't think I ever had a long conversation with a housemother. I was the president of Alpha Phi for my senior year, and I lived in the sorority house. We were an independent bunch, and I think some people considered us badly behaved. Pi Lambda Phi was the fraternity across the street. Residents of the two houses were known to invite

Clara Dickson Hall under construction, July 1946.

each other over for milk-punch parties in the basement. But I never got into serious trouble, except for once.

Alpha Phi's housemother had psychological problems, and she was causing a lot of disruption. I was the president, so I fired her. Then I informed the dean of women, Lucile Allen, what I had done. She hit the roof. She called me into her office and tried to break me down. I had no right to do that, she said. Disciplining housemothers was her job. But I had never met Lucile Allen before. I felt no responsibility to her whatsoever, and I wasn't about to cave in. Neither of us was very happy about this, but that's how we left it.

Marjorie Leigh Hart graduated with a degree in chemical engineering. She had a long career at Exxon as a senior executive in gas, energy policy, and corporate planning. She was the first woman executive to receive an overseas assignment from Exxon, and worked in Japan and London for years. She was also the first woman invited into the executive dining room at corporate headquarters. Marjorie served on the Cornell Board of Trustees from 1979 to 1985.

Marjorie Maddy Croop '50

I transferred to Cornell from Bowling Green State University and was elected president of Delta Gamma just a few months after that. I don't remember much about being president, though, so it must not have been a big deal. When I was president, I only heard of one case of a girl sneaking out at night after curfew. People told me about it and I was

angry, but I never confronted her.

I had other things on my mind besides the curfew. Cornell was hard. A few weeks after I arrived, I got a 75 on a test. I was upset about it, but my roommate came in and said just wait, pretty soon you'll be glad to get a 75. And she was right.

Because I was a transfer student, I still had to take courses to fulfill Cornell's freshman requirements. So I walked into the first meeting of a philosophy class, and here were all these freshmen talking about Spinoza and the other philosophers. I had no idea who they were talking about. It was a whole new world.

Marjorie Maddy received a BA, married Raymond Croop, and raised three children in Cincinnati, Ohio.

Elizabeth Severinghaus Warner '50

LETTER OF OCTOBER 13, 1948: We just finished dinner. Dean [of Women Lucile] Allen was here—she's a conceited, swaggering bag if I ever saw one. Just looking at her annoys me. A bunch of us sat at the farthest table from her and roared all through dinner. We shot water and spitballs at each other and had the best time. College time is making ladies out of us… I never knew there could be so much snow in a place.

Nancy Hubbard Brandt '50

I was fortunate that Louisville did not have co-educational public schools. When there were only girls

Lucile Allen was professor of personnel administration and dean of women from 1945 to 1952.

in the classroom, we didn't have to censor ourselves, so I got excellent grades. But when Louisville women went out in public in those days, we were supposed to be beautiful and dumb. Cornell was the first place where I ever had an unrestricted, friendly conversation with a man. At home, I never had that opportunity.

I was also lucky that Cornell started awarding National Scholarships in 1946. Their aim was to attract more students from outside of New York State. I would never have gone to Cornell if not for that program. I would have gone to the University of Louisville and lived at home. So I am quite grateful to Cornell. I think of it as the means of my escape.

Louisville back then was an overgrown small southern town, not a big city. I was fairly unsophisticated when I arrived, and I don't think I could have handled a big city like New York. Cornell was a good steppingstone. It was sophisticated, but at that time it was also much smaller and more isolated than it is now. I had to take three

Dorm room in Dickson.

trains to get there from Louisville. It was a safe place to be with your friends, and our friendships became very strong.

I never felt the slightest whiff of second-class citizenship in the classroom or in extracurricular activities. I was active at Cornell United Religious Work (CURW) and ran several programs there. And I remember a moment when I realized that things had changed for me. A group of faculty and administrators had proposed to abolish CURW. I was angry about it. I went to their meeting and told them, "Look, fellas, this is where I learned to think, not in your classes." I think they were kind of taken aback, but also amused. One of them said, "Well, that's an achievement," and pretty soon they abandoned the idea.

I was learning to have guts, and how to stand up to authority.

Nice girls from Louisville didn't act that way.

Nancy Hubbard earned a BA and married Jim Brandt '50, a navy veteran. In the 1970s, she served as an elected member of a suburban high school board of education. In 1980, she earned a master's degree in urban studies from Loyola University of Chicago and then became a banker and foundation officer in Chicago.

Ann Ellis Raynolds '50, M.Ed '53

The social rules at Cornell were mainstream for the United States, but I grew up in New York City and my parents gave me a lot of freedom. So when I was faced with the curfew and other rules, I just broke them, knowingly. Many of

the returning veterans lived off-campus, so if I was visiting them, I might spend the night rather than risk being late for the curfew. The curfew didn't give me a choice.

Two things gave me leeway. I started in the architecture program, where there were only a few women, and architects had special permission to stay out until 2:00 or 3:00 a.m. After I switched to an English major I worked at the *Sun*, where editors were allowed to stay out until we put the paper to bed, which could be midnight or 1:00 a.m. And I actually would have gone back to my room if it weren't for the stupid rule. I would have preferred to sleep in my own bed but when I missed the curfew, I couldn't go back.

My attitudes came from my background. My father was a liberal Republican from Vermont. He was a lawyer who handled some high-profile divorces. He saw how women were not treated equally, how they were totally dependent on their husbands because they had no way to make a living themselves. He told me that he wanted to make sure I had enough money so I would never be forced to stay with a man I didn't love.

I never joined a sorority, and I was totally opposed to the whole idea from the beginning. I saw girls going through rushing, and I saw the pain it caused to the ones who weren't chosen, and the exclusivity of it was appalling to me. I was rebelling against everything, and so I ran for president of the Women's Self-Government Association (WSGA). I was going to reform all these rules. I was spouting the whole feminist liturgy. I'm proud now that I was ahead of my time, but I also remember praying that I would not be elected. And when I was elected in the spring of 1949,

Dining room in Risley Hall.

I was shocked to realize that not everyone agreed with me.

A lot of women actually supported the rules. My proposals went over like a lead balloon. And I also had to stick to the curfew, of course, because suddenly I was the Queen of the Curfew. That was hard. All these great guys, and suddenly I had to cut my visits short. It seemed quite strange to me because I had been traveling all over Europe alone in the summer of 1949.

I thought about resigning, but my father advised me not to. He said it would be a good opportunity for me to have the experience of leadership. But it was the dean of women, Lucile Allen, who really got to me. She told me that not everyone had enjoyed as many opportunities as I had, and a lot of people resented me for my liberal ideas. She

made me feel like crawling into a hole, so I went through with it.

All of this made being head of the WSGA Judiciary Committee very interesting. The other women on the committee supported the rules, but they also understood my position. We only saw the worst of the worst cases, the ones the dorms referred to us, and we dismissed them whenever we could. I tried not to be punitive. We tried to be helpful in the letters we wrote, although I'm not sure we were successful. I remember encouraging one younger student to speak out, if she disagreed with these rules, and help change them. But most of the women we saw didn't want to take any responsibility for self-government.

I eventually realized that they weren't our rules, anyway. If I had

succeeded in organizing women to change the curfew, the administration would have taken our proposal to the Board of Trustees, and they would have squashed it. I was shocked when I realized that. But really, the whole idea of student government back then was almost always a farce.

The boys did something really wild to the WSGA at the end of our senior year. It was the last big meeting, and I was making my speech, and some boys put pepper in the air ducts. The women in the audience started getting restless, and then they started running out of the room. I was wondering why, because I had carefully edited my remarks to keep anyone from getting upset. It was actually the perfect way to end the year.

But this was really just a small

part of my experience. Overall, I thought Cornell was fabulous. I had only gone to girls' schools and then, suddenly, everything was wide open. There were only 350 freshmen women and all of these veterans in 1946. The veterans were very serious about their educations, and they also played hard. I had a ball.

Ann Ellis married Harold "Ron" Raynolds '48, MEd '53, an army combat veteran who had been editor in chief of *The Cornell Daily Sun.* She earned a second master's degree from Goddard College, as well as a doctorate in psychology in 1982. She was a clinical instructor in psychiatry on the Harvard Medical Faculty at Beth Israel Hospital in Boston, and an associate professor of child psychiatry and development at Boston University Medical School. She maintains a psychology practice in Queechee, Vermont.

Jane Haskins Marcham '51

I was women's editor of *The Cornell Daily Sun* in my senior year. I competed to be the managing editor, but nobody wanted to take orders from a woman back then, so a man got the job. John [Marcham '50] had been the editor in chief in 1949–50, and by the time he graduated, we had gotten serious about each other. He had taken a job with *Life* magazine in New York City, and it was not easy for us to spend time together. I had been exempt from the curfew when I was a night editor. But as women's editor, I was not exempt.

After a date with John, I would check back into my dorm at the last minute, and one time I slipped and I was quite late. I went before a

judicial review board of the Women's Self-Government Association (WSGA), and the experience just outraged me. I knew that some of the WSGA officers, the very same women who were judging me, had spent nights in Collegetown, which was off limits. They just had ways of getting away with it. The hypocrisy of that was infuriating.

I went to my typewriter and wrote several editorials for the *Sun* attacking the WSGA. After the second or third one ran, the dean of women called me into her office and urged me to stop. She asked me about my relationship with my father, and she said I had problems with authority, and I needed to work on my problems. She wasn't a psychoanalyst. It was ridiculous. I think I even knew that at the time.

Jane Haskins Marcham received her BA and married John Marcham '50, an army veteran. She was on the staff of *The Ithaca Journal* for twenty-nine years, including eleven as editor of the editorial page, after which she served four years on Ithaca's

Common Council and ten years on the city's planning board.

The Cornell Daily Sun elected a female editor-in-chief, Guinevere Griest '44, in 1943, shortly before suspending publication due to paper and personnel shortages. In 1943–44, Griest edited a university-owned weekly called *The Cornell Bulletin,* which described itself as "wartime successor to the *Cornell Daily Sun.*" Women held many of the senior positions there. When the *Sun* resumed publication in October 1946, Melba Levine Silver '47 was managing editor, the second-highest-ranking editorial position. Ron Raynolds '48 was editor-in-chief.

In 1950, Jane Haskins competed for the managing editor job but lost, she says, because "no one wanted to take orders from a woman." Ellen Shapiro '54 was named the first female managing editor in 1953. A woman was not named editor-in-chief of the *Sun* until Elizabeth Bass '72 got the nod twenty-five years later.

Lucile Allen and Frank Baldwin, Deans of Women and Men, meet with students.

THE CURFEW'S LINGERING SUNSET

The Cornell Daily Sun

February 25, 1954

Circle Cottage Two starts "an experiment in the sign-out system, under which the practice of giving minutes as punishment for late sign-ins has been discarded." Marlene Morack '55, president of the Circle Cottages, says that the old system was "petty and immature."

September 9, 1954

Sophomore women are permitted to stay out until midnight every night.

May 7, 1957

To the Editor: I am pleased to put forth a proposal that would…have a multiplied beneficial effect on the entire university. I suggest that the obsolete regulation that requires women to be in their dormitories by a certain hour each night be abandoned… There would be a marked decrease in hypertension on the campus, and the need for counseling would decrease, saving the university enormous sums each year. "Cornell woman" would become synonymous with "happy woman" and, in fact, everybody would be happy. I am sure that this proposal will be well taken and I look forward to its early adoption. Let's make Cornell happier!— Paul J. Peckar '60

May 23, 1958

One hundred and twenty-five women intentionally return late to their residences on a Friday night, touching off two days of riots. About 2,000 male students burn an effigy of university President Deane Malott outside of Sage Hall after the 12:30 a.m. curfew on Saturday morning.

Several students, including Richard Fariña, are suspended. Fariña drops out of Cornell and writes a fictionalized account of the demonstration in his novel, *Been Down So Long It Looks Like Up to Me* (1966).

October 18, 1961

To the Editor: The curfew and sign-out system for undergraduate women at Cornell is both unnecessary and degrading. If there is a cogent case to be made for having it, a parallel case can certainly be made for subjecting the undergraduate men to a curfew unless we, as undergraduate women, are assumed to be less responsible or somehow less able to take care of ourselves than our male contemporaries. If such an assumption is not based on the difference in physical strength between men and women, it is a gratuitous insult…we are confident in our ability to manage our own lives, [and] we urge that the curfew system be amended.— Nancy L. Phillips '62 and nineteen other women students

March 14, 1962

The WSGA votes to remove curfews for senior women. The Faculty Committee on Student Affairs (FCSA) approves the measure temporarily, and makes it permanent one year later.

February 1963

Betty Friedan publishes *The Feminine Mystique*.

January 1965

The FCSA approves the WSGA's vote to abolish curfews for juniors.

June 30, 1966

The National Organization for Women is founded, with a call to "confront, with concrete action, the conditions that now prevent women from enjoying the equality of opportunity and freedom of choice which is their right."

April 28, 1967

Curfews for second semester sophomores are abolished.

April 12, 1968

Curfews for first semester sophomores are abolished.

December 1968

Curfews are abolished for all women undergraduates.

Spring 1970

Controversy erupts over whether women's dorms would have 24-hour open house, a right that men's dorms had gained the year before. The decision is that each dorm decides its own hours by vote.

Fall 1970

Risley becomes the first co-ed dormitory, and the last panty raid takes place. "How can [men] get psyched to march on North Campus if there are women on the next floor?" writes Alicia Marsland in *The Cornell Daily Sun* of October 25, 1972. "In the midst of all these changes, WSGA, which had supported a good deal of the reform, died unnoticed. According to Ruth Darling, associate dean of students, the members of the 79-year-old institution had 'done themselves out of a function.'"

Chi Phi brothers relaxing in 1948.

CHAPTER 6

Friendly Places

Most Cornell students organized their social lives around clubs—sheltered, supervised organizations where they could safely have adventures and try out adult responsibilities. In 1950, the university registered 287 extracurricular student organizations, including fifty-five fraternities, thirteen sororities, and six other residence groups. Many more organizations were not officially registered.

Clubs, Class, and Student Power

Cornell had a men's glee club, a women's glee club, a dance club, a debate club, an outing club, a home economics club, a round-up club, a pilot's club, a poultry club, and an organization called YASNY, short for You Ain't Seen Nothing Yet, whose members adorned Barton Hall with elaborate decorations before the big dances. The job of uniting this diverse community fell to several representative organizations that met in a Student Council. Some students criticized their governance for its inefficiency, segregation, and immaturity. But at the Battle of Hoy Field, students organized a coalition that forced the Board of Trustees to back down. That had never happened before.

Nelson Schaenen Jr. '50, MBA '51

Cornell was like a bunch of small neighborhoods. If you didn't belong to at least a couple of clubs, you missed out. I socialized with classmates, but the fraternity and sorority houses were the major focus of my social life.

I was in basic training in the navy when they dropped the atomic bomb. When I was discharged in 1946, my father sent me one college application. The next thing I knew, I was sitting in a dorm room in

The junior varsity basketball team for 1947–48. Nels Schaenen is number 8.

Boldt Hall. But I don't think I ever saw my dorm roommate. My circle of friends was small, so I was alone a lot that first year.

I pledged Delta Upsilon (DU), where a lot of athletes lived. We had Henry Parker '47, captain of the heavyweight rowing team; Jim Farrell '50, JD '52, and a lot of others from the football team; and Bob Gale '49 and his brother Jim from the basketball team. I played freshman basketball with Dick Savitt '50. I think they might all have been veterans. I was never much of an athlete, but DU did expand my horizons.

The fraternities were sheltering places. I was pretty shy—in the years I lived in Ithaca, I had maybe two or three dates. But I did have friendly places to go.

Nelson Schaenen Jr. was an electronic technician's mate, third class, in the U.S. Navy. He is the son of Nelson Schaenen Sr. '23 (1903–1984), the first president of the investment firm Smith, Barney & Company. Nels Jr. became an investment manager at Weiss, Peck, & Greer. He also served as a Cornell trustee for twenty-four years, and was chair of the board's executive committee.

Alpha Delta Phi house at Cornell. Used by special permission.

Charles Torrington Thompson '51, MA '52
(1930–2001)

Charles Thompson is the author of *Halfway Down The Stairs* (1957), a novel partially set at postwar Cornell (see Chapter 12). In this excerpt, Thompson's blue-collar hero, Dave Pope, gets his first look at the place.

On my first day at Cornell I dropped my bags in a taxi and told the driver to take me to 300 West Avenue, where I was going to live. I pictured some ivy-covered rooming house, or a Tudor stone dormitory with guys leaning out the window singing the evening song and clinking beer glasses. I was naive. The taxi drove up a driveway hub deep in dust and let me out in front of a tarpaper shack. "What's this?" I said to the driver. "What are we doing here?'" He said, very gently, that this was 300 West Avenue. I got out, but I didn't believe him. How could I? There were no beer mugs and no songs, just dirt and this tarpaper shack, which crouched with nine or ten like it under the shadow of two great brick fraternity houses.

Well, I dropped my bags on the stoop of this hovel and looked up at the fraternity houses. They were huge, with diamond panes and lattice windows and about fifteen chimneys apiece. Each one had a cool flagstone terrace, and on one of these terraces a bunch of people were having a party. They were tall brown boys and girls in skirts and cashmere sweaters, in light flannels and white bucks, and they looked like something out of the Philip Yacht Club. They were drinking what looked like orange juice; they moved in and out of wide French doors to the terrace, and inside someone was playing good cocktail piano. I stood there and watched them for a long time, fascinated. They were all so pretty! Pretty boys and pretty girls. Laughing.and telling private jokes and using the slang. "Good deal," I heard people say. "Atta babe. How to go." And there I was down on the ratty stoop in my double-breasted gabardine suit and my long hair and my wing-toed shoes. "Jesus," I thought. "I've been through this before." It was not what I had expected from college, and I'd only been there ten minutes.

After a while a young man on the terrace turned away from his group and wandered over to the wall that protected his house from my dorm, and lounged against it, sipping his drink. I guess he wanted to look out over the town again, glad he was back. He stared over the dorms to the valley and the green opposite hill; he looked down at the roofs of the town, and north up the valley to the lake, which was very blue that day. Then he looked down at me—glanced away quickly, and looked again.

There was a funny mixture of reactions on his face. He saw my suit and my shoes and my long hair and my beat-up cardboard suitcases, but it wouldn't have bothered him if he hadn't caught the look on my face. I guess he saw pure envy there, and a bitter kind of lust, and even hatred. I was feeling hateful all right, but I was hating myself—and he couldn't know that. He thought I was hating him. He must have been a decent guy basically, because his glance had sympathy in it. I guess he knew what was going on inside me, maybe even that it was my first ten minutes at Cornell. Maybe it had happened to him, though the chances that it had are pretty slim. His clothes fit him too well. But the sympathy did not last long; behind it I could see in the uneasiness of his look and in the haste with which he moved away from the edge of the wall, back to his group, a swift "there-but-for-the-grace-of God" feeling. Maybe the son of a bitch felt guilty. Maybe he felt just a little scared.

I hope he did. Maybe if I hadn't stood there that first day watching his crappy party, or if he hadn't looked at me with his supe-rior pity, I could have gotten into it at Cornell, and maybe even made it. I don't think so. As I say, if you arrive a nebbish, you leave a nebbish. It was brought home to me that day that the West Avenue dorms were where I belonged. I stayed there.

Alan Brown '50
(1925–1970)

Whitney Balliett '51
(1927–2007)

Alan Brown   Whitney Balliett

Alan Brown illustrated and Whitney Balliett wrote "The Land of the Masque," which was published in the March 1949 issue of *Cornell Widow* and runs on the two following pages.

Alan Brown served in the U.S. Coast Guard during World War II and was editor in chief of the *Widow* in 1949-50. He received a bachelor's degree from Cornell and an MD from the University of Rochester in 1957. He was medical director of the hospital in Tompkins County, New York, from 1962 until 1968, when he developed amyotrophic lateral sclerosis (ALS). Alan was also a passionate fan of Cornell hockey, and the team still gives an annual cash award in his name to the student who scores the most goals against Harvard.

Whitney Balliett was drafted during his freshman year at Cornell in 1946. He returned a year later to complete his bachelor's degree. He was managing editor of the *Widow* in 1949-50. He was hired by *The New Yorker* and went on to publish more than 550 signed articles there between 1957 and 2001.

INADEQUATE RESTRICTIONS

FROM THE CORNELL INTRAFRATERNITY COUNCIL NEWSLETTER,
JANUARY 1950

A new committee was formed at the December 11 meeting of the IFC. Jim Brandt, Chi Psi, has been appointed chairman of this committee that has been formed to review the social by-laws. The first meeting was held just prior to the Christmas recess. At this time the by-laws were gone over and some of their inadequacies and ambiguities were discussed. Some of the problems encountered during fraternity social functions were brought up... It was pointed out at the National Inter-fraternity Conference that the Cornell IFC is lax in the restrictions it imposes on fraternities during social functions. This new committee will endeavor to determine the nature of the restrictions the IFC should impose...

The Land of The Masque

Being An Easy Primer
for Children of All Ages: With Lessons Concerning
The Glorious Days of College at Ithaca

This is Ithaca.

Cornell is in Ithaca.

Look at Cornell on the Hill.

These are boys and girls entering the University.

They are very young. They are brave.

Ithaca is a nice town.

Here is State Street. It is long.

See all the friendly hands.

The school week is over. It is Saturday night. The children are playing games, and everybody must wear a mask.

The big boys and girls have clubs. Their fathers are Republicans. See the Look-At-Me with the long necktie full of pins.

This is the teacher.

He is giving a lecture.

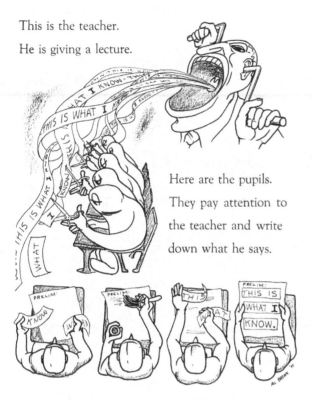

Here are the pupils.
They pay attention to
the teacher and write
down what he says.

This is a test. All pupils get 100.

Here is a merry-go-round. It is fun.

The teacher writes books for his pupils.

They are very polite. He is quite rich.

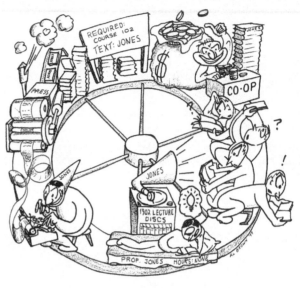

Do you see the funny man in his counting-house?

This merry-go-round never stops.

This building is for recess.
Some have milk. Others
have happy meetings.

They like to squash ants.

These are the boys and girls leaving the
University. They are brave and happy.

See the boy on the left. He has a job.

The other children still want to play their game.

They have even brought their masks.

Everyone is growing up.

Howard Loomis '49, MBA '50

The Student Council was made up of representatives from the seven largest campus organizations, the four class presidents, and members-at-large. The editor in chief of the *Sun* was a nonvoting member, which is why I was there. In 1948–49, Jack Sheinkman '49 was the president, and Dick Keegan '49 was there as President of the Interfraternity Council. They were both veterans of World War II, and Keegan had been in combat. The women members were a force, too. They weren't shy. They spoke up and had equal standing.

Dick Keegan had worked for President Day, I think as his chauffeur, before he left for the military. Then he got involved in student politics when he came back after the war. He was an excellent politician in the Irish, "Tip" O'Neill style. He

Richard Keegan

ran things with a firm hand. He was connected with everybody and he would constantly check with the heads of the fraternities, the faculty, and everybody else to make sure he wasn't too far out before he proposed something. He had dozens of people to keep in touch with, but he enjoyed doing it because he was an outgoing, gregarious person. After Cornell, he became an advertising and marketing executive.

I lived in Chi Psi and we were a fairly tight-knit group, but we could see Cornell changing. A lot of us were concerned about it growing so fast. We all shared a desire to see the university make progress, but I think we were also afraid that the student body might fall apart at the seams. We wanted to do something to make the campus cohesive, so we did whatever we could to keep people together. That was one of the reasons the Student Council welcomed the Independent Council, which was formed in 1947 for students who did not belong to a fraternity or sorority.

Cornell at that time had Jewish fraternities, a Catholic fraternity, and one black fraternity, and some other fraternities that explicitly barred Jews, blacks, or Catholics from joining. These restrictive clauses were a real bone of contention for Jack [Sheinkman]. He got the folks from the Independent Council really fired up about them. I was more neutral. I was all for the university's effort to get rid of restrictive clauses, but I also felt that the fraternities should handle it in their own way.

Jack was a good friend. We often disagreed, but we got along well. He knew where I stood, and I knew where he stood. And we all worked together on the battle to save Hoy Field, a campaign that came together fairly quickly. Dick Keegan worked with Jack Sheinkman to get the alumni to oppose

Jack Sheinkman

the trustees' plans. Everyone else joined in. It was all hands on deck, because our opponent was so powerful. See, the battle over Hoy Field wasn't just with the trustees. It was also with New York State. The powers that be in Albany really wanted the project, and it was very upsetting to them when we objected to it.

Howard Loomis is the son of Arthur L. Loomis 1918, who enlisted in the navy in 1917 and returned to Cornell as a soldier after World War One ended. "My mother, Genevieve Krey '20, was a mathematics major," Howard says. "She met him at a dance in Barton Hall—this handsome, tall man in uniform. Six months later, they were engaged." After Howard got his BA and MBA, he moved to Pratt, Kansas, and joined The People's Bank, which had $10 million in assets at the time. Now its assets are more than $300 million, and he is its chairman.

Jack Sheinkman '49, JD '52 (1927–2002) was a veteran of World War II who rose to the rank of lieutenant in the naval reserves. In addition to leading the Cornell Student Council, he was prominent in the Independent Council, a soccer star, and a founder of the Watermargin co-op (see Chapter 7).

The Battle Of Hoy Field

Cornell's baseball team had eight wins and seventeen losses in 1949, but its historic baseball field won big that year. An unprecedented coalition of student government leaders, athletes, faculty, and alumni united in opposition to a trustee plan to turn Hoy Field into the permanent home of the New York State School of Industrial and Labor Relations (ILR). It might have been the first time that the university's stakeholders successfully organized to reverse a decision of the trustees.

John Marcham: This was really a fight about tradition, and about respecting the students' point of view. We had been playing baseball there since 1922. The right-field fence was extremely deep, but Lou Gehrig had hit a home run over that fence when he was playing for Columbia, and we had marked the spot with a sign. The field is named for David F. Hoy, 1891, whom all the older alumni remembered because he was the registrar. He was famous for being a soft-hearted curmudgeon. The Cornell song, "Give My Regards to Davy," is named for Davy Hoy.

The ILR students were studying in Quonset huts that had housed the navy's diesel engine training program during the war. Everyone agreed that ILR needed a permanent home, and the State of New York was ready to pay for the building. It needed to be within walking distance of the arts quad, because the ILR students took many of their classes there. Hoy Field was in the right place, so the trustees went ahead with their plans. I suppose they assumed nobody would object.

I literally stumbled over the story. I was competing for a position on *The Cornell Daily Sun* in 1947, so I was eager to find good material. One day while walking across Hoy Field on my way to cover freshman football, I tripped over a surveyor's stake. So I went to see Bob Kane, the athletics director, and asked him what was going on.

Kane knew about the trustees' plan, and he didn't like it. He told me about it but asked that I not attribute the information to him. There were alternatives, but it seemed to me that the trustees had made their decision without consulting or even notifying students or alumni. So I wrote a column that was published on November 15, 1947.

The story simmered for a year. As expected, the athletes didn't like the plan. It was also unpopular with alumni because they had raised the money to buy the land in 1909, and at that time, a trustees' committee

Hoy Field in the 1980s.

had pledged that the field would stay in athletic use "in perpetuity." Trustees' meetings were not open to the public in those days, and they didn't publish their minutes, either. But the *Sun* kept checking on the story, and people within the administration kept complaining.

Things boiled over in early December 1948, when the trustees' buildings and grounds committee voted five to four to stick to the plan after a lot of people had asked them to reconsider. That's when we started organizing protests.

Robert Kane '34: Protesting the threat to the existence of Hoy as a playing field became an engrossing student cause. The Student Council, the *Sun*, and no fewer than sixty-nine student organizations coalesced in putting the pressure on... The Student Council, under the leadership of President Jack Sheinkman, a varsity soccer star, augmented by the strong support of the *Sun* and its editor in chief, Howard K. Loomis, were in the trenches together.

John Marcham wrote the first story on the proposal. The Student Council appointed a committee to apply pressure. Committee members were Bruce Davis (football), Richard Keegan (president of the Interfraternity Council), Ed Martin '49 (president of the Industrial and Labor Relations student committee), James Hazzard '50 (vice

HOY FIELD IS THREATENED

The Cornell Daily Sun, November 15, 1947

Cornellians may note with interest the engineers' stakes evident on Hoy Field for the past week. In the words of Superintendent of Buildings and Grounds Hugh E. Weatherlow 1906, the baseball field is "part of the proposed site of the State School of Industrial and Labor Relations."

One of the guilty pegs is located behind the pitcher's box, another in deep center field, placed there by the firm of Sprague and Hinwood, on contract from the state to examine the location of the proposed building. The two stakes mark the eastern edge of the future structure.

Funds for construction have not as yet been voted by the state, but erection of the edifice will see the end of Hoy Field, regarded by many as the finest college baseball park in the country.

Persons on the campus before 1941 can remember lush rolling lawns where Olin Hall, the diesel labs, veterinary, and ILR buildings now stand. Many grumbled when these beauty spots fell before the "advance of progress."

Far more than doing away with a beauty spot, the loss of Hoy Field will cut the available athletic fields to a point where intramural sports will be forced out into the country. In addition to the elimination of Hoy Field, Lower Alumni Field will fall before the steam shovel with the advent of the proposed $1,100,000 athletic plant on that ground.

At present, intramural football and softball have most of Upper Alumni Field to themselves in their seasons. In the fall, four separate football teams, two soccer squads, and two lacrosse teams overflow Hoy and Lower Alumni. Without these fields, the intercollegiate competitors would need so much of Upper Alumni that there would not be room for the many intramural contests now played there.

In the spring, the situation would be little improved, with the various baseball and lacrosse squads and spring football practice leaving far too little room for intramural football.

In addition to the large area which the intercollegiate teams would need upon which to practice, a sizeable part of the available space would be taken up with a new baseball park to replace Hoy Field. All the less room for the intramural program.

Where would the intramurals go? Planners would have us hike out to university land located near the radio transmitters across Kline Road. The spot is one mile on foot from Willard Straight Hall, at least thirty minutes of uphill walking from any of the [fraternity] houses behind the law school.

Superintendent Wetherlow indicated the new ILR building has "good priority" on the state building program. As such, Hoy Field might well be done away with while many of us are still on the campus. Many of us may yet witness the downfall of an excellent intramural program for want of playing fields within a reasonable distance of the campus.

—John Marcham

president of Student Council and head cheerleader), Sheinkman, and Loomis.

In a separate thrust, the varsity sports managers' club sent a strong letter to President Day, signed by Robert Corrigan '50, president of the club, and vice-president John Palmer '49. Corrigan was manager of tennis, Palmer manager of rowing. The *Sun* printed the letter on its front page, endorsed by a long list of student organizations.

Of all these organizations the most telling, perhaps, was the ILR student committee. Apparently the students themselves did not wish to see the baseball field appropriated for their new building.

Robert Kane (1911–92), a native of Ithaca, was a champion sprinter for Cornell and a member of the team that won the National AAU championships for 440, 880, and one-mile relays in 1933, '34, and '35. He joined the university's athletic department after receiving his Cornell law degree, and was Director of Athletics from 1941 to 1976. Kane directed the United States Olympic Committee from 1977 to 1981, and also served two terms as vice president of the National Collegiate Athletic Association.

Richard Pogue: The battle of Hoy Field. That was terrific. I didn't know why it was such a big deal, but my older fraternity brothers told me it was, and I took their word for it. I remember we had a production line down in the basement of Psi U where we printed mimeograph sheets and mailed them out to alumni all over the country. We all busted our tails.

The students organized to defeat a proposal from the university trustees, perhaps for the first time. I think the veterans had something to do with that. They knew how to get organized. They had more

An Open Letter to the President and Trustees

The Cornell Daily Sun, January 14, 1949

We believe student opinion can rightfully *demand* the following action:

1. That the President and the Board of Trustees make public their plans and intended action before the meeting of the board on January 29, 1949.

2. That the President and the Board of Trustees take into consideration the opinion and feeling of the student body in making their decisions.

3. That an intramural program, either the present one or one equal or better than the present one, be guaranteed to the student body. And also, that consideration be taken of student opinion in the formulation of such plans.

We have offered these proposals to you, feeling that you will deem it necessary to act upon them due to the vital role which they play in student life.

— Robert Corrigan and John Palmer

courage than kids just out of high school did. They knew how to get things done.

Bruce Davis, MBA '52: The Hoy Field campaign focused most of its efforts on getting support from as many of the alumni as possible. They knew that was the trustees' weak point, because Cornell was in the middle of a fundraising campaign. President Day and the trustees had organized a committee of 400 alumni and charged it with the goal of raising $12.5 million. It was the university's first foray into professional fundraising, and they couldn't afford bad publicity.

On January 29, 1949, the trustees voted to relocate the proposed site of the ILR school and leave Hoy Field alone. A few days later, President Day wrote to trustee Robert Treman 1909, "I was driven to the conclusion that emotional resistance to the enroachment on Hoy Field had risen to a point at which completely rational handling of the whole matter was no longer possible, and hence my decision to retreat from my earlier position."

Robert Kane: After President Day suffered a heart attack in the spring of 1949, he resigned and was made chancellor. He came back to his office after recovery. I went in to see him one day and we had a most pleasant chat. He was complimentary about my stewardship and as I was leaving his office he called out, "But don't think I don't know who engineered that whole controversy about Hoy Field." He did smile when he said it.

The ILR school moved into the old home of the Veterinary College, along Tower Road, in 1957. Ives Hall, its permanent home between Tower Road and Barton Hall, was not formally dedicated until 1962.

Eleanor Roosevelt arrives at the Watermargin co-op on February 21, 1950, accompanied by Jack Sheinkman (in hat) and greeted by Jim Gibbs.

CHAPTER 7

"Any Person"

Jews, Blacks, Greeks, and Watermargin

Cornell University uses a quote from its founder —"I would found an institution where any person can find instruction in any study"—to highlight its diversity. Yet there is a fine line separating diversity from discrimination, and some student organizations of the 1940s crossed it. Some fraternity and sorority houses had language in their charters barring blacks, Jews, and other groups from membership. Others discriminated through informal "gentlemen's agreements."

Although Cornell admitted only a handful of black students each year in the 1940s, there was no written quota for Jews, who made up 12 percent of the student body.

Jewish groups had been active at Cornell since the 1920s, and Jewish students there were far more integrated into campus life than were Jews elsewhere in the Ivy League.

Jewish faculty members, alumni, and some student veterans of World War II found discrimination repugnant and teamed up to attack it on campus. The veterans opened the Watermargin co-op in 1948 as a demonstration project in cross-cultural living, and they protested discrimination in housing and other areas. But postwar students did the most important work toward integration informally by forming cross-cultural friendships.

The vets were early converts to a civil rights movement that slogged through the 1940s and '50s before delivering widespread social change in the 1960s. Yet even as the movement percolated, the university's blatant discrimination against women in living arrangements, curfews, dress, and athletics went largely unnoticed.

Chosen People

M. H. Abrams: Everything had been so changed by the Second World War. The prejudice against Jews lessened greatly. When Cornell hired me to teach in 1945, the entire faculty might have had one or two or three Jews. Before the 1940s was out, about one-third of the English department was Jewish.

Sonia Pressman Fuentes '50: I grew up in a bungalow colony my parents owned in the Catskills, and all of my family's close friends were Jewish. We knew non-Jews, of course, but we didn't let them become too close. We were prejudiced.

My mother used to warn me about what would happen if I married a Gentile. She would say, "He might be nice to you for thirty years. Then one day, you'll be having a fight, and he will look right into your eyes and call you a dirty Jew." My parents felt that those lines should never be crossed, and while I was living in their home, I never questioned them.

When I came to Cornell, I saw a much larger world, and I wanted to be part of it. I met wonderful people and wondered why I had been cut off from them. For my second year in Balch, I asked someone to be my roommate because she was half Jewish. But as the year went on I became close friends with a Greek classmate, Florence Maragakes [Roukis], and eventually I asked her to be my roommate instead. I liked Flo better. She was a lovely person. The fact that she was not a Jew no longer seemed relevant.

Of course, there were ignorant people, too. I remember hearing a story about a woman from Texas who came to Cornell and was surprised when she met Jews because she thought we had tails. I would joke with my friends about this. I'd tell them how nice it was to have a tail.

Eve Weinschenker Paul '50: When I was a sophomore in January 1948, I rushed a sorority. We went to a meeting and they said, "Will the Jewish girls stand on one side of the room and the Christian girls on the other?" All the Jewish girls were wearing fur coats, so one side of the room suddenly got all furry.

There were two sororities for Jews, and I pledged to Sigma Delta Tau. I lived there for a year, and I frankly didn't like it. I had been in a segregated environment once before. Growing up, I had lived for a few years in Douglaston, out at the eastern edge of Queens. It was very anti-Semitic. We used to stay indoors during the Jewish holidays, and the boys in my neighborhood would throw rocks at me. I was much more comfortable on the Upper West Side [of Manhattan], where everyone mixed together. So the next year I moved back into a dorm.

HOW WOULD YOU FEEL?

The Cornell Daily Sun, May 24, 1948

In an attempt to discover to what extent racial discrimination [and anti-Semitism] exists among Cornell students, the Cornell Survey Committee asked this question of a representative sample of 500 Cornellians and got the following results: "How would you feel about having one of the following as a roommate?"

Responses were limited to,
(a) "Wouldn't like it at all";
(b) "Would prefer someone else, but it wouldn't matter much"; and
(c) "Would not make any difference."

	(a)	(b)	(c)
Negro	33%	28%	39%
Asiatic Indian	25	31	44
Oriental	20	32	48
Jew	16	27	57

The poll shows that background characteristics strongly influence attitude toward race [and Semitism]. Students coming from farms and towns with less than 2,500 population are more likely to be prejudiced than those coming from medium-sized cities, while those who live in metropolitan areas are by far the least likely to discriminate. Fifty-five percent of men and women affiliated with fraternities and sororities discriminate, compared with 41 percent of independents. And only one-quarter of Protestants and Catholics have no objection to living with other racial groups. Half of Jews at Cornell do not discriminate; nor do 80 percent of those with no religious preference.

David Kogan '50
(1929–1951)

David Kogan followed the teachings of Rabbi Mordecai Kaplan (1881-1983), who viewed Judaism as a progressively evolving civilization. The goal of Kaplan's Reconstructionist movement is to balance cultural integration with the distillation of values from traditional Jewish sources. These are excerpts from David's diary.

Monday, August 11, 1946: Obtained leave of absence from camp[1] and decided to hitchhike to New York. Was picked up in Stroudsburg by a lonely man traveling in my direction. He inquired whether

---

[1] Kogan had a summer job as a dishwasher at Massad, a Hebrew-speaking camp in the Pocono Mountains. Other Massad alumni include activist Noam Chomsky, lawyer Alan Dershowitz, and designer Ralph Lauren.

they were treating me well at that "Jewish camp," adding, "I don't like to do business with Jews, they are always trying to take advantage of you." I told him he evidently had some bad experiences, but it was not fair to generalize. He surprised me by saying, "If you would know Jews as well as I do, you would agree with me."

It is not unusual for me, being fair and blue-eyed, to be mistaken for an "Aryan." I told him I have been living with Jews all my life, that I am a Jew myself. The man looked at me closely. "Like hell you are, a nice kid like you." I asked him to stop the car and leave me off. I didn't think we were going to enjoy each other's company. He went on: "Let's not be too hasty. Perhaps you can enlighten me."

We had a long conversation on the way to New York, discussing various phases of Judaism. He asked me how our rabbis feel in regard to Palestine—"Are they all of the same opinion?" I told him that some of them believe Palestine should be a haven for refugees, but the majority think that it should be a Jewish Commonwealth. He gave me his card and offered to call for me at the camp the next time I decide to go to New York.

FRIDAY, OCTOBER 25, 1946 [TWO WEEKS AFTER ARRIVING AT CORNELL]: At the Oneg Shabbat[2] at Hillel. It was good to sing Palestinian songs and dance the Hora again.

I have been studying the Jews here on the campus. Of the approximately 1,500, about one hundred are truly tied to Jewish values and traditions in the modern sense of the term. Then there are about sixty who are Orthodox and do not have

Cornell chapter of the B'nai B'rith Hillel Foundation, 1949. President David Kogan is in the front row, third from right. Standing next to him (third from left) is Rabbi Morris Goldfarb (1914-2004), who arrived at Cornell in 1949 and led its Jewish community for more than 40 years.

EYE OF THE BEHOLDER

The Cornell Daily Sun, May 26, 1948

Jews and Gentiles seem to regard the problem of discrimination on campus quite differently. While only 10 percent of non-Jewish students feel that there is a great deal of discrimination at Cornell, fully 90 percent of the Jewish population (which totals about 1,275 students) feel that discrimination does exist. Jewish students are nearly unanimous in agreeing that more should be done to improve relations between Jews and Gentiles on campus. Only half of non-Jewish students agree.

---

[2] A social event held on Friday nights, the beginning of the Sabbath.

anything to do with Conservative Hillel House. Another 100 or 200 enjoy going to services and are sympathetic to Jewish traditions. A factor almost unknown among Yonkers youth are the 300-odd radicals who work for the Negroes and Russia, but have nothing to do with anything Jewish, even refusing to come to Hillel House for social activities. Nevertheless they hang together at meetings where Jews predominate. The remaining 900 are in-between. Some come to occasional services; most going to Hillel House, but not at all really concerned with Jews and Judaism.

SATURDAY, MAY 15, 1948: I am thrilled about the formation of the Jewish State. Last night the beautiful Cornell chimes played the songs of modern Jewish Palestine for a full half hour.

This weekend I was elected president of the Hillel Foundation for the coming school year. The work is most challenging, trying to minister to the 1,200 members of Hillel and the 200 members of Ithaca College. It involves myriad details—when to do the work, when to delegate it, conciliating, complimenting, introducing, arguing, studying. Offering suggestions to committee members and have the ideas appear to come from them.

So far I have risen to the test. Prepared a plan on reorganization; called a special meeting on the purposes of Hillel (vaguely, social and religio-cultural, etc.); got out some publicity.

Was one of the speakers at the Zionist prayer meeting for Israel at midnight. Things look bad for the new state. I wish the great nations of the world still knew the meaning of words like justice and responsibility.

WEDNESDAY, APRIL 19, 1950: A two-hour bull session on anti-Semitism and prejudice toward minorities. My position is that we must fight prejudice by not consciously, or worse, self-consciously doing so. The Jews are in a fine position to study technique, falling as they do between whites and Negroes. The solution is a basic realization of the importance of treating an individual as an individual—and then doing so, with as much play and insult as a married person would treat his better half.

Richard Ottinger '50

I was president of Zeta Beta Tau, one of the Jewish fraternities, in my senior year. We were the most affluent chapter in their entire system, but we nearly got kicked out because we admitted a black man as a member. He had been our houseman for many years and everyone loved him, so we decided to honor him by making him an official member. Someone from the front office came up to try to talk us out of doing it. Eventually the guy started threatening us, but we held firm and in the end they didn't do anything. It was a small step in the right direction.

After receiving his BA from the College of Arts and Sciences, the Hon. Richard Ottinger earned a law degree from Harvard in 1953. He was a founding staff member of the Peace Corps (1961–64) and a member of the U.S. Congress from 1965 to 1969 and again from 1975 to 1985, representing Westchester County as a Democrat. He was dean of Pace University's law school, and has been a professor there since 1985.

Hanging around at Zeta Beta Tau in 1950.

Jacob Sheinkman '49, JD '52
(1927–2004)

My transition in August 1946 from a nineteen-year-old navy veteran to a student at the School of Industrial and Labor Relations (ILR) at Cornell was an opportunity for me to fulfill my ambition to play a role in the American labor movement. It was also a challenge nurtured by the role played by my idol, Eugene Victor Debs, a union and political leader, as well as by my schooling in the Workmen's Circle schools.[3]

I always knew I wanted to work for the labor movement. I came to the ILR school with that idea in mind. Because my father was a Socialist, I become interested in the labor movement at an early age.

When I got to Cornell, I found it highly segregated on religious and racial grounds. There were Jewish fraternities, non-Jewish fraternities, some Catholic fraternities, and so forth. Even rooming assignments were made along those lines. One day Sam Sackman '49, another ILR student and an army combat veteran, and I started to talk about the situation, and we decided we ought to try to change it. The Watermargin co-op was the result.

When the Service Workers Union sought to organize the service employees at Cornell, I was serving as Student Council president. I called other student leaders together to meet with the union representative to try to gain their support for the organizing drive,

an attempt which ultimately failed. What I learned from that failure assisted me in organizing a paper bag plant in Brooklyn as a summer intern for the Pulp, Sulphite, and Paper Mill Workers, which helped launch me on my career.

Jack Sheinkman became a labor leader and served as president of the Amalgamated Clothing and Textile Workers Union from 1987 to 1995. He was also chair of Americans for Democratic Action, the liberal advocacy group. Yet he called himself a "true capitalist" because he was chair of the board of the Amalgamated Bank of New York. He was also a board-elected (labor) member of Cornell's Board of Trustees from 1970 to 1988.

Samuel Sackman '49
(1923–2007)

Jack Sheinkman and I met when we were boys in my hometown of Rockaway Beach, New York. It was a summer vacation spot, and I played softball and handball with boys who visited from every other place in New York City. Jack came from the Bronx, and after we got to know each other, we teamed up to sucker the big-city boys. We would play the other teams out of uniform at first, for a bet of fifty cents or a dollar per person, and we would intentionally lose. Then we would schedule another game for a two-dollar bet per player. We would show up fully uniformed, playing our regular positions, and we'd always win. We went through that routine many times, but the other teams never seemed to catch on.

Jack was a fierce competitor

and a great athlete. We parted ways during the war and then found ourselves together again at the School of Industrial and Labor Relations at Cornell… In May or June of 1947, after we had finished our final exams, Jack and I decided to go to a bar. After getting to the point when neither of us felt too much pain, we agreed with others we had met at Cornell that we didn't much like campus life.

The discrimination at Cornell fraternities was antithetical to everything we believed in and had taken from our families and our upbringing. We dreamed of an integrated living facility comprising all races, religions, and nationalities. And let me be clear: we weren't looking to build a new way of life on the Cornell campus called "tolerance." We didn't want to be tolerated. We wanted a house based on the full acceptance of our differences, not just tolerating them.

Jack and I spent the early part of 1948 recruiting people for this new residence. Dorothy Norman, a reporter for *The New York Post*, interviewed us, and we told her all about the discrimination we saw at Cornell. Shortly after she printed the story, we were notified that we were in danger of being expelled. So we called on Professors Maurice Newfield and Milton Konvitz of the ILR School to save our respective butts. They got us a meeting with President Day and brought him around. They also promised to watch over the house we wanted to open, if the university would just lease it to us. Day said he would do that if we raised the money.

We spent that summer in New York City, raising money and support, with the help of the Reverend Jim Robinson of the Morningside Community Center, and our mutual

---

[3] Eugene Victor Debs (1855–1926) was an American union leader, one of the founding members of the Industrial Workers of the World, and five times the presidential candidate of the Socialist Party of America. The Workmen's Circle is an American Jewish fraternal organization committed to social justice, community, and Ashkenazic culture.

Renovating at Watermargin, 1949. Toshio Sato '51 holds paint can, Scott Hamilton '50 scrubs the floor.

friend Lillian Poses. I remember she got us invited to a reception for Elia Kazan, who directed the film version of *Gentleman's Agreement*. We opened the house around the beginning of 1949.[4]

Now came the real tests. Could we live together without killing one another, especially at parties where

blacks and whites socialized and danced together? Would someone live up to the stereotype and become violent when a disagreement arose? And how would we attract new people?

We did it with sports. We fielded teams in the intramural athletics program, and they were successful enough that we could shop for the best athletes on campus. Our message was that men could live and work together, irrespective of race, religion, or nationality. By winning intramural sports tournaments, we helped to bring this message to the Cornell community. Because of the nature of Watermargin, we were also able to attract speakers and entertainers who agreed with what we were doing and felt comfortable hanging out with us. I remember the night Dizzy Gillespie and his group

played at the house after a concert on campus.

We played basketball and softball against fraternity teams, with a bet that the loser had to bring a keg of beer to the winner's house the next Saturday night. We had excellent teams and we won a lot, so we drank a lot of free beer. Those Saturday night parties also helped introduce Watermargin to fraternities in a non-threatening way. We made sure that those connections, as well as others, opened doors for us to spread the story of Watermargin up and down the East Coast.

One of our members, Scott Hamilton '50, was from Arkansas. He invited his father to attend a Watermargin meeting, and his father almost had apoplexy when he walked into the room and saw the black faces there. But he held up well. He didn't walk out. He swallowed hard, bit the bullet, and stayed with his son.

One thing we didn't understand was that some black organizations on campus viewed Watermargin as a threat to their own goals. We had some black members tell us that they received pressure from the National Association for the Advancement of Colored Persons (NAACP) not to be active in Watermargin. Integration was not their goal. It appeared as if their goal was strengthening their black identity.

Samuel Sackman was offered a contract to play center field for the New York Giants in 1942, but chose to enlist in the Army Air Forces instead. He served for three years in the United States, learning and teaching radio operations. After earning a BS from the ILR School, he worked in labor-management relations for the Ladies' Garment Workers Union, the Federal Mediation and Conciliation Service, and as a consultant.

---

[4] Alumni who were active in the anti-discrimination campaigns of the 1940s included Laura Z. Hobson '21, author of *Gentlemen's Agreement* (1947), a novel that became an Oscar-winning film about anti-Semitism; Edward Bernays 1912, nephew of Sigmund Freud and founder of public relations in the United States; the judge Samuel Liebowitz, LLB 1915; and Jerome "Brud" Holland '39, a native of nearby Auburn, New York, who was the first African-American to play football at Cornell. Holland became president of the Hampton Institute, held a seat on the board of the New York Stock Exchange, and was the US Ambassador to Sweden during the Nixon administration.

John Marcham '50
(1927–2014)

I was one of thirty-three founding members of Watermargin, and thirty of us were military veterans. Co-founder Jack Sheinkman was the quiet one. He was our first president, but he didn't ever live in the house. The other co-founder, Sam Sackman, was fiery. He was a member of the NAACP and the progressive American Veterans Committee. He lived in the house at 103 McGraw Place and shaped our early spirit.

Being brothers did not prove to be easy. I'm told at the first work party, two Jewish members self-consciously referred to one another as Yids and kikes. They quickly became comfortable enough with fellow Asian, Gentile, and black members to move beyond this. In time, more serious disagreements arose and factions formed.

Our parties were many and popular. I remember one clearly, centered downstairs in the crowded barroom. Jack Sheinkman and Harold "Ron" Raynolds '48, MA '53, who had been editor of *The Cornell Daily Sun* and lived in Theta Delt, the conservative fraternity across McGraw Place, were arm in arm doing a vigorous Russian Cossack squat dance on the basement floor to the shouts of the chanting partiers.

I also recall a houseparty date of mine (not my wife, Jane) who had started college in Washington, D.C. She told me she was uneasy with Negroes, whom she said jostled her on crowded sidewalks. What a surprise she had that first morning at 103, going into the women's bathroom to find the wife of black member Reggie Ingram '51 washing their baby son in one of the small sink bowls. Like others who came in touch with the vivacious Doris Ingram, my date came away a good deal more comfortable with all humanity.

Robert Kushell '50

I was just about ready to pledge a fraternity when I heard about Watermargin. After one visit I knew that this was where I belonged. Having just been discharged from the service, I had no patience with those aspects of society that represented un-American values. We had just returned from fighting a war to defeat countries that believed in the preservation of racial and religious purity. Yet campuses still had a fraternity system that selected its members from the same backgrounds as those who created these barriers. I not only did not want to be part of that state of mind. I wanted to do everything that I could to disprove this type of thinking.

Lots of people on campus looked at us with raised eyebrows and a sneer, and our house looked like the authorities might condemn it at any moment. We were not the kind of people you wanted to bring home to meet your parents. But thanks to the leadership of Sam Sackman, we stood proud and defiant next to those huge, well-manicured fraternity mansions. And we got them to respect us, because we were tough athletes and even tougher consumers of beer and whiskey. I ought to know. I was the house's bartender.

Robert Kushell was a corpsman in a naval hospital during World War II and received a BA from the College of Arts and Sciences. He is a business consultant.

Watermargin party.

Roger Wolcott '50

I considered myself something of a radical, so when I got to Cornell, I drifted into the Student League for Industrial Democracy, which was, at that time, a radical anti-Stalinist group. Some people called us Trotskyites. At one of those meetings, in my sophomore year, I encountered Jack Sheinkman. I joined Watermargin soon after.

One reason we succeeded was that Jack and Sam recruited such good people. They got Walt McNiece '50, sensible and steady, who became our first president. Jovial Reggie Ingram '51 was a conspicuous member, as was my good friend, the colorful Ted Sumner '50. Toshio Sato '51 educated me about the ways of the Hawaiian-Japanese community. Some other members who added an exotic element to the group were Harold Dale Shaw '50, an acrobat who kept a four-foot python in his room; Anastasios Cotsis '49, a citizen of Greece who was worried about being drafted into the Greek army, which was fighting a nasty guerilla war at the time; and Abdul from Afghanistan, who was famous for disregarding the usual American rules about driving motor vehicles.

Our parties had a variety of themes. I remember particularly one we called "behind the iron curtain," which featured an elaborate "Berlin airlift" to get into the house. You climbed up a ladder to get over a barrier and slid down the other side into a bunch of pillows. That was years before the Berlin Wall went up.

Roger Wolcott got a BA from the College of Arts and Sciences and earned a PhD in sociology from Columbia University. He became a sociology professor at Westminster College in New Wilmington, Pennsylvania.

Ted Sumner's Packard, which served as the Watermargin co-op's taxi.

Frederick O. B. "Ted" Sumner '50

Watermargin's float for the Spring Day parade in 1949 was notable. That was the year comic strip artists judged the floats, and to understand the float, you also have to remember that Alfred Kinsey's sensational book, *Sexual Behavior of the Human Male*, had come out just a few months earlier.

Walter Rutes, who got his architecture degree in 1950,[5] thought up our homage to Rube Goldberg. The float was a long platform, and at the far end was a bush. A hunter crouched, with his gun pointed at the bush. A guy was hiding in the bush with a bird on the end of a skinny pole. Roger Wolcott was dressed up as a huge, perpetually rocking bird, like the toy you used to see that would occasionally bend down to get a drink. Roger's tail would hit the bush, disturbing the bird, which flew upward. The hunter fired, and the shot activated a track runner to run the length of the float. The runner went through a string at the finish line, which was tied to a rocking chair where a pretty co-ed was sitting. She was reading a book we titled "Sexual Behavior of the Cornell Male." As she bent backward, the hero-runner came over and kissed her on the lips.

We had the cartoonists roaring, and we should have gotten first prize. We heard later that a fraternity beat us only because they had spent so much money on their Flash Gordon masks and suits.

Ted Sumner earned a BA from the College of Arts and Sciences. He has worked as an arborist, an inventor, and a toy maker.

Watermargin was entirely a men's project. When a group of Cornell women tried to start a similar residence project, they were rebuffed.

---

[5] Rutes later wrote *Hotel Design, Planning and Development* (W. W. Norton & Company, 2001) a classic in its field.

Lydia Cushman Schurman '50

I thought sororities were a lot of hokum, so I don't know why I pledged Kappa Alpha Theta in my sophomore year. I never should have done it. I liked the girls and was young and brainless, and so I joined. The next year, after realizing this was not something I wanted to do, I left. Mari Lund [Wright] '50 left with me. By that time I had gotten involved with a new organization called Credo, which was much closer to my beliefs. At Credo you didn't have to rush and be accepted and all that nonsense. We were looking at the example of Watermargin.

We felt that women should have an alternative to rushing. A lot of women were just devastated when sororities did not accept them. I couldn't stand that, and I had to do something. Credo means "I Believe" in Latin. We had a list of all the things we believed. We didn't have any social functions or parties or social service projects that I recall. We just believed things.

It was Ann Ellis [Raynolds], Marion Holley [Wijnberg], Eve Weinschenker [Paul], myself, and several others. We went to Lucile Allen, the dean of women, because we also wanted to set up a residence, like a women's version of Watermargin. So we went into our twenty-minute pitch about inclusiveness, Christians and Jews living together, and democracy and all these wonderful thoughts. She listened, and then she asked, "What is the difference between Credo and a dormitory?" And we didn't have a good answer in practical terms. It was a brilliant, incisive remark, and it took the wind out of our sails. We still held to our beliefs, but we didn't ever get our house.

FIRST LADY'S DAY AT CORNELL

FROM ELEANOR ROOSEVELT'S SYNDICATED NEWSPAPER COLUMN, FEBRUARY 22, 1950

Back from Ithaca, New York, this morning, two and a half hours late! I suppose the added load on the trains that do run—passenger and freight —contributes to the lagging schedules even more than the weather. However, the first real cold of the winter was noticed all through New York State. I went to Cornell at the invitation of a group that calls itself "Watermargin," a name taken from an old Chinese novel that means "all men are brothers."

Some of the boys met me at the train in Syracuse on Monday afternoon and, fortunately, I was only three-quarters of an hour late. The drive from there to Cornell had to be taken rather slowly, since the roads were somewhat slippery. We arrived in time for a reception in the boys' house, where thirty members of the group live and about sixty or seventy eat every day.

My speech in the evening came at the conclusion of a two-day conference at which [Watermargin had invited] forty delegates from seventeen schools and colleges to discuss the program they were carrying on and to find out whether they believed it was something that would be accepted on other campuses.

It seems to me very encouraging that these young people should take such an interest in human rights and freedoms. It is encouraging that they should recognize so quickly that our acceptance of these ideals is just a spelling out of the real ideals of democracy. They believe that only by putting them into practice will we demonstrate to the world what democracy really stands for and define more clearly for the average human being the world over the differences between the philosophy of democracy and of communism.

First Lady Eleanor Roosevelt (1884–1962) was the wife of Franklin D. Roosevelt, president of the United States from 1933 to 1945. She was also the U.S. delegate to the United Nations General Assembly from 1946 to 1952 and chair of the United Nations Commission on Human Rights from 1946 to 1951. This is an excerpt from her syndicated newspaper column "My Day," which ran six days a week from 1935 to 1962.

A QUALIFIED NEGRO

The Cornell Daily Sun, December 11, 1947

In recognition of the interest shown by several campus organizations, the Cornell chapter of the NAACP presents the following statement of the faculty survey made during the spring term, 1947... This survey is based on interviews of forty-nine department chairmen of various colleges of Cornell by members of the NAACP Educational Committee...

Would you have any hesitation about a qualified Negro on your staff? No, 71 percent; yes, 29 percent.

Do you think the students would object to being taught by a qualified Negro? No, 29 percent; some would, 27 percent; don't know, 43 percent; yes, 22 percent.

To gain further information on student objection, 461 students from three colleges were asked the following question:

"Would you object to being taught at Cornell by a qualified Negro instructor or professor, yes or no?" Yes, 5.5 percent; no, 92.5 percent.

Apparently students are more liberal than their teachers consider them to be...

Walter B. Lewis '46, JD '49, MPA '50
(1919–1991)

Cornell had an active chapter of the NAACP in the 1920s. The chapter became active again in 1946, after an Ithaca restaurant owner refused to serve two black students. The chapter's leader was Walter B. Lewis, a veteran of the Pacific war, who arrived at Cornell after receiving a degree from Tougaloo College in Tougaloo, Mississippi.

After receiving a BA and degrees from the law and business schools, Walter Lewis worked for the federal government and the Urban League. From 1964 to 1968 he was director of the federal program division of the U.S. Civil Rights Commission. He was director of equal opportunity for the Department of Housing and Urban Development in 1968 and 1969, and later a professor of city planning and associate dean at Howard University. He served on the Washington, D. C., zoning commission from 1975 to 1984, and was its chairman. At the time of his death, he was with the law firm Linowes & Blocker.

James Lowell Gibbs Jr. '52

Juanita Miller (Johnson) '52 and I were in Ithaca schools together, from the first grade on, and we went on to Cornell together. Other African-Americans from Ithaca had attended Cornell, but we were the first local black kids to graduate. Once we showed it could be done, several others followed us.

My father was the founding executive director of the Southside Community Center,[6] and later he was the first African-American to work in the Ithaca post office. He worked at the counter. From both of these jobs, he knew a lot of people. My family had friends who were on the Cornell faculty through the Democratic Party, the League of Women Voters, and St. John's Episcopal Church.

I thought of Cornell as the shining place on the hill. By the time I was in high school, I was convinced that a professor was the best thing you could possibly be.

When I was in high school I had jobs at Willard Straight Hall, first in the kitchen. This was before Statler Hall was built, so the faculty dining room was at the Straight. My job was to put the vegetables on the faculty members' plates. I also got to know my peers through youth fellowship groups at the Presbyterian and Methodist churches. And I had several exceptional teachers. Jane Stoutenberg,

---

[6] Southside Community Center opened in 1937 and paid off its mortgage in 1944 after a community fund-raising campaign supported by several Cornell faculty members, trustees, and alumni, including Mr. & Mrs. Robert H. Treman 1880 and Brud Holland '39. It remains open in 2015.

who taught social studies at Boynton Junior High School, was one. Elizabeth (Betty) Elliott, my high school English teacher, was an especially strong mentor.

But I did see racial discrimination, of course. I was a paper carrier until I was sixteen, when you had to give the job up. I went to the high school employment office to find another job. What I did not know was that they would call employers and ask them if they would take a "colored boy." I got a job as a part-time custodian for a second-floor photographer in an old building on State Street. I was supposed to sprinkle this green stuff on the floor and then sweep it up. That was the only time in my life I have ever been fired. I guess I was not very good at that.

Then I got hired at Feinstone Upholstery Shop, and that was partly what led me into anthropology. The owners were Mr. and Mrs. Hugh Chafin. She was Russian-born and they were Communists, really nice people. For Christmas in 1947, they gave me a copy of *African Journey* by Paul Robeson's wife, Eslanda Goode Robeson, about the fieldwork she had done in Uganda in the 1930s. The book made a big impression on me. I wrote a paper about it for Miss Elliot, whose praise and encouragement I remember well.

Sociology 101 at Cornell gave me a scheme, hooks to hang things on. I think the anthropologist who had the most impact on me was W. Lloyd Warner,[7] who most people thought of as a sociologist. He out-

---

[7] W. Lloyd Warner (1898–1970) was a socio-anthropologist who taught at the University of Chicago and Michigan State University. His five-volume study of Newburyport, Massachusetts, is a classic study of social class in the United States.

At a Watermargin group meeting around 1950. Jim Gibbs is second from left in the back row.

lined the six social classes he found in a small American town. That was revelatory. One of the advantages of growing up in Ithaca was there was only one high school, so I got to rub shoulders with people from all walks of life. Warner put all that into place.

My real understanding of social class, and of research, came in four summers, 1949 through 1952, when I worked as a researcher for Cornell's Department of Sociology and Anthropology. I worked in several capacities on a study of ethnic and race relations in Elmira, which resulted in the book *Strangers Next Door; Ethnic Relations in American Communities* (1964). The first two of those years I worked as an interviewer and participant observer. The second pair I was a coder of interviews and the operator of a pre-computer IBM counter sorter.

The two summers in the project office were particularly important. I rubbed shoulders with the graduate

students who worked on the project and, more importantly, with the faculty directors—Professors Robin Williams, Edward Suchman, and John Dean. I learned an enormous amount from them, and the experience led to my decision to enter academia.

It wasn't hard to be black at Cornell, socially, but there were very few of us, so we couldn't help but stand out. This could work in your favor. I was elected president of my junior class over someone who came from a prominent Cornell family—Barton Treman '52, the son of Alan Treman '21. One reason I won was that I had worked at the counter at the Johnny Parson Club[8] for three

---

[8] The Johnny Parson Club was a two-story facility on Beebe Lake where skaters and other students could eat, drink, and warm up. Parson (1870–1951) was an Engineering professor who is credited with establishing ice hockey and encouraging skating at Cornell. The Club closed after Lynah Rink opened in 1958.

years. Like my dad, I knew a lot of people. There were so few black faces that people remembered me. I also played drums in the Big Red Band. Out of town relatives would see the band at halftime, and there would be one black face in a sea of white ones. I was easy to spot.

I was also active in the Cornell chapter of the NAACP. We fought against housing discrimination in Ithaca and at the fraternities and sororities. We had a big campaign to abolish the requirement that applicants submit a photograph of themselves, because it gave the admissions folks a convenient way to discriminate against blacks and Jews. It's ironic, because years later, this position flipped completely. After affirmative action laws were passed, many people were eager to make their identity known.

I can remember being invited to apply to one fraternity. The person who invited me was Josiah (Jo) Dodds '51, whom I knew because he was the son of Ithaca's Presbyterian minister. He did it as a symbolic gesture, because he knew that my social life centered around Watermargin. I joined Watermargin the year it opened, which was also my freshman year, and even though I didn't live there. My mother used to say I only slept at home.

Jim Gibbs received a BA from the College of Arts and Sciences and a PhD from Harvard, where he was the first African-American resident tutor in the university's history. He became a professor of anthropology at Stanford and was the university's dean of undergraduate studies. He was also a senior fellow at the W. E. B. DuBois Institute for Afro-American Research at Harvard, and a Cornell Trustee from 1973 to 1977.

Gentlemen's Agreement

Prior to fraternity and sorority rushing in 1948–49, students from Watermargin were among those circulating a petition whose signers "declare opposition to discriminatory membership practices and rules based on racial and religious considerations for fraternities and sororities." Some Cornell chapters in the Greek system were required to discriminate by the bylaws of their national organizations. The petition asked signers to "actively work to delete such clauses," thereby "stopping a blight which threatens to undermine the whole [fraternity-sorority] structure." The petition's initial goal was to force the Interfraternity Council (IFC) to address the issue.

THE CORNELL DAILY SUN, EDITORIAL, FEBRUARY 7, 1949: The issue involved is not new. Can and will the fraternity and sorority system flourish to the maximum extent when some houses in it are forbidden to take persons of certain races and religions? It has been debated wherever the system has functioned and will be so long as blanket discriminatory rules are part of the system. The prevailing view in this country that requires individuals to be judged as individuals runs directly counter to the retention of such rules.

Even houses which are fortunate enough not to be hampered by restrictive clauses have been acting as though they did. It is squarely up to them to mend their ways and to pledge in the future after a consideration of the rushee as an individual.

Managers of *The Cornell Daily Sun* pose in 1950. FRONT ROW, L-R: Dick Pogue '50 (managing editor), John Marcham '50 (editor in chief), Lorraine Vogel [Klerman] '50 (news board). SECOND ROW: Marion Steinmann '50 (news board), Ellen Bigler [Harrison] '51 (business board), Tom McCune '51 (managing editor), Lydia Schurman '50 (women's editor), Pat Lovejoy [Stoddard] '52 (news board). Two in back row are unidentified.

THE CORNELL WIDOW

FEB. 25¢

SUN

SOAP

The February 1949 issue of the *Cornell Widow* poked fun at the sanctimonious tone of anti-discrimination editorials in *The Cornell Daily Sun.*

When a society permits the organization of groups within itself (as a democracy does), then that society must retain the right to have such groups constituted in such a way that they do not violate the principles of the larger institution. Fraternities and sororities should have the power to determine their own membership, but where restrictive clauses are present this right and duty is negated.

John Marcham '50
(1927–2014)

We *Sun* editors thought we were pretty hot stuff in those days. We drew from the best fraternities and sororities on the Hill, and from Telluride House. We had National Scholars and junior Phi Beta Kappas, pre-meds, and pre-laws in considerable numbers. Board members were bright, attractive, and sociable. The staff partied together, dated, and sometimes even married...

When we started going after discriminatory membership clauses in fraternity and sorority charters in the fall of 1948, it split our staff and made us many enemies among other students. We were so sure of our rightness that we asked editor in chief Howard Loomis '49, who was also vice president of the Interfraternity Council, to step aside as editor, but he didn't, and the *Sun* did not achieve any great changes that I can recall. The paper's righteousness brought it into direct and not surprising conflict with the *Cornell Widow*, defender of the status quo and the good life. And when the *Sun* spoke of minorities, chances are it was thinking of Jews rather than blacks as the people primarily aggrieved.

THE CORNELL DAILY SUN, APRIL 11, 1949: The Interfraternity Council (IFC) accepted unanimously last night a report on discriminatory restrictive clauses prepared by the executive committee of the council and based on a survey of Cornell chapters... the report concluded that "it is the considered opinion of the chapters here in general that discriminatory clauses should be removed..." Results of the survey indicated that most Cornell chapters believe action should come from member fraternities, and that "no united effort should be made to force fraternities to conform to a particular pattern."

The 1949 IFC report was the beginning of a long campaign to eliminate "categorical discrimination" at Cornell:

In 1952, the IFC's Discrimination Committee reported that twenty-one Cornell fraternities had restrictive clauses.

In 1954, a committee of faculty, IFC leaders, and Student Council members reported that thirteen fraternities still had discriminatory clauses.

In 1956, the Cornell chapter of the Sigma Kappa sorority was suspended by its national organization for pledging a black woman. The chapter decided to continue as an unaffiliated organization.

In 1957, a joint student-faculty committee appointed by President Deane Malott reported that eight fraternities still had formal restrictive clauses, and that others maintained unwritten "gentlemen's agreements" that restricted membership.

In 1961, the Student Council voted to end "categorical discrimination" in all student organizations and requested that the trustees make it the university's official policy.

In 1962, the university instituted random selection in rooming assignments.

In 1965, the university no longer allowed fraternities with restrictive clauses to remain on campus.

Watermargin is still operating at 103 McGraw Place. Although the founders' goal of starting a national movement was never realized, current residents say they "strive to live by their example."

Photographer Frederick Marcham recorded the reaction of Cornell fans as the ball cleared the goalposts to beat Dartmouth on November 13, 1948.

CHAPTER 8

Go Big Red

Championship Teams (Not for Women)

It was the biggest show in town. At Cornell home football games in the late 1940s, crowds of 30,000 or more packed Schoellkopf Field to cheer for teams that ranked among the best in the country. Football's Ivy League was not formally created until 1954, but competition among the eight Ivy schools (Brown, Columbia, Cornell, Dartmouth, Harvard, Penn, Princeton, and Yale) during the nine-game season was fierce.

In those pre-television, pre-NCAA division days, the game also had a more egalitarian spirit. President Edmund Ezra Day was a passionate football fan, but he also followed a 1945 Ivy League compact that banned direct athletic scholarships and urged players to "enjoy the game as participants in a form of recreational competition rather than as performers in a type of public spectacle." Cornell won the Ivy League football championship in 1948 and 1949 and ranked in the top twenty teams nationally.

Football wasn't the only show in town, however. The basketball and track teams drew thousands of spectators; the soccer team was a two-time Ivy League champion, the tennis team won the title three times, and the lightweight rowing team won the national championship in 1949. Yet amid all this action, women could only watch. They were largely excluded from athletic teams until Congress passed Title IX regulations in 1972.

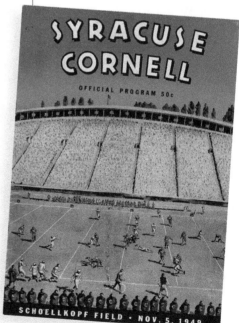

Football

Robert "Rip" Haley '51

"Rip" Haley was a starter on the 1948, 1949, and 1950 Cornell football teams.

I started as a defensive halfback at 165 pounds, and I was not considered small. Today, the average defensive back weighs about 200 pounds. Players today are also faster than we were, so the hits are much harder. The big differences are size and speed.

We wore hard leather helmets without an inner shell. Our pads weighed three or four pounds more, and they weren't as good. But the whole time I played I think I only got one concussion.

Training is different, too. Players now live in gyms year-round, and they always watch their diets. We could eat anything we wanted except for the day of a game. About two weeks before practice began in August, I'd go out and throw the football around a little. Several teammates were smokers, including some of our best

guys. The whole thing was much lower key. Still, the first two or three days of training were brutal.

Frank Kavanaugh was the trainer. Everyone called him Doc. He was a jovial Irishman, just as advertised. His main job was to get us in shape, but he also kept us loose by acting like one of the guys. He was always making jokes and leading us in songs that had titles like, "You worked all your life for me, dear mother, now go out and work for yourself." And he would dance when he sang.

My travel roommate was Hillary Chollet, one of our big stars, very bright and intense. The night before an away game, we'd go to our room after dinner and he'd sit right down and study for two or three hours. I would be so keyed up that I couldn't do anything.

The team had all kinds of guys. Hillary came from a Creole family in New Orleans. My father was a coal miner. One of my closest friends was Harvey Sampson Jr. '51, and his dad owned the Harvey Radio Company. Our different backgrounds didn't separate us, because we had football.

I did take my cues from the older guys who were war veterans,

like Paul Girolamo and Bob Dean, but there was no dividing line. Our quarterback, Pete Dorset, was a decorated veteran with incredible war stories, but I didn't know that until after I graduated.

The things I remember best about the games were the times I screwed up. We played New York University in one of my first games in 1948. They didn't have much of a team, but they did have a tight end named Irving "Moon" Mondschein who was also an Olympic decathlete. He took a short pass, and I had him completely trapped, but he did a juke on me that was so good that I fell down. He just kind of walked around me, and that was the only time they scored. It took me decades to live that down.

Haley worked for industrial supply firms and then became a development officer at Cornell, Clarkson, and Johns Hopkins Universities.

Meyer H. Abrams

I started going to Cornell football games in 1945, when I started teaching there. I didn't miss a Cornell home game until 2012. But I have very little interest in professional football. I like sports that are amateur and local.

Game days in the 1940s were extremely festive. The Schoellkopf Crescent would be decorated with banners; there would be music and cheerleaders, and people would get all dressed up. The stands were always full. A lot of people would bring alcohol, but the game and the athletes were intoxicating enough for me. I also remember a bear cub being led around on a chain. He clearly didn't like being there. My sympathies were with the bear.

Rip Haley intercepts a pass in the 1948 Cornell-Navy game as Hillary Chollet (r) looks on. Cornell won, 13 to 7.

Bob Dean '49 was a most attractive young man, with a shock of bright blonde hair. He was radiant. I think he must have colored it. And Hillary Chollet '50 was the best all-around athlete I have ever seen play. He ran with the ball, he could quarterback, and he was also on the basketball team. He could do anything.

Hillary came from a Creole family. He had curly hair and olive-colored skin. I think that the head coach, Lefty James, was suspicious that he was African-American trying to pass as white. The two of them didn't get along very well, but Hillary was always in the lineup because nobody was better than he was.

Kenneth Van Sickle
(1916–2000)

Kenny Van Sickle was the dean of Ithaca sportswriters.

The Ithaca Journal, October 27, 1947: The interest in Cornell has increased by leaps as a result of its great comeback victory at Princeton, to win 28–21…the chances are good that many fans will produce the $3.60, including tax, to [get into this weekend's game against Columbia] and get a glimpse of the new Cornell hero, Little Lynn (Pete) Dorset '50, a 160-pound, 5′8″ morsel of a man.

The home folks have had only fleeting glances of him this far, even in practice. By proving his worth as a pass pitcher and a field general, both far beyond Lefty James' wildest dreams, the fans can rest assured he will be used again.

1947 CORNELL FOOTBALL 4–5

Home games are capitalized, W = win, L = loss, T = tie

9/27	LEHIGH	W	27–0
10/4	at Yale	L	0–14
10/11	at Colgate	W	27–18
10/18	NAVY	L	19–38
10/25	at Princeton	W	28–21
11/1	COLUMBIA	L	0–22
11/8	SYRACUSE	W	12–6
11/15	at Dartmouth	L	13–21
11/27	at Penn	L	0–21

Don Diene '52 and his fraternity brothers at Tau Kappa Epsilon work on their mechanical "Beat Syracuse" sign the day before the Cornell-Syracuse game, November 1949.

Pete Dorset

late innings of a baseball game with a pitcher headed for a no-hitter, as Dorset had pass after pass completed. His last one, number ten, was a thirty-yard rainbow, which traveled even farther in the air, to Norm Dawson '48 in the end zone for the fourth touchdown...

The first two Cornell touchdowns were on identical sixty-four-yard marches with identical pass plays, Dorset to [Bernard] Babula '50, on the end of them... Cornell endeavored to grind out the yardage in its first second half offensive,

Bernie Babula

but it didn't work. But with Dorset interspersing ground plays with aerials, it began to bring results and Cornell marched sixty-one yards to its third tally. In all there were nine plays [in this scoring drive], three of them passes. On second down from the four-yard line, Babula cut wide around his left tackle for the six points.

Fred Westphal '48 recovered a fumble on the next play series, giving Cornell the ball on the Princeton thirty-yard line, and Cornell went in with a quickie. After a lengthy Princeton time out, Dorset heaved the high hard one to Dawson just inside the end zone. Norm somehow or other shook off the Tiger defender Sella, who was sprawled on the ground looking on as Norm made the catch. Sella looked pretty silly lying there.

Van Sickle started writing about local sports for *The Ithaca Journal* while in high school in 1931. When he retired in the late 1990s, he estimated that he had covered four hundred Cornell football games

Lynn "Pete" Dorset '50, LLB '53 (1925–97) was born in South Carolina and moved

Nobody in Palmer Stadium Saturday had their hopes rise an iota when Dorset entered the [Princeton] game in the second quarter. He was just another kid they called "Pete." The Big Red was virtually a wreck, snowed under by a seemingly insurmountable 14–0 deficit with only eighteen minutes of the game gone.

But just as easily as Princeton had amassed its two-touchdown lead with an assortment of plain and fancy plays, Dorset paved the way for an upset victory. His unerring accuracy with his passing arm, his play-calling, and the inspiration he gave the team was enough to give Cornell and not Princeton a fourteen-point advantage. It was a demoralized Tiger that sat back in wonderment until it was too late to do anything about it.

The tension was like that in the

to Miami, Florida, in 1930. He enrolled at Cornell in 1942 and left to become a staff sergeant in the Army Air Forces. He was a ball turret gunner for a B-17 that saw combat in Europe and was awarded the Distinguished Flying Cross, the Air Medal with three clusters, the Silver Star for exceptional gallantry, the Presidential Unit citation with one cluster, the ETO ribbon with four battle stars, and two Purple Hearts. He parachuted into enemy territory three times, each time escaping via the underground back to free country. In one case, it took him five months to make it home.

Dorset earned a BA from Cornell and a JD in 1953. He practiced law in Cortland, New York, and served as Cortland's city judge from 1971 until 1994. He was also a coach and director of the Cortland Small Fry Football League, where he mentored many players, including Gary Wood '64, who became Cornell's starting quarterback for three years and went on to play for the New York Giants.

"Pete was a nice Southern boy," says his wife, Diane. In 1979, after finding Thomas South, 20, guilty of shouting obscenities at police officers, Judge Dorset gave him a choice: a $50 fine, or having his mouth washed out with soap. "South chose the suds," reported *Time* magazine. The arresting officers took him "into the washroom of the police station and watched while he put some granular hand soap into his mouth and washed it out with water. Judge Dorset, who has offered the soaping to previous offenders, finds that none of the foul mouths who accept turn up again in court."

Walt Bruska '50

When I showed up for spring football practice in 1947, I was one of about 180 candidates. The competition for the position I wanted, halfback, was really tough. I wanted to make an impression, so I made sure that I was one of the first on the practice field every day, and I responded with great eagerness to every command. I even blocked a guy six inches taller and thirty pounds heavier than I was, using unnecessary force, in a one-on-one drill one afternoon. It made him furious and he came after me, but I fought back.

My eager beaver antics got some attention. Al Kelley '41, the end coach, suggested I try out for end, because there was less competition for that position. Al had played end for Cornell and was extremely intelligent, a Cornell engineer. He went on to be the head coach at Brown, Colgate, and Hobart. He spent some private time with me and taught me the moves. I had been a pretty fair halfback, but I had a lot to learn about other aspects of the game.

Al was a superior teacher, a great coach. Lefty James and the other coaches were outstanding, too. They worked hard and we were always well prepared. But the only players who got close to Lefty were the quarterbacks. Almost all of us ended up feeling that the assistant coach was our coach.

I made the team and played on the substitute squad in 1947. I was the backup player for Jack Rogers '49, but if the other starting end, Harry Cassel '50, was injured, I would start at left end. So I ended up learning the plays from both sides of the line. Then I was a starter in 1948 and '49, and a coach from 1950 to '53.

Walt Bruska, number 88.

Robert J. Kane '34, JD '37
(1911–1992)

Ed McKeever was Cornell's football coach in 1946, having arrived from Notre Dame a year earlier. Under my prodding, Ed hired as coaches Al Kelley '41 and Hal McCullough '39, who were members of the superior Cornell teams of 1939 and 1940 and had just been released from war service. McKeever brought Pat Filley and Bud Boerenger with him from Notre Dame. George K. "Lefty" James, E. B. "Speed" Wilson, and Mose Quinn remained from the previous head coach, Carl Snavely. With a worthy mix of youth and experience and a high quotient of brainpower, it was a good staff.

One winter evening I was sitting at the press table at a basketball game in Barton Hall. The stands were too crowded for comfort. As soon as the gun went off signaling halftime, a dignified, soft-spoken gentleman approached me and asked if he could speak with me for a few minutes. He identified himself as Wilbur Saunders, headmaster of Peddie School in Hightstown, New Jersey. He was on campus to attend a dinner gathering of Peddie School graduates at Cornell.

He acquainted me with the case of one Frank L. Bradley Jr., a Peddie graduate. Bradley was an Army Air Forces navigator, and he had just been turned down by our College of Engineering for the fall semester. Saunders asked me, "How could Cornell afford to reject the application of a young man who was cum laude at Peddie, president of his class, captain of the football team, all-state halfback, winner of

Head Coach George "Lefty" James with players.

the New Jersey one hundred yard dash title, and with two years of air forces experience behind him?" There were, he said, several good colleges that wanted him, including Ivy colleges, but Frank preferred Cornell because of its excellent engineering college and strong athletic program, and it was the only college to turn him down.

I had not heard of Frank Bradley, and being somewhat inured to overblown sales pitches in this vintage period of Cornell's sports appeal, I must confess I probably listened to Saunders with a degree of airy skepticism. But I made some notes and checked with our football coaches the next morning, and found out that Bradley was indeed all the headmaster said he was as a player and as a student.

Those were the days when the athletics director reported directly to the president, and one was care-

ful not to jeopardize this privilege by bothering him with trivia. Somehow, the more I thought about the Bradley situation, the less it seemed to be trivia. Next morning I called to see if I could talk with President Edmund Ezra Day. "Come on over," he said. I felt a little sheepish about it, but when I read off Frank Bradley's surpassing credentials, he was vexed.

President Day was a football fan, but he was also a man who was terribly bothered by things that didn't make good sense, and he could not find any sense in this one. Dean Hollister was also a Cornell football devotee. Day rang for his secretary, Frances Egan. "Get Dean Hollister for me," he called to her. He lit his pipe and set his jaw for some hard questioning. The phone buzzer on his desk soon sounded and the conversation with Solomon Hollister, dean of the Engineering

College, went something like this.

"Hello, Holly," he opened amiably enough, "I would like you to get out the mechanical engineering admissions folder of a young man named Frank L. Bradley. I want to talk to you about it." Dean Hollister left the phone for a few minutes and returned with the folder. Day read off the listing of credits I had given him. "Are those correct, Holly?" Holly must have said they were.

"How in the hell can we possibly turn down a fine student like that?" he zeroed in. Dean Hollister replied that the president had approved a quota of 175 entering students for mechanical engineering, and that was filled before Frank Bradley's application had come in. He explained that his application had been delayed until he was sure of the date of his release from the Army Air Forces. "We would have taken him, no doubt, if there had been a place for him. He's actually on the waiting list."

"Would you take him off the waiting list if there was an opening?" asked the president.

"Yes," responded the dean.

"You say the quota is 175. Let's make it 176. Does that do it?"

"That does it."

So Frank Bradley came to Cornell.

Robert Kane fired Ed McKeever after the 1946 Syracuse game because McKeever had asked alumni to cover the living expenses of football players, a violation of Cornell's athletic policies. Lefty James was promoted to head coach for the last two games of 1946 and remained in that position until the end of the 1960 season. James's lifetime record at Cornell was sixty-six wins, fifty-eight losses, and two ties. But between 1948 and 1951, he won twenty-eight games and lost only seven.

Ivy League Champs, 1948

Cornell and Dartmouth were contending for the title when they faced off in Ithaca on November 13, 1948.

Bob Kane: The 1948 Cornell-Dartmouth game will live in history as one of the most thrilling ever seen on Schoellkopf Field. One of Cornell's running backs, Frank Bradley '50, had broken his jaw in the Colgate game a week before. His jaw was wired shut and he survived on a liquid diet.

Everybody in Ithaca was thinking Cornell football in those days, and in the days before the game, Frankie's incapacitation aroused deep concern. Roland "Red" Fowler '22, vice president and superintendent of the National Cash Register plant in Ithaca, called me and said his technicians thought they could build a steel face mask to protect Frank, if the team physician would permit it, and perhaps allow him to play.

Dr. Alex Rachun gave his OK to try it. With the co-operation and advice of head trainer Doc Kavanagh, the mask was put together and then approved by Dr. Rachun, and Frankie started to work out. With his jaw wired tight it was tough to breathe and therefore difficult to run very much. Nevertheless, the following Saturday he was on the bench wearing his full-face metal mask, probably expecting to watch rather than participate. That wasn't quite the way it was.

Dartmouth scored first and led 6–0 until late in the first quarter. It was now Cornell's ball on its own twenty-yard line, and Coach Lefty James sent the masked man, Bradley, into the game. On the first play from scrimmage he was given the ball by quarterback Pete Dorset and raced around right tackle. Sprung loose by devastating blocking, two key ones downfield by Vincent Di-Grande '52 and Jack Jaso '50, Frank went the whole eighty yards for a touchdown, almost passing out at

1948 CORNELL FOOTBALL 8–1

Ivy League champions, ranked eighteenth nationally

Home games are capitalized, W = win, L = loss, T = tie

Date	Opponent	Result	Score
9/25	NEW YORK UNIVERSITY	W	47-6
10/2	vs Navy	W	13-7
10/9	HARVARD	W	40-6
10/16	at Syracuse	W	34-7
10/23	ARMY	L	6-27
10/30	at Columbia	W	20-13
11/6	COLGATE	W	14-6
11/13	DARTMOUTH	W	27-26
11/15	at Penn	W	23-14

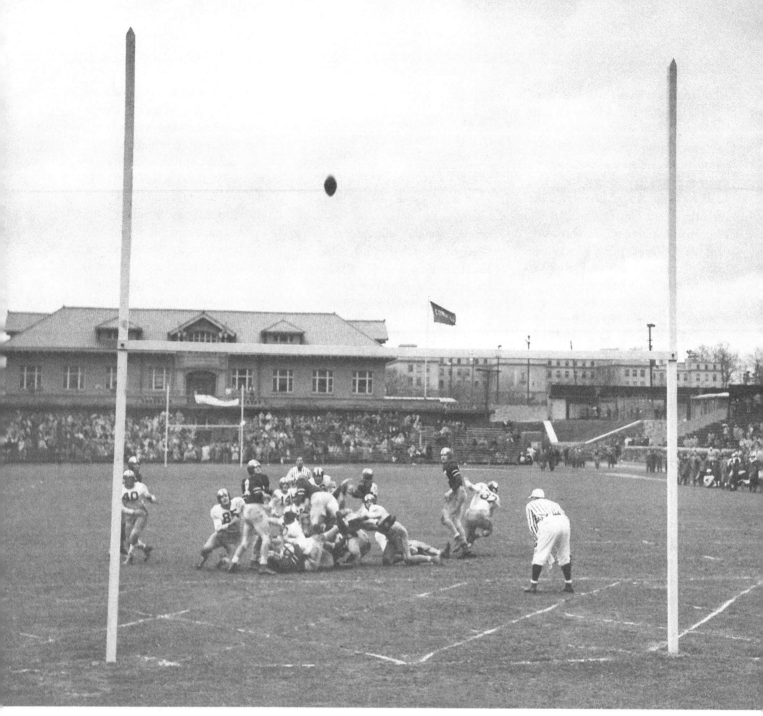

Rip Haley holds as Bob Dean kicks the extra point to beat Dartmouth, 27–26, on November 13, 1948.

the goal line because of his restricted breathing. The Cornellians among the 30,000 spectators went wild. The score was 7–6, Cornell.

In the box area of the crescent, a distinguished looking figure, hat askew, came racing up to box one, shouting breathlessly. "Ezra, Ezra, that's our boy." And the dean of engineering and president of the university exuberantly embraced each other.

THE CORNELL DAILY SUN, MONDAY, NOVEMBER 15, 1948: Cornell proved to 30,000 roaring fans and the football world Saturday that it is a fierce and fighting never-say-die football team, as Lefty James's inspired lads swept from a two-touchdown disadvantage going into the last quarter and slipped by the Green of Dartmouth, 27–26, in a dramatic, swirling Ivy League battle…

What made the victory even more impressive to Cornell enthusiasts was that the comeback was accomplished without the ramming services of Jeff Fleishmann, the high-powered sophomore fullback who has done so much for the Big Red cause this year.

Fleischmann was carried off the field on a stretcher in the

second quarter, just as a light rain began to fall, with a simple fracture of the left leg…but Bob Dean came through for big Jeff with a terrific game of fullback, smacking the line for [an average of] 7.6 yards in a smash, getting away punts in a whipping crosswind for a 45.7 yard average, bucking over for the tying touchdown with two minutes and forty seconds left on the big clock, and, finally, with cool precision, kicking his third point-after-touchdown for the victory that set the stands into chaotic jubilance.

Frank Bradley '50

After the Colgate game, they x-rayed me and the doctor told me I had a broken jaw, that's it. I didn't accept that. See, back in those days, football helmets didn't have cages over the face. So they wired my jaw shut, and then they put two iron bars across the front of my helmet so nobody could get to my jaw or my nose. It was really a prototype for the kind of helmets everybody wears today.

People still ask me why I played with a broken jaw. It's an excellent question. I had gotten married in 1947, and we had a child when I played that game. I probably shouldn't have done it. But I just loved being on that team. I think it may have been the greatest football team Cornell ever put together. And it might have been foolish, but I felt that I just had to play.

Frank Bradley served as a B-17 navigator in the Army Air Forces. A mechanical engineer, he worked in power plants and then joined the consulting firm Stone and Webster, eventually becoming its president.

Bob Kane: Bob Dean continued his intrepidity in a victory over Penn on Thanksgiving Day, 1948. It was his final exploit in an unselfish, notable career, and it happened before 78,000 spectators at Franklin Field. Dean kicked a thirty-yard field goal, two conversions, booming punts, and long kickoffs. He also scored a touchdown, running from the fullback position. Jack Rogers '49, also in his final appearance with Cornell, caught a fifteen-yard pass from Dorset and ran the remaining ten yards for the score, ensuring the Ivy League title. Lefty James's jubilant players carried him off the field on their shoulders, ending one of the most sterling years in the history of Cornell football.

Frank Bradley

1949 CORNELL FOOTBALL 8–1

Ivy League champions, ranked twelfth nationally

Home games are capitalized, W = win, L = loss, T = tie

9/24	NIAGARA	W	27-0
10/1	COLGATE	W	39-27
10/8	at Harvard	W	33-14
10/15	at Yale	W	48-14
10/22	PRINCETON	W	14-12
10/29	COLUMBIA	W	54-0
11/5	SYRACUSE	W	33-7
11/12	at Dartmouth	L	7-16
11/24	at Penn	W	29-21

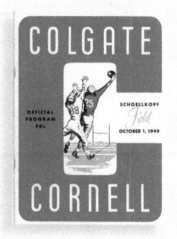

Richard Loynd '50

The most memorable experience I had as a defensive end at Cornell was on November 24, 1949, the last game I played. We were losing to our archrival, Penn, 21 to 6, at half-time. But I noticed a weakness in their blocking scheme, so I told the linebacker, Harvey Sampson '51, to change his route and loop in behind me. I was going to make my move and block the first punt of the second half. The punt was blocked, we scored a touchdown, and we went on to beat Penn, 29–21. It was a great way to end my football career.

When I was approaching graduation, the New York Giants were showing interest in me. I decided to

SLEEPING IT OFF

Cornell Alumni News, December 1948

The Colgate contest [Cornell 14, Colgate 6, November 6, 1948] was played under weather conditions calculated to make the most critical professor palliate occasional lapses from complete sobriety on the part of visiting alumni. That game, played throughout in a heavy downpour, produced but one known case of overindulgence. And that single lapse would have remained undiscovered, no doubt, but for the report of a conscientious night watchman, who, making his appointed rounds at 2 a.m., had been startled by screams, protests, and entreaties which he finally located as coming from the gentlemen's comfort station serving Sections EG and EH under the Cornell Crescent. A gentleman had been locked in there, according to the report.

It was the night watchman's theory, concurred in by the gentleman, that the latter had stepped out between the halves and had gone to sleep there. Nor had he been aroused by Mr. Floyd Darling of the Athletic Association making his final inspection and locking up at 7 p.m. It was not until after midnight that the gentleman's potations had worn off, and the chill of his wet clothes had sunk in, sufficiently to wake him up and start him calling upon his Alma Mater for assistance while attempting to kick the hell out of a concrete comfort station in indignant protest.

The night watchman and the gentleman had ample opportunity to develop the facts of the case in a leisurely chat, because the comfort stations, like the football ticket department, still remain under the jurisdiction of the Athletic Association, and the universal passkey carried by the night watchman fitted neither the situation nor the lock. It took a full hour for Mr. Floyd Darling, summoned by telephone, to get up there and let the gentleman out. —Rym Berry

"Rym" Berry's column, "Now, in *My Time!*," ran in the *Cornell Alumni News* from 1936 to 1950.

give that a try, so I did not actively interview for other jobs. One of my professors in electrical engineering, either Everett Strong or Bill Erickson, called me and asked me to come in for an interview. A man from Lincoln Electric was coming, he said, and I was just the kind of guy he was looking for. At the professor's insistence, I went for the interview. I told Leonard Giles, the Lincoln rep, that I planned to try to play professional football. He convinced me it would be a great experience to come to Cleveland for interviews at their expense, however, so I agreed to do that.

I met a number of their key people, including a man by the name of Buck Persons who offered me a job. I reminded Buck that I was going to try to be a professional football player. Thank God, through their continuing insistence and further discussion with both my professors and coaches, I changed my mind and took the job with Lincoln. That man, Buck Persons, later left Lincoln and went on to build Emerson Electric in St. Louis. I went with him.

Richard Loynd, an army veteran who earned his bachelor's degree in electrical entgineering, worked for Emerson Electric for decades and served on its board of directors until the mid-2000s. He is president of Loynd Capital Management in Short Hills, New Jersey, and is also on the board of directors at Joy Global. He has also served as an executive or director at several other companies, including group vice president of the Allied Corporation.

Richard Loynd

Benjamin Mintz '43
(1921–1991)

Benjamin Mintz, a native of Ithaca, was Cornell's sports information director from 1949 to 1976. He wrote this profile in January 1950.

Hillary Chollet was [more than just a football player. He was also] captain and the outstanding all-around basketball player on the 1948–49 team. On February 23, 1949, he smashed the all-time Cornell scoring record with thirty-seven points against Syracuse University at Syracuse. In so doing he scored nineteen out of twenty-three foul shots, and this constituted a national collegiate record.

In [1949], his final season of football, he played offensive left halfback and was safety man on defense. Though Cornell used the two-platoon system, Hillary played in practically every minute of all nine games, and for the second season was highly instrumental in Cornell's gaining the Ivy League championship.

Among the individual honors he received after the season were the following: first-team All-Television and *Chicago Tribune*

Hillary Chollet hands the 1949 Cornell-Penn game ball to Cornell President Edmund Ezra Day as Mrs. Day looks on.

All-American, Associated Press and Collier's All-East, and All-Ivy. He was also named a second-team AP and Grantland Rice All-American.

Although he was outstanding in every game, Hillary's performance against Yale on October 15, 1948, at the Yale Bowl, was called by Coach James "one of the most brilliant displays of offensive and defensive football I have ever seen." This is what he did: without throwing a single pass, he accounted personally for 242 yards in the following manner: fifty-four yards on eleven rushing attempts, forty-five yards receiving three passes, fifty-seven yards returning two intercepted passes, thirty-one yards on two punt returns, and fifty-five yards returning the opening kick-off. He scored one touchdown and set up two others in the Big Red's 48–14 victory. He played about three-quarters of the game on both offense and defense.

Other highlights of his career: he was the football team's leading scorer in 1946. He was injured in preseason practice in 1947 and did not play that season. He was the basketball team's leading scorer in 1946–47.

In fall 1949, he was the football team's leading scorer and ground gainer until the fifth game, when unbeaten Cornell faced unbeaten Army at Ithaca. In receiving a pass that led directly to Cornell's only touchdown in the second quarter, Hillary suffered a sprained ankle that prevented his playing until the Penn game on Thanksgiving Day, when he appeared only as safety man. His performance helped Cornell defeat Penn.

He was regarded as the most effective safety man in the East in 1949. He concluded his college football career in the annual East-West All-Star game at San Francisco. Chollet's long pass to Leon Hart of Notre Dame counted for the East's first touchdown and was, according to Coach Frank Leahy, "the turning point of the game." The event raised money to help children afflicted with polio.

Hillary had already been helping polio victims for the previous two years in Ithaca. During summers he was an orderly at the Reconstruction Home. His work with youngsters was invaluable, according to Lawrence Gaurnier, the director of the Reconstruction Home.

It is fair to say that the people of central New York will remember Hillary as one of the legendary figures in athletics in the region. Though his individual accomplishments surpassed those of his teammates, it was his team play that has made him popular among them. His modesty, coolness under fire, and ability to perform at his best when the pressure is greatest established him as Cornell's greatest modern athlete, and put his name among such legendary Cornell football figures as All-Americans Chuck Barrett 1916, George Pfann '24, and Eddie Kaw '23.

Hillary Chollet '49, MD '54 (1926–89) was a star scholar-athlete in his New Orleans high school. He was accepted by Tulane and Louisiana State University, but then disinvited after the press reported that one of his grandparents was black. Cornell accepted him, and Tulane paid his first-year tuition and fees to Cornell. He arrived in Ithaca in October 1945 and is identified as a graduating senior in Cornell's 1950 yearbook.

Chollet was the chief executive of two cancer surgery clinics in West Covina and Nogales, California, until he developed amyotrophic lateral sclerosis (ALS). His son, Hillary Chollet Jr., is a trauma and vascular surgeon in Los Angeles.

Soccer

Ivy League Champs

The Cornell football team secured their second straight Ivy League title on Thanksgiving Day, 1949, the last day of the season, by beating Penn in Philadelphia. A short distance away, the Cornell soccer team did the same thing, securing their second Ivy League title. But the soccer game went into overtime.

The Cornell Daily Sun, November 28, 1949: Gunter Meng '51 neatly placed a shot in the early moments of the first overtime period that brought [coach] Jim Smith's spirited soccermen a hard-earned 4–3 victory over Penn and their second straight Ivy League championship in a game played before 300 excited fans on Penn's River Field Thursday...

Played to a 3–3 tie during the regulation eighty-eight minutes, the game broke wide open in the overtime periods. Meng's winning goal, scored at 2:05 of the first five-minute period, served as an added incentive for the already-inspired Cornellians who went on to completely outclass and outhustle the fading Pennsylvanians in the waning moments of the game...

[Trailing 2–1 at the beginning of the second half], Anthony "Tony" Tappin '50 took a pass from Gordie Gardiner at 21:40, and fired the ball netward. It deflected off Penn's Don Cavanaugh into the Quaker goal, tying the score at two-all.

Penn controlled the ball at the outset of the fourth period, but Deri Derr solved the Quaker's defenses, passing skillfully to Guntar Meng, who netted the ball from five yards out at 2:35. The Quakers knotted the count a scarce forty seconds later as Pat Welsh scored from fifteen yards out.

Tension increased as time ran out, and the struggle for the ball involved close contact resulting in penalties for both sides.

Cornell took three shots to Penn's one in the first overtime period, making good on one, while in the second overtime the Big Red completely dominated play, allowing Penn to have the ball only once.

The two-time Ivy League Champion Cornell soccer team in 1949. KNEELING: Deri Derr '51, Joe McKinney '50, Bob Robinson '50. STANDING: Tony Tappin '50, Len Fahs '51, Frank Schwenke '50, Richard Myers '50, coach Jim Smith, Jack Rose '50, Gordon Gardiner '50, Jack Scheinkman '49, Jim Ballew '51, John Coffin '50.

Tennis

The Cornell tennis team did the soccer and football squads one better, winning three straight Ivy League titles in 1947, 1948, and 1949. Coach Richard Lewis led his squad to within one game of a perfect record in 1949, losing only to William & Mary, the best team in the country. Cornell's leader was Richard Savitt '50, an arts college graduate, who posted a career singles record of 57-2, won the Eastern Intercollegiate singles title in 1949 and '50, and paired with Leonard Steiner '51 to win the doubles title in 1948, '49 and '50. Dick Savitt was a seaman second class for the navy. After receiving his Bachelor's degree from the arts college, he won the singles title at Wimbledon and the

Australian Championships in 1951. He was inducted into the International Tennis Hall of Fame in 1973. He is a financial advisor for Morgan Stanley Smith Barney.

Richard Savitt

Basketball

John Rose '50, MD '54

The basketball team would play home games before 7,500 people in Barton Hall. The place was packed. People would come up from town in the afternoon and mix with students. It was a wonderful scene. Cornell did not have a reliable hockey team back then, because it did not have indoor ice until Lynah Rink opened in 1957. The hockey team played on the natural ice of Beebe Lake, which had a tendency to melt unpredictably. So in the winter, basketball was the big show.

I came to Cornell straight from boarding school in 1946 and never went into the service. I don't remember any veterans being on the freshman basketball team. I moved up to the junior varsity team at the end of my freshman year, and there were four or five veterans on it. And when I got to the varsity team as a sophomore, everyone was a veteran except for myself and Hillary Chollet '50.

I was in the first group of Cornell students who were awarded National Scholarships, and my only thought when I arrived was to get into medical school. But I had also been on New Jersey's all-state high school basketball team for two years, and I was about 6′3″, and you know how these things go. Coach Roy Greene signed me up almost as soon as I arrived, and the season went from mid-October to mid-March.

I was a chemistry major, and I also played basketball all four years. That was tough. The practices took at least two hours a day. By the time the seasons were over, I would be so far behind in my classwork that I

had to spend the whole weekend in the lab for the rest of the year. But I didn't care. I was captain of the Cornell basketball team in 1949–50, and it was one of the best things that ever happened to me.

I started every game for three years. Some guys on the varsity team were taller than I was—Ed Peterson '49, for example, was 6′9″. So the coach asked me to take the ball downcourt, and he switched me from guard to forward. I remember Bob Gale '49 and I

Jack Rose

double-teaming Ernie Vandeweghe when we played Colgate. I played in Madison Square Garden against Newark University, and I played against Dolph Schayes when we took on NYU.[1]

I didn't play on a team that won the league title, but we came in second in 1947–48 and 1949–50. We would go to the midwest and play the Big Ten schools over Christmas break, and we held our own. They had a much more physical style of play than we did. It was almost like football. But we came within one point of beating Ohio State in 1949, even without our best scorer, Walt Ashbaugh '51. Ohio State was the second-best team in the country that year.

Winning games was great, but it isn't what I remember. So many good things in my life came to me because of basketball. In my junior year, I made friends with a member of the freshman squad, Joe Hinsey '53. We were in Willard Straight Hall one day, and he asked me to come over and meet his father. I wasn't eager to do it, but I said all right. So I shook this man's hand, and he said, "I am Dr. Joseph Hinsey, dean of the Cornell Medical School." I thought to myself, oh, my God! And then he said, "I want to thank you for being so good to my son, and also let you know that we have a spot for you at the medical school. Just keep working hard, and you'll be fine." Well, I was flying!

The next year, my senior year, we were going to play Yale on December 17. A team from the

medical school was coming up to interview candidates that afternoon. It was pretty intimidating. They were all big-time doctors. One of them said, "Jack, we have a major problem with you." I thought, holy Jeez, what could that be?

"The New York Knickerbockers are asking several Cornell players to join the team," he said. "In fact, someone you know has already joined them. We are wondering whether you plan to play for the Knicks while you are in medical school."

I said, "Doc, I have not heard from the Knicks, and I do want to go to medical school. But if the Knicks get in touch with me before I hear from you, I will have to call you back." At that point we all laughed, and I said, "I sure would like to hear from you first." The interview ended with them asking me to please beat Yale that night, which we did.

A lot of Cornell athletes from

Barton Hall Official Program 15c

Cornell vs. Rutgers

December 19, 1949

the Class of 1950—Hillary Chollet, Ralph C. "Cooly" Williams, Harry Daniell, and I—ended up going to Cornell Medical School and studying together.

Jack Rose became a urologist at the Geisinger Medical Center in Dansville, Pennsylvania.

BIG RED TOPS BULLDOGS, 60–57

The Cornell Daily Sun, December 19, 1949

[The Yale game] was probably as exciting a contest as ever witnessed in Barton Hall, an Ivy meeting not decided until the final seventeen seconds of sizzling action... It was a veteran [player], Jack Rose, who made the plays that saved the victory.

Jack, who had done a brilliant passing job throughout that hectic night, came through, stealing the ball and sending it into a Cornell freeze that was broken when [Yale captain] Bob Joyce fouled Roger "Red" Chadwick '52 with seventeen seconds to play. The cool redhead swished the ball cleanly and the fans and players went wild as the clock ran out.

---

[1] Ernie Vandeweghe played for the New York Knicks for six seasons. Adolph Schayes was a twelve-time NBA all-star and a member of the 1955 NBA Champions Syracuse Nationals.

Lightweight Rowing

Carl Ullrich '50, Robert Post '50, and Dick Elmendorf '50

Carl Ullrich

Robert Post

Dick Elmendorf

Carl remembers driving down Gunshop Hill in his Model A Ford in the fall of 1946 as a freshman, with Dick in the passenger's seat. They turned onto the railroad tracks at the base of the hill and continued on to the Cornell Boathouse. They were checking out the lightweight rowing team, and it looked interesting enough that they showed up for practice the next day.

Bob Post had rowed at prep school, and he remembers meeting head coach R. Harrison "Stork" Sanford at registration. Stork was 6' 5" and looked like a giant to Bob, who was 5' 9" and 145 pounds. Stork told Bob to report to the lightweight crew coach, Bob Tallman '41, at the boathouse on Monday.

The lightweight team practiced on a wooden barge that had oars set up on either side, so that the coach could walk up and down the middle and observe his galley slaves. It was hard work, but as the weeks went by, we began to enjoy it. In the winter we ran down Forest Home Road and around Beebe Lake, up and down some terrible hills, and then

The varsity lightweight crew being passed by a Cornell yacht club sailboat, spring 1949. "Most of us were looking over at the sailboat and undoubtedly having mixed thoughts about our contrasting situations," writes Dick Elmendorf. "My hands, resting below my oar at #8, seem to be wrapped in something. It is because the oar handles in those days were just bare wood, and in the cold and wet conditions of early spring, our hands became badly blistered manipulating the oars. Each day before practice we would wrap them in gauze and tape to try to minimize the pain, sop up the blood, and provide some cushioning against the rough wood. Later in the season our hands developed calluses and we could discard the bandages, but in this and many other ways we learned to suffer together uncomplainingly for the sake of a larger goal: winning races."

worked out on rowing machines on the third floor of the Old Armory until our legs and arms were aching. After the ice went out from the Cayuga Lake inlet we got back on the water, looking something like a crew.

We finished fourth at the Eastern Association of Rowing Colleges (EARC) 150 lb. regatta in 1946. As sophomores, we were separated—Dick moved up to the varsity team, and Carl rowed for junior varsity—but all three of us were in the varsity boat for our junior year, under coach Al Bock '49.

We weren't sure of our chances at the EARC regatta in 1949. In the morning heat against Princeton, Yale, and Columbia, Princeton finished first and we were second. The first two finishers qualified for the finals in the afternoon. Bob Post remembers that as we approached the finish line, the Princeton coxswain yelled to his crew, "We're not going to sprint!" Hearing this, our coxswain, Dana Brooks '49, yelled back, "We're not going to, either!" Both teams were saving themselves for the afternoon.

And what an afternoon it was! As we approached the finish line in the afternoon final, there was a tremendous clap of thunder and a strike of lightning. That's when we moved ahead of Princeton to win the race and the Joseph Wright Trophy. Princeton claimed that the thunderclap was the only reason why we won. We had to wait a week to prove them wrong.

We were scheduled to row against Princeton in a dual meet in Ithaca the following Saturday. To make it even more dramatic, the coach of the Princeton lightweight crew was Chuck Von Wrangell '48, who had been commodore of the Cornell heavyweights the previous year. To say that it was a grudge match is an understatement.

The race was scheduled for the west shore course on Cayuga Lake, but rough water forced it on to the inlet course. In those days, Cayuga Inlet had not been straightened yet, so there was a turn in the middle of the course. We asked our coxswain, Dana Brooks, to tell the story. He was the only one who could see where we were going.

"The boat started in the left hand lane, which placed us three or four seats ahead of Princeton," Dana said. "Despite that handicap, we were sure that the turn would give them an advantage. So I told the guys we were going to try something risky. We were going to turn the boat without using the rudder, by getting the port guys to pull harder. That way there wouldn't be any drag on the boat.

"The race started in the canal by the Buffalo Street bridge, which was very narrow. It would have been easy to lock oars or go off course, but somehow we didn't. The turn was a moment of high drama. Our oars cleared the marker by just a couple of feet—but we did it! Princeton never led us, and we beat them by two to four seats at the end. Everyone was totally exhausted—more so than any race I can recall—but eventually we made our way back to the boathouse. It was a moment never to be forgotten. We had done it twice in a row. We were the best!"

That's the way the rest of us felt, too. But there is one more twist to this tale. Before that race, Princeton had already decided to compete in the Henley Royal Regatta in England, which is held in late June and early July. So, if Princeton was going to go and we had already beaten them twice, why shouldn't we go, too? It wasn't easy to raise the money, but we all chipped in. We also asked alumni for more help, and things looked hopeful enough that we started making preparations. We kept practicing and applied for passports, and we got more and more excited.

Then came the worst day of our young lives. We had arranged to ship our shell in a baggage car to New York, to be put on a ship for England. We all joined in taking the shell to the baggage car, and it looked like we really were going to go. Just before we loaded it, though, Al Bock showed up and gave us terrible news. Our entry to the Henley Regatta had been received two days late, and had been refused. We had made entreaties. Princeton had even spoken up for us. But the Henley governors would not budge. A few weeks later, Princeton did go to Henley, and they won.

Who knows what might have been? We came close to a repeat in 1950, but finished second to Yale in the EARC regatta by one-third of a length.

Five members of the Class of 1950 were on the 1949 championship crew boat: Carl (at bow); Bob (at position number two); Dick (position eight); Larry Christensen (three), and Paul Zimmerman (five). In addition, Bob Collins '50 was our starboard spare for the aborted Henley trip. The other members of the crew were Chuck Warren '51 (position four), Norm Baker '49 (six), Towner Buckley '49 (seven), and Dana Brooks '49 (coxswain). "Chuck" Taylor '50 was an alternate.

The bonds formed among us on that crew have lasted a long time, and even though we have lived quite different lives and have different viewpoints on many things, the warm fellowship, mutual respect, and deference to each other that we learned in the boat remain. Cornell's academic program taught us to be independent, clear thinkers. But Cornell crew taught us that there are lots of times in life when the best thing to do is just to shut up and keep rowing. We are very grateful for both.

Carl Ullrich, a navy veteran and mechanical engineer, coached the Cornell freshman heavyweights, then went on to coach the varsity teams at Columbia, Boston University, and the United States Naval Academy. He was the first civilian athletics director at the United States Military Academy (1980 to 1990) and received the James Lynah Award for distinguished achievement.

Bob Post, a mechanical engineer, worked at the American Brake Shoe Company.

Dick Elmendorf, another navy veteran and mechanical engineer, is the founder and former president of a mechanical engineering firm in Bairdford, Pennsylvania.

Women's Athletics

Patricia Carry Stewart '50

Women in the 1940s were far more docile than they are today. Many of the men in our classes were older and more experienced than we were, because they were veterans of World War II. We respected them, and we often may have deferred to them.

There were no female cheerleaders then, and no women played in the Big Red Band until 1969. The 1950 Yearbook devotes fifty-eight pages to athletics, but just two of these show women. And the women who did play sports were not taken seriously.

Every woman who enrolled at Cornell in 1946 was required to take an entrance physical that was highly intrusive, and which many of us found insulting. We had to take off all of our clothes and stand behind a screen for a silhouette photo—for our posture, we were told, although no one ever gave me any feedback about whether or not my posture was good. I am also told that more than one man tried to steal these photos. Then we had to take a swimming test in a dinky pool in the Old Armory, which was built in 1885 and stood on the current site of the engineering quad.

We were required to take what was called physical training, or "PT," for two years, but our choices were limited. Every girl had to attend a course called Rhythmics, which was essentially calisthenics. But women did not have any athletic facilities of their own until Helen Newman Hall opened in

1963, so they taught rhythmics in the common rooms of the dorms. We were not allowed to play in Barton Hall or on the fields in the lower campus, where many of the men's events were held.

The PT electives available to women included field hockey, softball, bowling in an alley in Collegetown, tennis, golf, archery, crew, swimming, and basketball, which we played with six players on each team—three forwards and three guards, none of whom were allowed to cross the center line. The women I talked to said that all of the team play for women was intramural, although the 1950 and 1951 yearbooks mention some intercollegiate competitions, but never with Ivy League schools. Most of our games happened in the Old Armory, or in Risley or Sage Halls, which had gyms, or on the field behind Balch Hall.

There were some bright spots.

Letitia Ann Hayes '52, national women's riflery champion.

Our riflery instructors were top-notch military men from the ROTC unit, and Letitia Ann Hays '52 became the national women's riflery champion with a perfect score. Women did not have organized fencing teams, but one of my classmates reports that the

The women's riflery team, around 1944.

men's team allowed her to play. Horseback riding was co-ed, with army cavalry officers as instructors. One woman reported that the men's rowing team adopted her and made her their mascot.

Still, the opportunities for women athletes in those days were so limited that it is hard for women today to imagine what we were up against. Charlotte Conable '51 recalled getting a man on the crew team to lend women a shell and shirts for the Spring Weekend interfraternity boat race. She said the women actually won the race, but were denied the prize. Another woman I corresponded with said that she and others gave up golf because the men made them so unwelcome at the links. Another recalled that she and others offered men dancing lessons to raise money for women's athletics. Times certainly have changed for the better.

About half of the women I talked to wondered why we had just accepted all of the restrictions on women's participation in athletics. Why didn't we try to change things? The best answer I can give is that it was a sign of the times. In the late 1940s, women were discriminated against in business, the professions, academia, politics, and almost every other part of life.

Patricia Carry Stewart, who has a BA from the College of Arts and Sciences, surveyed several dozen women from her era while writing this essay. She played basketball while at Cornell and also served on the board of the Women's Athletic Association. She married Charles T. Stewart '40 (1918–2008), a navy veteran, and had a long career in business and finance, including stints as president of a New York Stock Exchange firm and as vice president of the Edna McConnell Clark Foundation. She also served on several corporate boards, including Borden Inc. and Trans World Airlines, and was a Cornell trustee for twenty-eight years.

Charlotte Williams [Conable] '51 (right) and her crewmates. She said they won the Spring Weekend interfraternity boat race but were denied the prize because of their sex.

Women's athletics began approaching equality when Congress passed Title IX of the United States Education Amendments in 1972. The law states (in part) that "No person in the United States shall, on the basis of sex, be excluded from participation in, be denied the benefits of, or be subjected to discrimination under any education program or activity receiving federal financial assistance." The number of women competing in intercollegiate athletics increased from 16,000 in 1966 to more than 150,000 in 2001, when women were 43 percent of all college athletes.

Detail from J. O. Mahoney mural in Clinton House bar.

CHAPTER 9

Pastimes

Parties, Dating, Drinking, and Sex

Cornell's social calendar peaked on three weekends that featured big-name performers, lavish parties, student performances, and high-stakes athletics. During these "houseparty" weekends, fraternity men moved out of their usual sleeping places so their weekend dates could move in. The parties went around the clock.

The overriding fact of social life in the 1940s was "The Ratio" of 4.5 male students for every female. Few students had cars, and those who did led expeditions to nearby women's colleges. Sex was limited by supply and demand, and also by curfews, chaperones, and poor access to contraception. But the drinking age was eighteen, so spirits flowed freely. Fraternity houses had their own barrooms, beer was served at the Willard Straight Hall cafeteria, and no one asked anyone for proof of age. By the early 1950s, open lawn parties featuring orgies of binge drinking had become a regular feature of campus life.

The Mural Lounge in downtown Ithaca's historic Clinton House.

James Owen Mahoney
(1907–1987)

J. O. Mahoney was a captain in the Army Air Forces who served in Europe during World War II. He became a Professor of Art at Cornell in 1939. In 1949, he completed a mural in the lounge of the Clinton House, a historic landmark in downtown Ithaca, and wrote this description of it.

The painting's primary function is to decorate the room, to harmonize with and to enhance the architecture in design, color, theme, and spirit, and to induce a mood of discreet fantasy and restrained gaiety in the clientele of the bar. It is not a story-telling picture, i.e., one with a definite anecdote. It is subject to ideation, more than just perception.

[The mural] depicts a spirited but refined bacchanal involving numerous figures, some nude and allegorical, and some in contemporary attire, against a romanticized version of Ithaca's gorges, waterfalls, lakes, and architecture, all as if idealized by slightly alcoholic fancy. In this connection, one must bear in mind that Dionysus, the god of wine depicted in the central group of figures, represented not only its intoxicating power, but its social and beneficent influences likewise, so that he was viewed as the promoter of civilization, a lawgiver, and a lover of peace.

Thus the painting suggests that recreation, sport, and creative activities of all kinds are more pleasant with alcohol as a stimulus. This is its theme. The effect of the painting will depend on the direct appeal of color and design to the particular individual. This cannot be described generally. It will be felt only by actual perception.

Kirk Reid '50

They called her Genevieve, and she was a real mess when I first saw her. She had a cracked engine block. They had painted her gray, and they were using her as a chicken coop. It was 1943, I was sixteen, and she was the most beautiful thing I had ever seen in my life. I bought her and dragged her over to our house. We got new parts and she ran fine.

Cornell freshmen were not allowed to have cars, so I took the

Kirk Reid driving Genevieve in 1948.

train from Cleveland to Ithaca in 1946. There wasn't much time for partying, anyway. I was discharged from the navy in June 1946, but I stayed in the reserves, so I had to put on a uniform several times a week and go to Barton Hall and do drills. On top of that, I was also studying mechanical engineering. I really had to bear down. Theta Xi used to have something called the 2:30 club. That meant whoever was up and studying at 2:30 a.m. would come downstairs for a gab session. I would usually be there. But I think working so hard made going out even better. A night out was special.

Genevieve is a 1929 Model A wagon. It's the first year Ford made them in a factory. In September 1947 I painted her red and white, Cornell colors, and drove her to Ithaca. I brought some canvas to cover her up in the winter, and I went into the woods behind the Theta Xi house and built a frame out of tree branches and put the canvas over that to make a garage. She lived there for three years.

Cars were scarce in 1947, and that made me popular. On Sunday

night we'd go to Joe's for pizza, and occasionally we'd go to Zinck's for a drink on Saturday night. Those old Model A wagons never had glass in the windows. You could get isinglass that snapped into the window frames, but I never had that. We didn't care how cold it was, or how much ice there was on the roads. Genevieve could carry eight people, and she was always full. There were usually three or four people hanging off the running board, and three or four people stuffed into the front seat.

The year I brought her to Cornell, Genevieve towed Theta Xi's float in the Spring Day parade. She has no back bumper, so I had to hook the hitch up to the front bumper and drive her down the street backwards. The next fall, she was in the halftime show at a home football game. We packed her with maybe eighteen people hanging all over her, and drove her onto the field and got out and ran around. People were smaller back then.

In those days the Cornell co-eds booked their Saturday night dates weeks in advance, and if you didn't get one, you were out of luck. That's what the photo is about. It shows a group of weekend procrastinators who are heading to Elmira College [a women's school] for date night in 1948. I am behind the wheel holding a cup of water. It is water. That is our story, and we're sticking to it.

The Elmira co-eds were always so appreciative that we made the trip. When we pulled in, they always gave us a big reception. We would go to their dances, and they would invite us to picnics. Don Hayes, in the back seat, ended up marrying one of those Elmira College girls.

Kirk Reid served in the navy in 1945–46. After receiving his bachelor's degree in mechanical engineering, he worked for General Motors and Terex Corporation as a test engineer for off-highway vehicles.

David Dingle '50

I was the campus piano guy. My father, Howard Dingle 1904, was a trustee of the Cleveland Orchestra, and he always made sure I had good piano teachers. My fraternity, Theta Delta Chi, had a grand piano that I would play at parties and whenever people gathered to sing. Group singing was a big deal back then. Veterans and non-veterans, students and faculty, it didn't matter. It was how you bonded. We would sing at Jim's Place (later the Chapter House), Zinck's, you name it. These days, people don't know the second verse of Cornell's "Alma Mater." Back then, everybody knew the words.

SPRING DAYS

Cornell Alumni News, June 1, 1947

The first symptoms of spring fever on campus appeared on May Day, when a week of student ballyhoo blossomed into a mammoth Apollo Contest sponsored by the Octagon Club, supposedly to pick the handsomest Cornell male. Twelve candidates vied for the grand prize: tickets to all Spring Day events, a loving cup, and a bottle of Scotch. Before a crowd of shirt-sleeved and baby-toting students which thronged the Willard Straight steps, Central Avenue, and the lawn between Sage Chapel and Barnes Hall, the terrific twelve made their glorious entrances: one in a rowboat, borne aloft by his cohorts; one flag-draped on a bier; one astride a cow labeled "This is no bull! Vote for Gilbert"; and others in vehicles ranging from a Model T Ford to a '47 Buick. Their costumes were splendid, and eight pretty co-eds from the cast of the Octagon show, *Maid to Order,* chose the winner, Thomas D. Wells '43 of Farmington, Connecticut.

Howard Heinsius '50, master of ceremonies, introduces E. Whitney Mitchell '52, a contestant in the 1950 Apollo Contest. Mitchell, who portrays "Hector the Golden Fleecer," disembarked from a mammoth wooden horse drawn by "slaves" and populated by students dressed as Greek warriors and maidens. TOP: Otto Soglow's illustration for the 1949 Spring Day program. The parade that year honored Soglow and other prominent cartoonists who attended to judge the floats. Among the contenders were a Rube Goldberg kissing machine (see Chapter 7), Soglow's "Little King," a purple dinosaur more than sixty feet long ridden by an undergraduate dressed as Alley Oop, and the winner—a Buck Rogers float that included a rocket ship with a lifelike radio broadcasting flight instructions and a cortege of futuristic "soldiers," scantily clad co-eds, wearing plastic oxygen helmets with tanks strapped to their backs.

I was also the piano accompanist for the Glee Club from 1948 to 1950. That was more about putting on a performance than teaching a group to sing, although we certainly encouraged people to sing along with us at points in the program.

Tom Tracy, the director of the club, was very much in charge. John Timmerman and I would do a spot on the program where we would play duets, either on a single board with four hands, or on two pianos. We would do standards, like "Lover" by Rodgers and Hart. Rusty Davis and Howard Heinsius '50 were our star soloists.

I was not a World War II veteran, but Timmerman, Davis, and Heinsius definitely were. Having them around was a wonderful thing. A lot of these guys had gone through some challenging stuff. They had grown up fast, and they gave non-veterans the benefit of their maturity. They didn't lord it over us, but they did set a serious tone. In music, you always want to play with people who are a little better than you are. They make you better.

Dave Dingle majored in economics and earned a BA from the College of Arts and Sciences. During the 1950s, he worked in marketing for Scott Paper Company. He then co-owned a travel agency and became a financial planner and a mortgage broker. During these business ventures, he usually held down a "night job" as a jazz piano player. He also led the Cornell Songbook Project, which combines vintage recordings of Glee Club performances from the late 1940s with lyric sheets and piano tracks to encourage sing-alongs.[1]

---

[1] The Project's CD was uploaded to the Cornell website in 2013. The web address is http://www.alumni.cornell.edu/remember/songs.

Erwin C. "Rusty" Davis '50

The years after the war were a golden age for the Glee Club. The veterans were several years older than college students had been before the war, so their voices were often much stronger. The recordings from that time are extraordinary.

I was a soloist with the club in 1949. Tom Tracy asked me to form a triple quartet along the lines of Yale's Whiffenpoofs or Princeton's Tiger Tones. He wanted the twelve of us to step off the risers during the Glee Club concert and do our numbers from the front of the stage.

I suggested that we call the group Cayuga's Waiters. The name evoked Cornell because everybody knows the line in the "Alma Mater" about Cayuga's waters, and we could signal the start of our routine by putting little towels over our arms when we stepped forward. Cayuga's Waiters has changed a lot since then. We never used microphones, for one thing, and now they do. But it's still going strong.

The Glee Club traveled a lot back then, all over the country, and even to Bermuda and other countries. One day the student manager of the Glee Club, Robert "Pat" Landon '48, came by and asked

Howard Heinsius solos at a Glee Club concert as Duncan Sells '49 waits for his turn.

me how high I could sing. I said I supposed I could hit a high C. He came back a few days later with an arrangement of "Over The Rainbow." I was stunned and flattered, and I said I'd give it a try.

We ended up singing it in Bailey Hall, at a joint concert we gave with the Glee Club from West Point. When we finished, the applause was so overwhelming that we had to repeat it.

I had a ball singing at Cornell. After I left, I was having lunch at the Automat in New York City. A Texan came up to me, wearing a ten-gallon hat, and he said, "Hey! You're that tenor from Cornell, aintcha?"

Rusty Davis served in the Army Air Forces during World War II. After receiving his bachelor of arts degree, he earned a master's from Boston University and became a school psychologist there and at other colleges. He also continued singing, appearing at the Opera Company of Boston with stars like Joan Sutherland and Marilyn Horne.

David Kogan '50
(1929–1951)

Saturday, October 19, 1946: Went to my first Cornell dance—taking the stocky girl from Rochester I met last night. I can't understand the morals of her position. We dance so closely. I am continually hot. The dips and hand-holdings are breathtaking. We then go out. I kiss her and it falls flat! She then feeds me a line about she "didn't think I was that type." I devoted the next ninety minutes to brilliantly talking. At 12:29 a.m., I had completely won her heart! I

IMMATURE BEHAVIOR

The Cornell Daily Sun, PAGE ONE, NOVEMBER 24, 1947

All plans for the Penn [football] rally were called off following the complete burning of the pile of wood set up in the Myron Taylor lot for the freshman cap-burning. The fire department was summoned at 2:55 a.m. to extinguish the blaze which had been started by some Cornellian shortly before…

OPEN LETTER TO CORNELL

The Cornellians, and they were Cornellians, if only by registration, who Saturday night burned the thirteen-foot pile of wood for tonight's rally bonfire, should feel proud of their timely contribution to the team… However, these men should not take all the credit for the apathy which has been prevalent throughout this school year. The entire student body is responsible for the overall lack of support and poor spirit displayed to date.

The letter was signed by the presidents of three student honorary organizations: Curtis Morehouse '48 of Quill and Dagger, Norman Dawson '48 of Aleph Samach, and Daniel C. McCarthy Jr. '49 of Red Key.

Notice

Then be it Known that on the Dreade and Fearful Nighte of November 22nd, in the Yeare of our Lord, 1947, the Treasure Shippe, Tau Delta Phi, will dock at 8 Bells under the Sign of the Jolly Roger.

Be it also Known that onlie those True and Brave Members of the Pirate Order will be admitted who exemplifie their Brotherhood in appropriate garbe.

Failure to complye with above regulations will be subjected to Tortures too horrible to mention, suche as eye-gouging, flogging on the quarterdeck (with rat o' nine tails, natcherly) or in case of severe violations, the supreme penalty -- walking the plank -- will be meted out.

Writ by my Hand this 10th day of November

Pistol Pete Barotz,
Ye Olde Social Chairman
Tau Delta Phirates

Say thee the word
(R.S.V.P.)

The Pirate Party happened a few hours before vandals torched the woodpile set up for the rally.

have come to the conclusion (a) either I don't know the art of kissing or (b) I am not emotionally responsive to it or (c) both.

Sunday, October 20, 1946: Sally found out I was Jewish today by watching me write a Hebrew letter. No words were exchanged. We just looked at each other.

Saturday, May 8, 1948: Phi Sig served over a hundred tonight, and what caught my eye was Josh Greenwald's sister Julie, sixteenish. Hung around her until I wangled an introduction. Was awkward for a few minutes, and then asked her for the date.

We went to the Dutch with two other couples. She ordered a daiquiri. While there we sang. I showed off with my notebook and hit it off with Julie. She is tall, dark-haired, intelligent, has been around; has curiosity, wit, congeniality, and we were rapidly falling in love. Things were getting too beery, so we went to Leonardo's. Low lights, soft music—and we danced and danced, very slowly, very closely, and got along famously. Another daiquiri—I switched to rye and ginger.

We went to Beta Sig, but they had a formal. So back home to Phi Sig—it was most crowded. Julie and I put our arms around each other, and danced dance after dance to "Beyond the Sea."

Sunday, May 9, 1948: Couldn't sleep much all through the night. I fall in love so easily. Got up at eight—wrote home—puttered, and then to the House. Julie looked almost as pretty as last night—but she will never look that pretty again. Her folks were hard for me to reach. I went with them, and we brunched at ten.

Then began three hours which dragged. We were both tired, hadn't much to say to each other, and just sat. She would talk to the folks. I would go and come back in ten minutes. I did, though, develop

Junior Week houseparty at Alpha Delta Phi, February 1948.

an appreciation for good piano. She played, Josh and Ben dueted, and recordings of Rubinstein and Horowitz were heard.

I asked Josh if I should ask Julie to houseparty, and he was noncommittal. I did it, she asked her folks, and it's O.K. It has been so long since I have met parents of girls I have been out with. At Cornell they are orphans, and in Yonkers I know them all.

Friday, May 21, 1948: The Bacchanalia began today. There is no institution in dating which has such a terrific impact upon the individual as houseparty.

David Kogan earned a bachelor of arts degree. He was president of the Hillel Foundation, marched with the Big Red Band, joined the Debate Club, and tried out for 150-pound crew. In his diary, he notes that most of the women he dated were Jewish. He died of lymphoma in 1951.

Eve Weinschenker Paul '50

I was just sixteen when I got to Cornell, and I was completely naive about sex. Soon after I arrived, a guy asked me to be his date to a fraternity party, which basically turned out to be an orgy. Everybody was getting drunk and going upstairs. But my date was a decent guy. When he realized I had no idea why people were going upstairs, he gave me a book called *Sane Sex Life and Sane Sex Living,* by H. W. Long, MD. He said, "Go home and read the book!"

After a while, I'm afraid I started acting badly. I was not a beauty, but women were a scarce resource at Cornell, so we all got the rush. The boys would call and call, asking for dates, and I got greedy. I wanted to have as many dates as

possible, so I strung people along. I was terrible.

You did have to be careful, how you conducted yourself. I don't think women drank quite as much alcohol as men did, but there were still a lot of scandals. Remember, contraceptive pills were not available until the 1960s. One girl I knew, a very good reporter for the *Sun,* got pregnant. I suppose you could have found a doctor who would quietly do an abortion, but this girl didn't do that. She ended up delivering her own baby in a sorority house. Her father rushed up to get her, and then she disappeared. It was such a tragedy. It seemed to us that her life was over.

Harland William Long, MD
(1869–1943)

From Sane Sex Life and Sane Sex Living (1919): Let it be said that all sane and intelligent men and women agree that anything even approaching infanticide is nothing short of a crime, and that abortion,

except for the purpose of saving the life of the mother, is practically murder. But, while this is all true, to prevent the contact of two germs which, if permitted to unite, would be liable to result in a living human form, is quite another affair . . .

It should be the constant aim and endeavor of both parties to continually lift all sex affairs above the plane of animality, mere physical gratification, into the realm of mental and spiritual delight. To this end, let it be said at once that such a condition can be reached, in the greatest degree, by the practice of what is known, in scientific terms, as "coitus reservatus," which, translated, means going only part of the way in the act, and not carrying it to its climax, the orgasm . . .

In this act, the lovers simply drift, petting each other, chatting with each other, visiting, loving, caressing in any one or all of a thousand ways. The hands "wander idly over the body," the husband's right hand being specially free and in perfect position to stroke his wife's back, her hips, her legs, and

Cooking and serving was part of the curriculum for women in the "Homemaking apartment" course in the School of Home Economics. This photo shows "student husbands and wives having dinner."

pet her from top to toe . . .

To go back a little: In speaking of mutual masturbation on the part of the husband and wife, this method of satisfying the sex nature is of great value, sometimes, especially for use during the "unfree time." If, during this time, the parties get "waked up," and feel the need of sex exercise, they can satisfy each other with their hands in a way that will be a great relief to each. This is especially true for the husband; and a wife, who is enough of a woman to thus meet her husband's sex-needs, with her hand, when it is not expedient for him to meet her otherwise, is a wife to worship! . . . Let love direct the way here, and all will be well.

Sane Sex Life and Sane Sex Living was one of the most popular and forthright books about human sexuality written before the 1960s. Although it is written for couples, it risked violating obscenity laws when it was released, so it was officially sold only to physicians. It is still in print.

Sandy Bangilsdorf Klein '53

I was a freshman competing to get onto the staff of the *Sun*. The game was to get as many column inches printed as you could. The people who published the most got on the staff, and inches on the editorial page counted double. So I decided I'd write a letter to the editor about

THE CO-ED'S CREED

FROM A BOOKLET DISTRIBUTED BY THE WSGA EXECUTIVE COMMITTEE TO INCOMING WOMEN IN 1950

News and gossip travel fast. That boy sitting next to you in English, in whom you confided your secrets, may very well be the roommate of the man of the moment—and don't think he won't run right home to give him the news. When you tell the girl down the hall how you would love to go out with Johnny—it just may happen that the girl you tell knows Johnny. More friendships are broken that way.

Sometime at the party where you flirted with a couple of cute boys, they just might turn out to be the fraternity brothers of your date. They won't like you so much, and they'll be sure to bring you up in gab sessions so your date will undoubtedly know! News travels fast, and gossip travels even faster, so watch your step and see that only good news travels about you!

Poise is an indefinable quality which you may cultivate with experience. As we see it, it is the ability to meet and cope with any sort of

situation gracefully and with tact. All sorts of problems may come up, and it's up to you to meet them well…if your date is a fizzle, if he becomes slightly inebriated before the evening is over, or if you don't care for the party in general—hold your head up, keep your common sense, be a good sport—and carry it off as well as possible. But make a mental note for next time. Be tolerant of others, BUT KEEP YOUR OWN PRINCIPLES [emphasis in original]…

Houseparty is the time when you "party" from morn 'til night and have a wonderful time or a rather unhappy experience. To avoid the latter calamity, just be sure your date is the kind of person you enjoy being with, and that he belongs to a house you enjoy going to. Don't jump at just any invitation to houseparty that you get just so you can say, "Yes, I went to houseparty." It isn't worth it.

Remember that some of the girls are "imports" and that you and your reputation have to stick around long after houseparty is a thing of the past… Be careful of your drinking, if you drink at all (and you will find drinking is not necessary; some of the most popular girls on the hill do not drink)… Enjoy yourself thoroughly, and show it. Your date has probably spent a good deal of trouble and money to make houseparty a success, so be a good sport and have a thoroughly tremendous time. But don't do anything you wouldn't want people to find out about because, like it or not, they're bound to, sooner or later.

the ratio of 4.5 guys to every girl.

I had been picking up rancor from guys who thought the co-eds were all so spoiled and unfair, and then I heard stories about guys who had been unfair themselves. So I gathered all the stories I had heard, put them together, and used a pseudonym. My phone started ringing the day the paper came out, and it literally rang around the clock for weeks. Some guys just wanted to insult me, but some of them wanted dates. I still don't know how the word got out that I was Name Withheld, because I told the editor not to give out my name. I wasn't bitter about it, just amazed.

That letter changed my life. I heard that for weeks after it was published, boys would call up radio stations, request "Take Me Out to the Ballgame," and dedicate the song to Name Withheld. An English teacher read it aloud in class and said it was the best rhetoric he had ever seen in the Sun. Wherever I went, I saw people pointing at me and whispering. I had become a public figure. I didn't like it. And in a way, it hasn't ever stopped.

I was at a concert last year with several Cornell alumni, and I was introduced to these two old geezers from my class. I told them my maiden name and they both said, "we know."

Sandy Bagilsdorf Klein worked as an advertising copywriter. Neither her first nor her second husband attended Cornell.

Jane Haskins Marcham '51

I was the women's editor of the Sun when the "Name Withheld" letter came in. There was a big, immediate reaction from both men and women that continued for weeks.

A lot of them were joking, but some of them thought it had raised issues that were worth hearing. And everybody wanted to know who the writer was.

The editor in chief said he wasn't interested in printing all the reactions. So a dozen Sun staffers, nine of them men, took up a collection and published them in a sixteen-page booklet with a blood-red cover. We had boxes and boxes of them. Then the university decided it didn't want the booklets on campus. We were told they were banned because the administration didn't want a sex scandal at Cornell.

We found someone to drive the boxes up to my dorm, and we snuck them in through a basement

window. Then we went around and sold them for fifteen cents each, under the table. They sold out immediately, because now it had become a free speech issue. People were buying four and five copies at a time.

The inside back cover of the "Name Withheld" booklet.

Ann Ellis Raynolds '50, MEd '53

I remember hearing about the woman who worked with us at the Sun who had a baby in her sorority bedroom. How did she hide it from everybody? Back in those days, women didn't have their own contraception, and my friends and I were scared to death of getting pregnant. I knew several girls besides the Sun reporter who also got pregnant. Someone living down the hall would just disappear, and you'd hear the story at breakfast.

Looking back, I don't know how I got through Cornell without getting raped. I always said no to sexual intercourse, but was frequently drinking so much and engaging in so much "necking," as we called it, that the lines were hard to draw. I can only say that the men I was with were honorable. Perhaps there really was a code of conduct in those days.

Most of my dates were either veterans or faculty members, and I think I learned something from every one of them. But the most memorable of all of them was Richard Feynman, the physicist. I heard rumors that he had tons of women at Cornell, but he made me feel special, which was fine because I already knew I was.

Dick never touched alcohol, which was refreshing at Cornell. I

NAME WITHHELD

The Cornell Daily Sun, April 7, 1950

Many's the gripe I've heard from Cornell men on the dating situation and co-eds in general, but as a frosh co-ed, I would like to offer a few complaints from the better fifth of the student body. It is high time that a popular Cornell tradition receives a well-deserved squelching from one of the group that has long borne the brunt of its abuse. The tradition in question is the ignoble status of the Cornell co-ed, the myth of popularity which surrounds her, and the resulting behavior of Cornell men toward us.

Far and wide, Cornell co-eds are known as "dogs" or "pigs." Years before I came here, I had heard that they were not only by far the world's ugliest women, but that they further disgraced their sex by their scandalously loose morals. On campus we are told that we are conceited, spoiled snobs, prudes, or frigid women who are getting away with repeated outrages, who are living in an ideal set-up, and who are taking unfair advantage of an unfortunate situation—namely, the Ratio [of 4.6 male students to every female].

Proof of our fabulous popularity and the desperate shortage of girls may be seen in the large number of girls who stay home on weekends in Clara Dickson Hall alone. These co-eds are not just the "ugly 30 percent," but include an amazing amount of cute and "popular" girls. Several weeks ago, one of my corridor mates held a formal funeral for her telephone, complete with candles and epitaph. "It died," she mourned solemnly as I passed her darkened room.

The hardest thing to grin at and bear, however, is the assortment of low, vile tricks commonly employed by the male population hereabouts in dating techniques.

The most lovable of these is used by the smoothie who selfishly attaches himself to a new co-ed to tide him over, then calmly drops her, leaving her with scanty dating prospects. Closely related to him is the type who also goes practically steady with a co-ed, then shows up at houseparty with an import. Imports, we note bitterly, are given sickeningly special consideration over co-eds at every opportunity. This is usually to "teach her a lesson."

Still griping, we are especially repelled by the tender lover who carries on an elaborate courtship, with or without a line, then reveals with a sheepish grin after several months that he's really engaged. This leaves us speechless with laughter.

Then there's the lad (often a first date) who, after wearing an unmasked leer for half the evening, suggests to his date that they spend the remaining two hours of a cold and windy night on the bleachers of Hoy Field, "to talk." Should the girl display any doubts as to the conversational conduciveness of a snow covered wooden bench, he becomes mortally wounded and bitterly disillusioned as to the moral simplicity of women.

The third thing that a freshman co-ed is told by the helpful upperclassmen who are eager to orient her (after she has been warned about the sophomore slump and the size her legs will be in two years) is that she has got to "give." Not only does everyone else "give," but if she doesn't, she is doomed to social failure. Plainly, we are expected to be sex machines for the satisfaction of adolescent male libidos. Nobody bothers to mention how such generosity is received by fraternity bull sessions and bulletin boards. "Kiss and tell" may not be a practice exclusive to Cornell men, but it is not the less obnoxious for its popularity.

I'm tired of drying the tears and patting the crewcuts of the men on this campus who are heaped with abuse from co-eds. If the social situation is not ideal, let them consider the possibility that it is not all our fault. They can learn to live with the Ratio and like it. —Name Withheld liked beer, but I never drank when I was around him. He loved to dance, and I did, too. We'd be at a party, dancing. He'd pick a book off the shelf and hand it to me and say, "What's this about?" I might tell him that it was a reproduction of the first folio of Shakespeare. He'd say, "I can't believe you know so much," and I'd say, "Well, I can't believe you know so much!"

One night, we were dancing and he suddenly stopped and said, "Do you mind, I have a formula running through my head and I have to go straight home and write it down before I forget it." Well, what do you do? Physics came first.

Yet Dick was also a wonderfully sensitive person. He told me about the hydrogen bomb before it was developed. He was clearly bothered about nuclear weapons, especially since he had helped get them started. But he always approached things from the scientific angle. Once I skipped a class to go with him to visit his mother, who was visiting friends nearby. Dick was hooked on the idea of finding formulas that could describe the ways human beings interacted. I was disdainful of that idea. We argued all the way

LOVE CHILD

The Cornell Daily Sun, February 18, 1949

A newborn baby girl, found Wednesday night in the basement of a Cornell sorority, was doing well in Tompkins County Memorial Hospital last night. A physician estimated her age at three days and said she was in "good shape." The finding of the baby was reported to police at 8:18 p.m. Wednesday [February 16]. The baby was found lying on a blanket and was taken immediately to the hospital.

back and forth to Syracuse.

I got engaged to Harold "Ron" Raynolds '48 in November of my senior year. Ron had been the editor in chief of the *Sun* when I was a sophomore trying to get on the staff there. He was a combat veteran, and he converted my politics. All the Ellises were expected to be Yankee Republicans, but Ron turned my head with stories about working conditions and unions. I had never come into contact with that point of view before.

Dick Feynman was horrified when I got engaged to Ron. I was also fairly confused about it,

to be truthful. Then, at the end of the year, Dick took me to Buttermilk Falls and asked me to marry him and go with him to Brazil that summer, where he would be teaching. That made me even more confused. Dick had lost his wife, Arline, to tuberculosis in 1945. She had been his high school sweetheart, and he had adored her. It was clear to me that he was still suffering, and it was all too complicated for me. I could also see that if I married Dick, my life would have to fit into his life. I wanted to carve out a life of my own.

I saw Ron as my partner and

From *Cornell Widow*, November 1948.

the man I wanted as the father of my children. The ethos at that time was very strong—you were expected to become a mother. Everyone around me was getting married with this intention, and I wanted to be a mother, too.

Richard Pogue '50

I played freshman basketball, and six of the seven starters on the varsity team lived at my fraternity. My roommate was a fantastic player. He had been all-state in Ohio. The problem was, he would go out every night. He partied so much that he started dropping out of class. He'd beg me to get him up in the morning. I'd throw water on his face, pull him onto the floor, anything I

could think of, but he just couldn't make it. By the end of the first year, he was gone. It was a tragedy.

People did flunk out because of drinking. It didn't happen a lot, but it happened. There was a guy who lost his clothes in Ithaca and at 3 a.m. walked up the hill wearing a barrel. So there was a lot of partying.

I never drank, it just didn't appeal to me, although it wasn't a philosophical thing. I was happy to tend the bar. And there were limits, informally set, but you knew them. You weren't supposed to drink during the week. And there were no other recreational drugs in those days. I had never even heard of marijuana. That was something jazz musicians did, and they were in a different world.

John Marcham '50

Watermargin members frequented an after-hours black nightclub in downtown Ithaca called The Golfers Club. It was upstairs in the Clinton Block, a brick building on the west side of the 100 block of North Cayuga Street. The Mural Lounge was in the Clinton House, on the same block. If you closed down that place, you could go to Golfers and keep drinking.

Harold "Cookie" Cook, a well-known black Ithaca trumpet player, told me that his friends started the club. They played golf at the local courses, but they didn't feel welcome at the clubhouses where they played. So they formed their own club and called it The Golfers. The drinks were potent, the entertainment raucous, and the pork chop sandwiches a delicacy.

There was a lot of drinking at Cornell, particularly in the later years. The fraternities would put kegs and punchbowls out on their lawns, so you could get free drinks and wander around all night. I remember going for a walk with Jane [Haskins '51] one Sunday morning on Thurston Avenue, and people were still out there drinking in the morning sunshine.

It got pretty bad. On the Friday of Junior Week in February 1950, the police pulled a body of out of Cascadilla Gorge, just under the Stewart Avenue Bridge. It was Lawrence Woodworth '50. He was on the lacrosse team, a leader at Delta Upsilon, and a National Scholar, so his death really shocked people. As far as anyone could tell, he had fallen while trying to cross the bridge. I suppose that he was stumbling around drunk in the dark.

Sam Johnson '50 was a good

Interfraternity Council president Richard Keegan (behind keg in dark suit jacket) partying with the brothers of Alpha Tau Omega in 1949.

From *Cornell Widow*, October 1948.

friend. One night he arrived at a party with all the makings for a pitcher of something strong, like martinis or Moscow Mules. We thought, oh, great, these will be good to share. But that wasn't Sam's intent. He drank it all himself.

Samuel C. Johnson Jr.
(1928–2004)

FROM *CARNAUBA: A SON'S MEMOIR* (2001): My earliest memory is of not understanding why my father and mother couldn't be together for the long term. Years later, my father told me the reason they got a divorce. My mother was an alcoholic, and he didn't know what to do…

In the very early days, I couldn't understand why she couldn't be all the time the way she was when she was sober, which was wonderful. But most of the time, she wasn't. And that was the biggest disappointment.

Eventually, I developed my mother's disease after many years. I had a hard time admitting it to myself. When I was a child, I said the one thing I never want to be is like my mother, in terms of this problem. But I did develop it. And after denying it several times, in confrontations with members of my family, I finally—they finally got me to admit that I had a problem, and they got me into a hospital where I needed to be in order to get well again.

Alcoholics have difficulty recognizing that they have a disease. And that's why it creates such a

sense of internal frustration. You know that you have to get this monkey off your back, the alcohol off you, and you cannot do it. And that is why a lot of alcoholics suffer from severe depression. They cannot figure out what to do!

It was very difficult for me because I was the chairman of the board of the Mayo Clinic, and had been for seven years. They were trying to get me to go to the Mayo Clinic for treatment. How can I go there? I'm the chairman of the board, and I'm walking into the addiction center for treatment? How do I do that? So I called up one of the top doctors at the Mayo Clinic, and he said, "well, my brother's daughter just got out of the addiction center here." That kind of softened the blow.

I walked in there one day, and twenty-eight days later, I walked out. I am forever grateful that my family pushed me into it. I think one of the great values of a family is to help a member get over a problem like I had. When I signed into that hospital, I thought I would never have fun again. I was wrong.

Sam Johnson was the fourth generation of his family to lead S. C. Johnson & Son, Inc., a global, privately held manufacturer of common household products such as Windex window cleaner and Ziploc plastic bags. As a Cornell student, he was on the staff of the *Cornell Daily Sun* for three years and was its advertising director in 1949-50. After receiving his bachelor of arts degree from Cornell, Sam went on to an MBA from Harvard in 1952. Under his leadership, S. C. Johnson & Son's estimated annual sales grew from $171 million to $6 billion.

Johnson was a leading environmentalist, philanthropist, and proponent of corporate social responsibility. He served as a Cornell trustee and, with his family, endowed the Samuel Curtis Johnson Graduate School of Management, named after his great-grandfather. The family also endowed Cornell's Herbert Fisk Johnson Museum of Art (named for Sam's father) and its Center for Birds and Biodiversity (named for his spouse, Imogene Powers Johnson '52).

William Joy '50
(1928–1988)

After receiving his BA degree from Cornell, William Joy became the fourth generation in his family to serve as editor and publisher of the *Evening Sentinel* in Centralia, Illinois. His love of the Cornell chimes inspired him to lead a drive that built the Centralia Carillon, a 160-foot tower featuring 65 bells, some weighing five and a half tons.

THE LAST BEER

By William Joy
CORNELL WIDOW, FEBRUARY 1949

In Zinck's the beer shall ever flow
Between the Bustees, row on row
While mid those aged, graven walls
The lush beside his bretheren falls
Scarce heard above the din below.

We are the Drunk. Short hours ago,
We busted finals, packed portmanteau,
Loved and were loved, and now we lie
In Zinck's Saloon.

Take up your fight with this under-tow:
To you with trembling hands we throw
A glass of beer, a life of lust—
Break not the faith with us who bust.
Sing us a song as out we go
From Zinck's Saloon.

Zinck's at its 1947 location on Aurora Street, at the base of South Hill.

Paul Joslin '50

Willie Joy was a real character, and his pranks were legendary. *The Great Gatsby* fascinated him. Every year, about a week before spring break, he would go downtown to a fancy haberdashery and purchase a new pair of white buck shoes, white flannel pants, the appropriate jazzy shirt and, if necessary, a new sport coat. He bought the outfit to wear on the annual train trip he took to his family's winter home in the Florida Keys. I was just a destitute farmboy, and he dazzled me.

In 1948–49, Will and I moved to the top floor of Baker Tower, the Gothic stone dorm in West Campus. We had a fine view of the city, and Will liked nothing better than to crank up an old tabletop Victrola he had bought at an estate sale, put on some 78 rpm records from the 1920s, and study while looking out the window. The music was seriously out of fashion, but he didn't care. Enrico Caruso, the great tenor of that era, was Will's favorite.

One warm, still evening in June, all the windows in the dormitories along the courtyard below Baker Tower were open, and all residents were polishing up term papers and otherwise earnestly studying for final exams. Will was also reading for a final exam, so he cranked his Victrola to the max and blasted out some Caruso. His neighbors became seriously agitated and began leaning out of their windows, hurling curses at Will and making one-finger salutes.

Will went to his open window, high above the courtyard. In a brief but eloquent lecture, he suggested that true students at a fine Ivy League university should study in the same manner as he, and should also acquire a taste for fine music, which he, without obligation, was providing so freely to them. The rebuttal was extensive and immediate. After the chorus of jeers had died down, Will made a grand and magnanimous gesture. He yelled, "OK, have it your way! Here's your Caruso," and he hurled his phonograph out the window. It made a deafening crash on the stone courtyard, five stories below! Cheers arose from the courtyard, and silence reigned till dawn.

The *Cornell Widow* was Will's main extracurricular activity. But in February 1949, he was caught setting off cherry bombs and doing all kinds of damage to Baker Dorm, including blowing the doors off a lavatory. I was implicated because I knew he was doing it, and I hadn't done anything to stop him. We were caught, summoned before the campus authorities, and told that we would be immediately expelled. But an unexpected event saved our hides.

Will threw the cherry bombs on the afternoon of February 16. This was also the day that Proctor Manning, the campus security officer and a dreaded authority figure, was arrested for shooting the lock off the front door of the Ithaca Country Club. He was drunk and allegedly trying to get into the liquor cabinet. The administration was shocked. Compared to his crime, ours was considered minor. We got off with probation and were banned from participating in extracurricular activities.

Our narrow escape meant that Will had to work at the *Widow* under a pen name. So he chose to become Pearl White, the silent film star from the *Perils of Pauline* serials, who had once lived and worked in Ithaca. She appeared on the *Widow*'s masthead in 1949 and 1950.

LOST WEEKENDS

The Cornell Daily Sun, May 15, 1951

As of late Sunday evening, the revelry and the fancy had passed, and reality had returned. The upturned beer kegs marked the end of the weekend, as did the freshly cleaned houses. What was left were empty glasses, empty visions, and emptier heads. And engraved in our weekend memories was the recurring picture of crowds of people standing and trampling on lawns all over the campus, while a dull, cloud-covered sun rose over Cayuga Lake Sunday morning.

The people were at once funny and pathetic. They were screaming and raving at each other. The crowds were generally spaced in widening concentric circles, with the heart or center group clutching at beer glasses and other drinking paraphernalia as they sought desperately to take a quick swipe at the keg. The other crowds and circles watched the central group and their antics. Faces were expressionless, except for the twisted contours required for yelling. Now a new howl, a ting-a-ling of an alarm bell, and the whistle of a siren split the air. Here and there someone would slip and [collapse, or] "crump out." The blare of the Dixieland jazz band was shrill and heavy as the music spread over the lawn in rising and falling tones.

Inside the houses, the dancing continued. The aim of the dancers was physical exhaustion and nothing less. In the rooms, the men and a few women were asleep, their breaths and bodies filled with hair tonic gin or cheap Imperial. Outside, the stumbling bodies with the raised glasses continued to rave and scream. Slowly the sun rose higher in a now less-clouded sky. All in all, the scene portrayed a feverish chaos and confusion that was a sad testimonial to a social weekend at Cornell.

The "Arabian Nights" party at Phi Sigma Kappa, 1948.

Charles D. Manning

(1907–1982)

Charles Manning was Proctor of Cornell University from 1935 to 1949, with responsibility for student discipline and campus security. According to the annual reports of the dean of men, Proctor Manning dealt with fifty-four cases of "student problems" in 1946–47 and eighty-three cases in 1947–48.

THE CORNELL DAILY SUN, FEBRUARY 18, 1947: A mysterious note was found on the third floor of the Plant Sciences Building. The note read, "*Eutaxocrinus ithacensis* (Williams) Sherburne, foot of falls in Fall Creek Gorge." Fearful that the note indicated a possible suicide, the campus patrol and Proctor Manning searched the gorge and are reported to have found nothing except water and ice—and oh yes, some *Eutaxocrinus ithacensis.* Proctor Manning is supposed to have been much chagrined the following morning on having the note translated to discover it referred to a fossil…

THE CORNELL DAILY SUN, EDITORIAL, JANUARY 12, 1949: Within the last month, Proctor Manning entered the room of a male student living off-campus in Collegetown early one morning to catch the student and a co-ed in rather extenuating circumstances. On the basis of the evidence obtained through this "raid," both students have been expelled from the university… [but] does an officer of the school administration have the right to enter the room of a student living OFF-CAMPUS to investigate his conduct at any particular moment?

In 1948–49, the dean of men and dean of

women jointly reported "a marked increase in the number of students who visited this office for help with serious problems of emotional adjustment. Of these, approximately 110 were found to have [psychological] implications. The data on these cases were organized and most of the students were referred to the medical department for psychiatric treatment."

Richard Pogue '50

I was busy putting out the *Sun* at about 11 p.m. on February 16, 1949. That was when we heard that Proctor Manning had been arrested for trying to break into the Ithaca Country Club. So we all roared over to the police station and sure enough, there he was.

We talked to the cops, who said that Manning and a former state trooper were both being

PROCTOR MANNING ARRAIGNED

THE CORNELL DAILY SUN, FEBRUARY 17, 1949

University Proctor Charles Manning was arraigned last night before Justice of the Peace T. B. Maxfield on the charge of third degree burglary (breaking and entering).

At 1 a.m. this morning Manning was released on $200 bail produced by his attorney Edward J. Casey after a hearing by Special Judge Louis K. Thaler. The arrest at 9 p.m. followed the forced entry into the Country Club of Ithaca clubhouse early yesterday morning. Revolvers had been fired into locks at the club, but nothing was removed from the clubhouse…

Proctor Manning was arrested by state troopers last night in the company of George Lawrenson, a former state trooper with 20 years service, who was also released on $200 bail. At the hearing before Justice Maxfield, no testimony was recorded. Proctor Manning will remain on bail until Friday. When interviewed by the *Cornell Daily Sun* upon his release, Proctor Manning had no comments for publication.

charged with breaking and entering. We tried to talk to Manning, but he didn't say anything. This was a huge deal, because Manning was so roundly disliked for busting so many people. So we raced back to the *Sun* and wrote up what we knew and put it in a box on the front page, in bold typeface.

Just before we put the paper to bed, someone asked whether or not printing the name of an accused criminal on the front page had any legal implications. No one knew, but someone said, "Dick, your father's a lawyer. Call him up!" So I called my dad, who was an aviation lawyer in Washington, DC, at 2 a.m. He said, "I don't do libel law. Just tell the truth, and you'll be OK." And we were ok.

Manning had obviously gone off his rocker, and he had taken his friend with him. The next day they were both charged with impersonating police officers, along with burglary. They had tried to make it look like a raid, but they were really after the contents of a locked box, maybe containing money. They had been drinking and playing poker up there after hours. They came back at five in the morning and told the night watchman that they were plainclothes police officers, and when they couldn't pry the lock off, Manning shot it with his revolver. But they still couldn't get into the box, so they left. The police picked them up at the bar of the Alhambra Hotel that night.

Manning pled guilty to the impersonation charge and not guilty to burglary. He was found guilty of impersonation and was sentenced to six months in jail, but the judge suspended the sentence because of his service to Cornell, and the grand jury didn't indict him on the burglary charge. I guess they felt that the poor guy deserved a break.

Charles Manning left Ithaca in 1949, worked as a bartender in Newark, New Jersey, and returned to Ithaca to retire. In 1949, the number of students referred for psychiatric evaluation exceeded 200.

Rose K. Goldsen
(1917–1985)

Rose K. Goldsen came to Cornell as a researcher in sociology in 1949 and quickly advanced to full professor. She became a nationally known commentator on the effect of the mass media on American life, and especially on the lives of children. Her first job at the university was to survey 2,758 Cornell students in seven colleges.

During the spring term of 1950, when the present study was made, one-fourth of all undergraduates were veterans—in contrast to the previous year, when 40 percent had come out of the services…since veterans are usually older than nonveteran students, their presence on the campus raises the median age of Cornell undergraduates. Veterans are about four years older than nonveterans, on the average… The declining proportion of veterans in each college becomes even clearer when their representation in each class, senior [Class of '50] through freshman ['54], is compared:

In the College of Agriculture, 57 percent of seniors are veterans, compared with 11 percent of freshmen. The declines are also pronounced in Architecture (55 percent, 18 percent), Arts & Sciences (39 percent, 5 percent), Engineering (69 percent, 11 percent), Home Economics (6 percent, 1 percent), Hotel (69 percent, 11 percent), and Industrial and Labor Relations (53 percent, 9 percent).

Favorite Drinks of Postwar Cornell

Bourbon Milk Punch
Adapted from French 75 Bar, New Orleans

1 ¼ ounces bourbon

½ ounce dark rum

2 ounces milk (use cream or half-and-half for a richer drink)

⅛ ounce vanilla extract

½ ounce simple syrup

Dash of grated nutmeg

In a mixing glass three-quarters filled with ice, pour the bourbon, rum, milk or cream, vanilla and syrup. Shake vigorously until chilled, about 30 seconds. Strain into a rocks glass. Dust with nutmeg.

Orange Blossom
Made famous by the rapper Snoop Dogg as "Gin 'n' Juice"

1 ½ ounces gin

1 ½ ounces orange juice

Shake well with cracked ice, then strain into a chilled cocktail glass. For Gin 'n' Juice, use rocks and a Collins glass.

Timeline of World Events

1944

JUNE 6
D-Day. More than 160,000 Allied troops land on the beaches of Normandy to begin the re-conquest of Europe.

JUNE 22
The Servicemen's Readjustment Act of 1944, commonly known as the G.I. Bill of Rights, is signed into law by President Roosevelt.

1945

MAY 8
Victory in Europe (V-E) Day.

AUGUST 6
The *Enola Gay* detonates a nuclear weapon over Hiroshima, Japan, killing one-third of the city's residents and injuring another one-third.

SEPTEMBER 2
Victory over Japan (V-J) Day.

1946

MARCH 5
Speaking in Fulton, Missouri, Winston Churchill describes Soviet expansion into Europe as an "iron curtain" and warns of secret "fifth columns" expanding Soviet influence in democratic countries.

JULY 1 AND 25
The U.S. military detonates two twenty-three-kiloton atomic bombs over Bikini Atoll. Films and reports of the events receive wide publicity.

AUGUST 1
The U.S. Atomic Energy Commission is established.

AUGUST 31
John Hersey's *Hiroshima* is published and becomes an international bestseller.

NOVEMBER 5
U.S. Senate and House elections give majority control of both houses to the Republican Party.

1947

JANUARY 31
Communists take power in Poland.

MARCH 12
President Harry S. Truman announces a new U.S. foreign policy aimed at containing the expansion of the Soviet Union.

APRIL 16
Bernard Baruch describes U.S.-Soviet relations as a "cold war."

JULY 26
The National Security Act creates the Central Intelligence Agency, the Department of Defense, the Air Force, the Joint Chiefs of Staff, and the National Security Council.

AUGUST 31
Communists seize power in Hungary.

NOVEMBER 24

Ten screenwriters and directors are "blacklisted" after refusing to cooperate with a House Un-American Activities Committee (HUAC) investigation of communist influence in the movie industry.

1948

FEBRUARY 25
The Communist Party seizes control of Czechoslovakia.

APRIL 3
The Marshall Plan becomes law, sending $5 billion in aid to sixteen European countries.

MAY 14
The Israeli Declaration of Independence marks the birth of the State of Israel, and also the beginning of the first Arab-Israeli War.

JUNE 24
The Soviet blockade of Berlin begins. American planes supply essentials for the next year.

JULY 20
Truman issues America's second peacetime military draft.

AUGUST 25
In a televised Congressional hearing, Whittaker Chambers accuses State Department official Alger Hiss of being a member of the Communist Party. Hiss's first trial ends in a deadlocked jury. He is later convicted of perjury.

NOVEMBER 2
Truman is re-elected, defeating Republican Thomas E. Dewey, "Dixiecrat" Strom Thurmond, and Progressive Henry Wallace.

CORNELL UNDERGRADUATE ENROLLMENT/PERCENTAGE OF VETERANS | 1944–45: 4152/na | 1945–46: 6322/42%

CHAPTER 10

1949

JANUARY 31

Forces from the Communist Party of China enter Beijing.

JUNE 8

George Orwell publishes *1984*.

AUGUST 24

The North Atlantic Treaty Organization is established.

SEPTEMBER 23

Truman announces that the Soviet Union has tested an atomic bomb.

OCTOBER 1

Mao-Tse tung proclaims the People's Republic of China (PRC). The Soviet Union recognizes the PRC and signs a non-aggression pact.

OCTOBER 14

Eugene Dennis and ten other leaders of the Communist Party U.S.A. are convicted of advocating the violent overthrow of the government. All but one are sentenced to prison.

1950

FEBRUARY 9

Senator Joseph McCarthy accuses the U.S. State Department of harboring 205 Communists.

JUNE 25

Kim Il-sung's army crosses the 38th parallel behind artillery fire at dawn, starting the Korean War with support from China and the Soviet Union.

JULY 17

Julius Rosenberg is arrested (while shaving) on charges of spying for the Soviet Union.

1951

SEPTEMBER 9

Chinese Communist forces move into Lhasa, Tibet.

APRIL 6

Ethel and Julius Rosenberg are sentenced to death for espionage against the United States.

JUNE 14

The U.S. Census Bureau begins using the UNIVAC I computer.

NOVEMBER 1

The first military exercises for nuclear war, with infantry troops, are held in the Nevada desert.

DECEMBER 31

The Marshall Plan expires after distributing more than $13.3 billion US in foreign aid to Europe.

1952

APRIL 15

A U.S. B-52 Stratofortress flies for the first time.

JUNE 15

Anne Frank's *The Diary of a Young Girl* is published.

OCTOBER 3

The first British nuclear weapon is detonated in Australia.

OCTOBER 14

The United Nations begins work on its headquarters in New York City.

NOVEMBER 1

The U.S. successfully detonates the first hydrogen bomb, with a yield of 10.4 megatons.

NOVEMBER 4

Dwight D. Eisenhower is elected President. Republicans control the Presidency and both houses of Congress for the first time since 1929.

1946–47: 9021/64% | 1947–48: 9124/60% | 1948–49: 8849/52% | 1949–50: 8749/37% | 1950–51: 8492/28%

The World War II memorial in Anabel Taylor Hall.

CHAPTER 11

Outside Worlds

The Cold War on Campus

As Cornell got bigger, the world got smaller. The opening of the New York State School of Industrial and Labor Relations in 1945 introduced hundreds of students and faculty whose primary concerns were workers' rights and social justice. Expanding Soviet influence in Europe gave new urgency to international news. Although most Cornell students identified as Republicans, *The Cornell Daily Sun* endorsed the Progressive Party's presidential candidate, Henry Wallace, in 1948. A small, vocal Communist discussion group was a constant irritation to alumni and trustees.

As international tension mounted, students made earnest efforts to promote cross-cultural understanding, from clearing rubble in Europe to enthusiastically participating in a model United Nations. Many believed that the fate of the world depended on their efforts: President Truman announced that the Soviets had exploded an atomic bomb on September 23, 1949, a few days after the start of fall classes. Shortly after graduation, on June 25, 1950, South Korea was invaded and the US sent soldiers back into battle. With hot and cold wars raging overseas, Cornell students of the early 1950s grew increasingly wary of Communists at home—both real and imagined.

OPERATION CROSSROADS

The Cornell Daily Sun, November 8, 1946

"In five to ten years any major industrial country will be able to make enough atomic bombs to completely wipe out life in any other country," warned Philip W. Swain, editor of the magazine *Power*, who addressed the American Institute of Electrical Engineers here last night.

Mr. Swain supplemented his lecture on nuclear physics with an official Technicolor movie of the Bikini experiment, which vivified his ardent statements that the bomb's tremendous power must be harnessed through national diplomacy. Mr. Swain witnessed the Bikini tests and is one of the few journalists with a background in physics and engineering. He has taught mechanical engineering at Yale University.

Richard Feynman

During World War II, before he began teaching at Cornell, Feynman worked on the development of the atomic bomb.

Did I tell you what I thought about the atomic bomb and everything right after the war? I couldn't look at New York City and people building a new building without thinking that they're crazy. When I came to New York, I would eat in a restaurant at 52nd Street and look down the street, and think of what would happen if a bomb went off at 34th Street. It's less than a mile. All those bricks.

I realized the terrible thing the atomic bomb represented. I had a feeling—possibly because my wife had just died,[1] and so I had some feeling of impermanence of things—and also, a general prejudice that human beings were doing exactly the same thing as they had done before. It looked to me like history was not getting anywhere, and that people were holding the same kinds of stupid, selfish, national views that they had before. It seemed to me inevitable that they would be led into a war, that it was just a matter of time.

And so, I couldn't accept the idea that there was really a future. I thought that [the end of the world] was imminent. I even thought that people were crazy because they didn't understand this. I mean, why would you bother to build a new bridge or tunnel?

I'm glad not everybody believed the way I did, or the whole damn thing would have stopped. But [after I arrived at Cornell in November 1945], I spent a lot of time explaining the bomb to

[1] Arline Feynman died of tuberculosis in June 1945.

Tom Dewey after speaking at Cornell during the 1948 presidential campaign. Rick Diamond '50 (right, in sweater) approached him to ask whether he thought he could win in New York State, traditionally a Democratic stronghold. Dewey, the Republican candidate, said that he could do it, and he did, beating Truman by 60,000 votes. Henry Wallace of the Progressive Party received more than 500,000 votes in New York, many of which would have otherwise gone to Truman.

people in lectures. I felt that I knew something about the bomb, and that citizens should know more, because, thinking idealistically, decisions are made by citizens.

Doing Something

THE CORNELL BULLETIN, NOVEMBER 9, 1945: We have received a communication from the student leaders of Bennington College, requesting that the editors of this paper consider the grave consequences of the atomic bomb, and that we enlist the aid of all university organizations in urging congressional action that would make the few remaining "secrets" of this weapon common scientific knowledge… We hope that campus groups will accept the suggestion of Bennington College students. If we are to take the places

of educated people in the world of tomorrow, now is the time to form the habits of keeping abreast of the news, and taking action, to the best of our ability, in the direction that seems right to us.

World Federalists

THE CORNELL DAILY SUN, OCTOBER 23, 1946: Students interested in world federation met last night at 217 West Avenue, Ithaca, to form a Cornell Chapter of World Federalists, USA. World Federalists believe that a world government is as necessary as local and national government; that there can be no permanent peace without justice, no justice without law, and no law without governmental institutions to make, administer, interpret, and enforce it…

Thomas Dewey
(1902–1971)

Thomas Dewey was governor of New York from 1943 to 1954 and the Republican candidate for president in 1948. These are excerpts from his remarks at the dedication of the New York State School of Industrial and Labor Relations, November 12, 1945.

This is no labor school where dogma will be taught, from which trained zealots will go forth. This is no management school where students will learn only to think of working men and women as items on a balance sheet. This is a state school under the sponsorship of our great, progressive land grant university and under the direct control of a board of trustees selected from all walks of life; from education, from business, from labor, from agriculture, and from the professions.

It is a school which denies the alien theory that there are classes in our society and that they must wage war against each other. This is a school dedicated to the common interest of employer and employee and of the whole of the American people. It is dedicated to the concept that when men understand each other and work together harmoniously, then and only then do they succeed.

Edmund Ezra Day
(1883–1951)

From the introduction of Governor Dewey at the ILR School Dedication ceremony:

We are fully aware of the complications that face the life of this new school. We are familiar with the controversy that today envelops the industrial field. We know that forces will play upon the school which will not be wholly rational nor disinterested. We realize that administration of the school will be a very exacting responsibility.

But the responsibilities involved in the operation of this school are the very ones which a great university should be prepared to assume. In higher education, soundly conceived and wisely directed, the existence of deep controversy must be regarded not as a warning to keep out, but as a summons to move in…

Barbara Cole Feiden '48

I was in the first class that graduated from the New York State School of Industrial and Labor Relations (ILR) in 1948. A lot of us had transferred from other colleges or within Cornell. Our backgrounds were also unusual because a lot of us were veterans and had done interesting things. My roommate, Helvi Selkee '48, had worked for the United Nations.

We ILR students felt like pioneers, because we were. It was an ideal position. We were a small, tight group, but we could also take advantage of a large university. Our classes and offices were housed in Quonset huts that stood where the Engineering Quad is today. The best word to describe them is "functional," but I have fond memories. I loved that most of our professors were not career academicians. They came to Cornell with practical experiences in unions, government, or industry.

A lot of ILR students benefitted enormously from the GI Bill. My future husband, Barry Feiden '49, had been in the army infantry. Max Finestone '49 came from the merchant marine. Bill Carroll '48 had attended three colleges before he got to ILR, and he had also been in the navy.

A lot of veterans were keenly interested in politics. I was a member of the American Veterans Committee (AVC), which was

Quonset huts that housed the ILR school, under construction in 1945.

141

a progressive alternative to the American Legion. We were active in civil rights, world peace, and similar things. Barry and I would have long political discussions as we studied on Library Slope and in Goldwin Smith Hall. Our friends sang folk songs and discussed plays. Barry courted me by bicycle, riding from his apartment in Collegetown to my living quarters. We made our own fun.

Alan Towbin '50

Thanks to the housing shortage, I moved six times during my time at Cornell. In my junior year I rented a room in a private home in Ithaca's west end, near the railroad station. My job was washing dishes at Balch Hall, two and a half miles away. I had no car, and I had to make it to work every morning by 7 a.m. The rule was, be there before the second hand crosses the hour mark, or you get no food, and you have to work anyway.

The grim-faced elderly ladies stood in front of the table with the breakfast meal, with a hand on a plate and an eye on the clock above them, ready to snatch the plate away as soon as the second hand completed its journey. On this particular icy morning, I had run up the street from my room to the bus stop, and when the bus dropped me off outside of Balch, I ran into the food-service area, in time to miss breakfast by a few seconds. I knew I was supposed to stay and work the meal, but I turned and left to buy breakfast elsewhere.

When I returned for lunch, the dietician in charge summoned me and put me on notice. If this happened again, she said, I would be fired. It was obvious I needed to find another job that included meals and was closer to my room. Within a day or two, I was working at Willard Straight Hall.

I enjoyed working at the Straight. It offered more varied employment and cash pay. There was a cafeteria, with an alcove adjoining the cafeteria that provided short-order service on Sunday mornings. The Ivy Room had an informal atmosphere with picnic tables and benches. It was open every afternoon and served beer, with a soda fountain and a short-order kitchen on the premises. Another student employee and I staffed these short-order stations. It was a lot like being in business for ourselves, except we didn't handle cash. We just took orders and cooked, essentially unsupervised.

Mrs. Weaver, the assistant manager, seemed to like me. I thought that was a plus for my prospects for promotion. She wandered around the cafeteria service a good deal. But I never saw Mr. Ryan, the manager, outside of his office.

A few weeks into the fall semester of my senior year, I had a visit from one of my colleagues at the dining service, Richard Keesee '50. We had exchanged a few words, and I knew he was a combat veteran, but that was all I knew about him. He came to my room, which was now in the student laundry building on College Avenue. He was upset. He said that Mrs. Weaver had accused him of stealing food.

I had seen other student employees reach up to the tray they were carrying from the kitchen, take a plate and pop a dessert into their mouth. I was never bold enough to try that trick. Keesee didn't even bother to deny the charge, but he felt humiliated that she had charged him with a crime. He wanted to form a union of the student employees at the Straight. The students needed representation in the matter of wages and the inferior meals that we were offered by management, he said. A union would also give us protection from unwarranted charges and criticism from management. Would I help him organize it?

I don't believe Keesee knew it, but labor activism was in my family background. My mother was a shop steward in the International Ladies Garment Workers Union. Her younger brother, my uncle Morris, was the business agent for the Waiters, Waitresses, and Bartenders Union in the Times Square area of New York City. So of course I agreed to help him, and we called a meeting of the student employees.

I only vaguely recall that meeting. I can picture perhaps ten to fifteen men and women (none of them waitresses) sitting around tables in what may have been Sage Hall. We presented our plan to the group and asked them to endorse it, and to elect Keesee and myself as their representatives to management. We had two immediate goals. First, we wanted a raise in pay—I believe it was by ten cents an hour. We also felt that that the low priced meals served to us in the late afternoon, before we worked the evening shift, were unacceptable. They were leftovers, for the most part. All present agreed, and they authorized Keesee and me to seek a meeting with management.

The end of the story is anticlimactic. Mr. Ryan and Mrs. Weaver immediately agreed to meet with us. They were cordial, and they seemed pleased that we had organized ourselves. Later, someone told me they believed that a union would make students more disciplined and thereby reduce the theft of food. This seemed weird to me, because we students knew that the major food losses happened when chefs walked off with hams and roasts. We were happy to take advantage of their wishful thinking. They agreed to our demands, and, incidentally, they were right about the students. I never heard any more complaints about students stealing food.

Alan Towbin earned a bachelor of arts degree at Cornell, and a master's degree and PhD in 1955 from Yale. He has a psychology practice in Bethany, Connecticut.

The Willard Straight Hall Student Employees Association was an early stirring of the postwar labor movement at Cornell. In the autumn semester of 1950, between 500 and 800 employees staged an eleven-day walkout organized by the Ithaca chapter of the Building Service Employees Union. The university ended the strike by agreeing to bargain with the union, while the union agreed that membership would remain voluntary so that non-union employees could continue working without penalty. During the strike, James Gibbs '52 and five other students walked off their jobs rather than do the jobs of striking workers.

Paul Rosenblum '48

I grew up in the Allerton co-ops, in the northeast Bronx, in the 1930s. My father was a garment worker. Everyone in my housing complex was working-class, Jewish, and left-wing, so I was very comfortable with the Communist Party. It was what the grown-ups argued about, because it had so many factions and was always falling apart. People kept telling me, "don't play with him, he isn't from the right faction." I just ignored them. At the same time, I was very comfortable with the left and very pro-union.

I had vision problems that made me ineligible for the military when I graduated from high school in 1944, so I went on to college. I was attracted to the School of Industrial and Labor Relations because it was such a revolutionary idea, and also because it was a state school, so tuition was free. I was in the first class. It was quite a change for me. All of a sudden I was in upstate New York, surrounded by cows and people from all different backgrounds.

Jack Sheinkman '49, JD '52 and I were classmates and friends. I was associated with the Communist students, and he was associated with the Socialists. I remember once we rode home to New York City together on a bus, and we had an argument. I remember it vividly because it reminds me of how stupid I was back then. We were arguing about laundry. Like a lot of

---

STALIN, TROTSKY DEBATE AT CORNELL

THE CORNELL DAILY SUN, MAY 22, 1947

Robert Fogel '48, arguing from a standpoint of economic inequities under the capitalist system, and John Roche, graduate, basing his opposing views on the loss of individual freedom, debated the desirability of Communism in America last night.

Addressing the last meeting of the Marxist discussion group, Fogel, president of the organization, declared that "while we have tremendous resources, our present society is so constructed that we have lavishness for the few and discrimination, poverty, and war for the many." Quoting from Lenin, he pointed out that there is no conflict between Communism and Socialism in the classical sense.

Communists in this country and in most countries throughout the world are actually working for socialism, he said. Citing the Communist Party stand in favor of such legislation as the housing and national health bills, Fogel declared, "Anything that aids the majority of the people brings the country that much closer to socialism."

Deploring the use of "barbaric expedients," John Roche, president of the Student League for Industrial Democracy, said that he was in favor of eliminating the class system, but that a government dominated by Communists "would establish a despotism which would make the present capitalistic system, with its admitted inequalities, seem like utopia. In the name of classless society, Communists would enslave the people they came to liberate."

us, I was sending my laundry back to New York City for my mother to do and send back to me.

I said to Jack that Stalin should not have to do his own laundry, because he was such an important guy. Jack said that was all wrong. He said that in a just society, we should all be responsible for doing our own laundry. My argument was so naive. I was a victim of the cult of personality that surrounded Stalin, and Jack saw through it. I remember that so well.

Robert Fogel was the most strident Communist on campus, and I knew how to talk to Communists because I had grown up around them. I would go on walks with him, and listen to him, and be a sort of friend to him because I'd let him vent and rant all he wanted. His ambition was to be an organizer for the Communist Party. I said, "Bob, you can't do that. You're far too dogmatic and overbearing." I have a mental image of Bob Fogel with a copy of *Das Kapital* under his arm, backing a little co-ed into a corner and hectoring her. An organizer? This is impossible! Forget about it!

All of a sudden, we heard that Bob was going to get a job as a Communist organizer in New York City. We actually sent a couple of people down there to tell the Party guys that they shouldn't hire him, because he really needed to learn some humility. We told these bureaucrats that he needed to work at a factory for a while. I mean, his father owned a factory! But they turned us down, and off he went.

Paul Rosenblum earned a BS from the ILR School. He worked as a typesetter for *The New York Times* and other newspapers in New York City, as a member of the International Typographical Union.

Robert W. Fogel '48
(1926–2013)

Robert Fogel entered Cornell to study physics and chemistry, but switched to economics and history and became a strident advocate of Soviet-style Communism from the mid-1940s to the mid-1950s. In a 2008 article in *Cornell Alumni Magazine,* Fogel reflected on his young adulthood.

Marxism and Communism loomed large in Fogel's world, even before he was born. The outbreak of the Russian Civil War prompted his parents to flee from Odessa in 1922. An affluent family, they bribed their way to Constantinople, where his father almost died of typhus and gangrene. Having spent most of their money to keep him alive, the Fogel family arrived at Ellis Island in steerage. Robert was born four years later. For a time the family lived in a tenement on Manhattan's Lower East Side that lacked electric lights. They later moved to the Bronx. "Although I lived through the Great Depression, I remember it as a golden age, because I knew I was loved," Fogel says.

Fogel has said his greatest intellectual influence was his brother Ephim (1920–1992), who was six years older. (Ephim Fogel would join Cornell's faculty in 1949 and chair the English department from 1966 to 1970.) Robert Fogel remembers lying in bed at night listening to Ephim and his friends debate what to do for a date when one had only a dime, as well as ask questions about the economy and politics. For a date, visit a girl at her babysitting job. For the rest, "They said, 'The answers to all that

are in Marx,'" Fogel remembers. "For years after that, I thought Marx must be the name of an encyclopedia."

The U.S.S.R. was an American ally then, and Hollywood films framed Communists as freedom fighters while newsreels lauded the heroic struggles of the Russians beating back the Nazi invasion during World War II. "Marxism was colorful," Fogel remembers. "It was the snobbery of the young intelligentsia to know these arcane works about the analysis of capitalism and its imperfections." By the time he entered Cornell in 1944, he was a devoted Marxist.

It was an ironic philosophical choice, given his father's capitalist success. By then his father, an engineer by training, owned a profitable meat wholesale business. "I didn't become a radical through my own experience of how terrible capitalism was. It was purely intellectual," Fogel says. "I was a rich boy, the son of rich parents. And I believed that Marxism was the science of society and Marxists were the social scientists of the time." He joined the Cornell chapters of the NAACP, American Youth for Democracy (the Communist Party's youth wing), and the Young Progressive Citizens of America. He also chaired the Marxist discussion group, and he spent half of his sizable allowance to bring radical speakers to campus.[2]

"My father thought American capitalism was God's gift to the Earth," Fogel says. "I had a big argument with him about how

---

[2] Robert Fogel's relatives point out that he did not actually come from a wealthy family. "Uncle Bob liked to talk and act like he was privileged, but his father was a middle-class businessman," said his nephew, David Fogel '72.

Robert Fogel, with his mother and his pipe, on the trail through Cascadilla Gorge.

capitalism corrupts and oppresses people. He said, 'Look at me. I came here with nothing. Anyone who works hard and who is bright can make a good living in America.' And I said, 'No, Papa, you're the exception that proves the rule.' Sometime afterward, he said his attitude toward me was that with some kids, it's sex, but with me, it was politics. He was just waiting for me to grow up."

As Marxists' predictions of severe unemployment failed to materialize, Fogel began to question if they understood capitalism at all. "They couldn't even get a business cycle forecast right. They were Johnny One Note," he says, referring to a 1937 show tune. "The one note was, 'It's going to get terrible.' And if it didn't get terrible, they didn't have an answer." In 1956, Fogel left the Communist Party and enrolled at Columbia, borrowing money from a Cornell friend to pay tuition. "I decided that I wanted to go back to school," he says, "because I had glibly accepted a lot of things."

Fogel received a BA from Cornell. He earned a master's degree in economics from Columbia in 1960, a PhD from Johns Hopkins in 1963, and became director of the Center for Population Economics at the University of Chicago. His research revolutionized understanding of the role of railways in the economic development of the United States, the economic role of slavery, and long-term changes in the health status of older Americans. In 1993, he shared the Nobel Prize in Economics "for having renewed research in economic history by applying economic theory and quantitative methods."

William Kay '51

Everybody thought that ILR was the Communist school. It wasn't—it was a very diverse place—but I would get called a Communist all the time because I was an ILR student. I am a complete capitalist and always have been, so I just ignored them.

Of course, there were Communists around. The Lubell twins, David and Jonathan, were the reddest of them all. They smoked pipes. Bob Fogel did, too. This wasn't unusual, but I was also told that they did it because Joseph Stalin smoked a pipe, and they wanted to be just like him. My roommate, John Marqusee '51, was also a

David Lubell   Jonathan Lubell

Communist. I would drive him to Party meetings at an apartment somewhere in Collegetown.

I thought this was all completely ridiculous. I told John and every other left-wing person I met that they were enjoying the benefits of a capitalist system, and that they were all going to go on and make good livings, and nobody was making a good living in Russia. They would just *hate* that. But lo and behold, John later became my business partner. He was a good businessman, too. I tried not to be too hard on him about it.

Bill Kay served in the merchant marine during World War II as an engineer third class, running the electrically powered tankers that fueled aircraft carriers. He went to New York University before transferring to the ILR School in 1948, where he earned a BS degree and became a founding member of the Watermargin co-op. He is a real estate developer and investor in Philadelphia.

Rose K. Goldsen
(1917–1985)

As a new sociology instructor at Cornell in 1949, Goldsen surveyed 2,758 members of the Cornell student body. She quickly rose to the position of professor.

The campus is predominantly Republican. Over half the students (57 percent) reported that in the 1948 presidential campaign their sympathies were with Dewey or the Republican Party. Less than a third (29 percent) were sympathetic to Truman or the Democratic Party. Four percent were in favor of Wallace or the Progressive Party; another 4 percent indicated other political loyalties; and 6 percent indicated that they had had no political opinion on the 1948 presidential election.

The only campuses where the Republicans are not in the majority are the College of Architecture and the School of Industrial and Labor Relations (ILR). In the former college, a plurality (45 percent) indicated Republican sympathies in 1948. In the ILR School, on the other hand, more than half the students (52 percent) said they were sympathetic to Truman or the Democrats, and only a third (32 percent) were in favor of the Republican candidate. Aside from these two campuses, variations are minor in the other colleges.

Political Leanings

In the spring of 1948, the student council's survey committee polled a representative sample of Cornell students on political issues. It summarized the results in *The Cornell Daily Sun* on May 21, 1948.

Cornellians seem rather pessimistic about the future. Sixty-two percent felt that the United States would find itself in another war within twenty years. Only 10 percent definitely saw no war in the near future. However, women were a little more optimistic than men. Only 54 percent of the women saw war ahead, whereas 65 percent of the men did. Looking at the communities from which students came, the survey committee found that the most optimistic group was from the big cities.

The large majority of those polled wanted a world federation. Seventy-five percent said that a "democratic world government of all nations" was "desirable," whereas only one quarter were either undecided or against it. However, very few thought that such a world federation was feasible. Even among those who thought that it was "very desirable," only one-quarter believed it possible. As a government major said, "Most of us want a world federation, but very few think we can get it.'"

Concerning cooperation with Russia in a world organization, 70 percent said that "we should continue to try to cooperate with Russia," while 30 percent held that "we should go ahead with other nations and leave out Russia."

May Day Hijinks

Cornell Alumni News, May 15, 1949: A May Day chimes program, which jokingly followed the "party line" with left-wing songs and red kites flying from the library tower, received mixed comments from the public on May 2. Starting an hour early in honor of the occasion, the morning concert planned to last from 6:50 to 8:00 a.m. was soon stopped by the Campus Patrol, which refused to believe that students up that early could be doing anything legal.

Student letters to *The Cornell Daily Sun* included protests from men in Sage College, who objected to being awakened an hour early; praise from women in Risley Hall, who enjoyed the concert; and a note

European Tour, 1948

Jane Wigsten [McGonigal Crispell] '50, Kitty Rusack [Adams] '50, and Agnes Ronaldson [Poole] '51 joined forty American college students doing relief work in Germany in the summer of 1948. The trip was organized by Lee Clare, pastor of Cornell's Presbyterian youth group.

The group spent most of its time clearing rubble from the grounds of the University Hospital in Hamburg, Germany. They lived in tents and Jane cooked in a field kitchen, where the food was mostly potatoes, bread, and a few dried vegetables. On the way home, the group visited the founding convention of the World Council of Churches in Amsterdam.

"The way the Germans felt when we left them was unforgettable," Jane said. "They seemed to be sure it was the last time, maybe forever, that they would have regular meals and a little fun with people their own age. They firmly believe that a terrible war with Russia will break out within a year."

On board the ship, Jane (center of photo) wrote to her parents that she, Kitty (right of Jane), and 710 other students spent most of their time on deck, weather permitting. The Americans mixed freely with German, Dutch, and Malaysian fellow travelers. Conditions were "extremely informal," she wrote.

of warning from a resident of the West Avenue temporary dormitories, who denounced the whole thing as "another sad example of the lethargic attitude of the majority of Americans toward the insidious threat of communism in this country."

William vanden Heuvel '50, JD '52

My parents were working-class immigrants from Holland and Belgium who spoke broken English. As far as they were concerned, Franklin Roosevelt was the working man's best friend and the savior of the Western world. My parents were not involved in politics, but they were very patriotic and proud of being Americans. On the other hand, I was always interested in politics.

I transferred to Cornell from Deep Springs College[3] and was also admitted to Telluride House, which was sophisticated, intellectually rigorous, and a major influence on my life. It was also a long way from the boardinghouse in a working-class Italian neighborhood in Rochester, New York, where I grew up.

As soon as I arrived at Cornell in September 1948, I became a member of the Young Democrats. Democrats were rare in upstate New York in those days. The

[3] Deep Springs College is extremely small (twenty-four students) and isolated, and it gives students primary responsibility for managing the college and cattle ranch in eastern California. Its founder, LL Nunn, also founded Telluride House at Cornell, which was fashioned along the lines of an Oxford College.

Democratic Club at Cornell had a couple dozen members at most. We had so few resources that, at the age of eighteen, I became the campaign manager for the Democratic candidate for Congress, a wonderful man and labor leader named Donald O'Connor, who was running against a well-financed Republican incumbent. O'Connor lost, as expected, and for me it was a most valuable experience. I saw the losing end of politics, how difficult the process is, and the importance of money. It reaffirmed my interest in the democratic process.

In October 1948, things looked so bad for Harry Truman that the pollsters stopped measuring public attitudes. Everyone just assumed he was going to lose to Thomas Dewey, especially in New York, where Dewey was governor. And then President Truman came through upstate New York on his famous campaign train. Don O'Connor and I were invited to join him for the trip. So a month after I arrived at Cornell, I spent half a day with the president of the United States.

We ended the day in Auburn, New York, where President Truman gave a great stump speech against the "do-nothing Congress." A crowd of twenty thousand was there. It rained hard, but nobody ran for cover. When we moved back into the train, President Truman looked up at the sky and said, "God may be with the Republicans, but I know the people are with me." He was right.

I was also on the Cornell debate team. Shortly after that campaign trip, I was in a public debate at Cornell with Sandy Lankler JD '51, a law student whose family was close to Governor Dewey. I said that I believed President Truman was going to win. Sandy

Harry Truman addressing the crowd in Rome, New York on October 8, 1948. The train went on to Syracuse before stopping in Auburn. Photo by Mrs. William R. Johnson.

sarcastically invited me to come to Republican headquarters on election night "to celebrate Truman's victory." So I did. It was one of the greatest parties I ever attended. It was one smiling, happy young man surrounded by hundreds of gloomy Republicans.

The following year I organized the young Democrats at Cornell to go door-to-door in a campaign to elect Lee Daniels, a Democrat, as mayor of Ithaca. The Democrats were successful for the first time in decades. It was a wonderful, idealistic, productive time.

The Korean War really changed things, though. I remember that a harshness came into the debate competition. The witch hunts led by Senator Joseph McCarthy that blew up in the early 1950s—I don't remember very many people at Cornell taking them seriously. I had many friends who were conservative and Republican and who also found McCarthyism abhorrent. At the same time, there was pressure.

I remember people objecting to left-wing speakers who would come onto campus. And the alumni and trustees objected strenuously to a Cornell physics professor, Philip Morrison, who had attended Communist Party meetings when he was younger. To their credit, the administration let him stay and did not silence him, but there was a lot of talk and behind-the-scenes negotiations.

I had a show on WVBR [the student radio station] where I commented on the news and interviewed people. In May 1952, just at the end of my time at the law school, some students came in and seized the radio station as a prank. It was during the time when everybody was staying up late to study for exams. They took over late at night and said that Soviet warplanes were headed our way, and that everyone should take shelter. Many students and townspeople just lost it. They tore up their term papers and called the police and so on. The cold war had begun in earnest.

William vanden Heuvel earned a BA from the College of Arts and Sciences and was editor in chief of the *Cornell Law Review*.

In the 1950s, he was executive assistant to William Donovan, founder of the Office of Strategic Services. In the 1960s, he was an assistant to Attorney General Robert F. Kennedy and a member of Kennedy's presidential campaign. He was also U.S. Ambassador to the European office of the United Nations in Geneva and United States Deputy Ambassador to the United Nations during the Carter Administration. He has been a director at several large corporations and, since 1984, senior advisor to the investment banking firm Allen & Company. He has also been chairman of the Franklin and Eleanor Roosevelt Institute since 1984.

WVBR RAIDED: FALSE BOMB SCARE BULLETINS AIRED

Ithaca Journal, May 29, 1952

Identity of the masked marauders who invaded radio station WVBR's studio in the Willard Straight Hall Wednesday night, overpowered the staff, and broadcast fake war bulletins, is expected to be established late this afternoon...

After overpowering and trussing up the station attendants (at 11:09 pm), one of the band wearing a rubber mask took over the control room as another moved to the microphone in the broadcasting booth. This "announcer" interrupted a 24-hour program of study music with a "special bulletin" to the effect that Russian type planes had bombed Paris, Marseilles, and London.

The music was then resumed only to be interrupted again with a "bulletin" announcing that unidentified planes had been picked up by radar at Gander, Newfoundland, and appeared headed for Bangor, Maine. A third "bulletin" called upon all ROTC personnel at Cornell to report in uniform at Barton Hall at 9am today.

Subsequent activities by the masked band included the playing of a recording dealing with the atom bomb and a candy bar advertisement. "If all listeners had stayed with the program to the end," a Cornell spokesman said today, "they would have realized it was a prank."

Evidently many of them didn't for approximately 50 students appeared in person at the station around midnight when all phones were busy with incoming calls... Late Wednesday night and early this morning, long distance lines out of Ithaca were said to be "tied up" with students calling to their homes.

WVBR is a so-called "pipe station" with a limited range that may be picked up only on the campus and in some places in the city proper... The student-operated station is not [WCHU], the official Cornell University station, which has greater range and power.

Judicial hearings implicated 25 students in the raid, including five editors from *The Cornell Daily Sun* and several officers at the ROTC program. All of them were juniors or seniors. All were immediately suspended from the university, a move that endangered their scholarships, their ability to graduate, and their post-Cornell jobs. After appeals and heartfelt apologies, the suspensions were not carried out and the perpetrators were allowed to graduate on June 9.

Lee Daniels's Fate

Cornell Alumni News, February 1950: Ithaca elected a new mayor on January 10 in a special election called by Governor Thomas E. Dewey. He is Stanley C. Shaw, Republican, forty-four-year-old veteran of twelve years in the NY State Assembly. The special election was made necessary by the unexpected death of the mayor-elect, Lee H. Daniels, Democrat [on November 21, 1949].

Volunteers from Cornell's Young Republicans Club worked against Bill vanden Heuvel and the Democrats in the special election to replace Lee Daniels. Among the club members was Houston "Hugh" Flournoy '50 (1930-2008), who went on to have a distinguished career in politics.

Hugh Flournoy

Flournoy was elected to the California State Assembly for two terms, was California state controller in the 1960s and early 1970s, and ran unsuccessfully for governor. In 1974, a particularly bad year for Republicans, Flournoy came within two percentage points of beating Democrat Jerry Brown in the governor's race.

International Students

According to the Report of the University Registrar for 1949–50, Cornell had just 346 international students, or 3.5 percent of the student body. Eighty-nine students came from Canada, fifty-one from China, twenty-two from India, and thirteen apiece from England and Mexico.

Although international students in the class of 1950 were rare, several went on to distinguished careers at home. Ernst Albrecht '50 became prime minister of the German state of Lower Saxony from 1976

Ernst Albrecht

to 1990. Akhlaqur Rahman Kidwai PhD '50, a member of Watermargin House, became a political leader in India; he was governor of the states of Bihar, West Bengal, and Haryana, and a member of the upper house of parliament from 2000 to 2004. And Jamshid Amouzegar, PhD '51, held several high government positions in Iran, including prime minister from 1977 to 1978.

An Interfaith Memorial

From Proceedings of the Board of Trustees, January 26, 1950: Chairman John S. Parke of the Buildings and Grounds Committee presented for the consideration of this Executive Committee the latest sketches and plans for the proposed Anabel Taylor Hall, as well as a model of the building. He stated that these plans are satisfactory to all persons concerned; that the designs for the chapel, the war memorial, and the founders' room have been completed, but the plans for the rest of the building for the use of Cornell United Religious Work have not yet been fully developed.

The chairman invited trustee Myron Taylor to speak to the committee about this building, which is his gift to the university. Trustee Taylor said that he wants this particular memorial to represent to the future generations at Cornell something that means perfection, something that is not a mere passing phase. It is to be a memorial to those men who died in World War II—some six hundred Cornellians in all. It is also to be built as an interfaith center.

Religion is the greatest force in

the world today, [Mr. Taylor said]. There are some misguided peoples whose leaders try to make them believe that atheism is better for them than religious faith. Disregard for religion is the one big fault in the world today. A great question is whether the Chinese can be made to adopt atheism through communism. Mr. Taylor stated that he doubts it can be done. We must fight the attempt with all our resources, as these people are being misled by greed and politics.

Mr. Taylor expressed his idea of this memorial building as a religious faith center. It will be built on the simple conception that we all believe in God and human liberty, and that we must stand together to resist evil… Nothing else can save us from destruction. This is no time for division, but rather for a united action. That idea is the inspiration of this memorial at the present time. Nothing else being done at Cornell today is more important than the building of an interfaith center.

Anabel Taylor Hall opened in October 1952.

Myron and Anabel Taylor leaving the building he named for her.

Ellington Invades Bailey

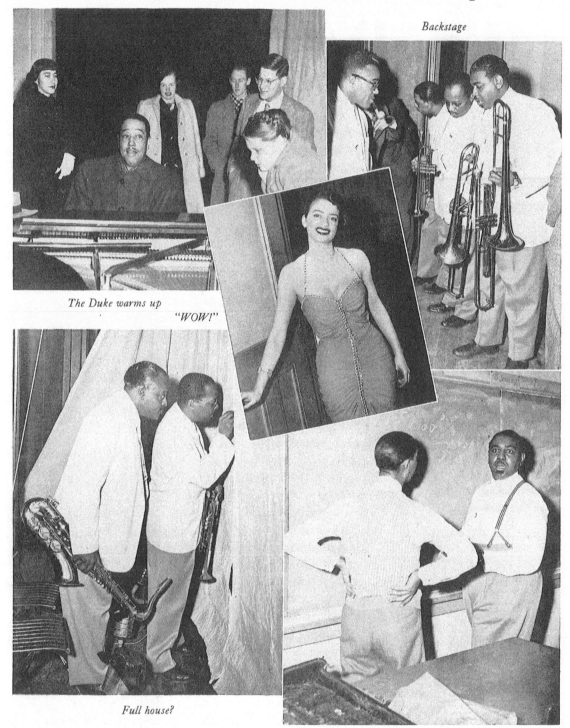

Backstage

The Duke warms up

"WOW!"

Full house?

Who says?

Critics rank the concert Duke Ellington and his Orchestra gave at Cornell's Bailey Hall on December 10, 1948, among his best performances. It was also one of Whitney Balliett's first published jazz reviews (see p. 156).

CHAPTER 12

Jazzniks

The After-Party

Cornell freshmen of the late 1940s were younger and less experienced than the World War II veterans they replaced. They were also more likely to believe that the best way to get ahead was to fit in. But if Cornell's mainstream became more socially conservative in the early 1950s, it had a counterweight. A small group of students disregarded conventions and sought ecstatic experiences through alcohol, jazz, and sex.

One person came to exemplify this new attitude. Larry Cunningham enrolled at Cornell in 1948 as a 24-year-old freshman; he was a veteran of the war who had done time in an army stockade and had barely escaped a dishonorable discharge. Cunningham came from wealth and was uninterested in classes, but he was passionate about fast cars, women, drinking, and jazz. Like Jay Gatsby and Neal Cassady,[1] Cunningham became a muse for three young writers who portrayed a Cornell campus where postwar idealism was ebbing away.

Larry Cunningham and his friends weren't beatniks, but their wild times gave the beatniks of the late 1950s something to look up to. Their scene foreshadowed the social and sexual revolutions of the 1960s.

---

[1] Jay Gatsby is the fictional hero of *The Great Gatsby*, which was revered in the Cornell English department during Cunningham's era. Neal Cassady was a real person who met two Columbia students, Alan Ginsberg and Jack Kerouac, in 1947.

Charles Thompson '51

Charles Thompson's novel *Halfway Down the Stairs* (1957) tells the story of Dave Pope, a Cornell freshman and budding jazz saxophonist from a blue-collar family in Philip, Massachusetts. After finishing high school, Dave has a summer romance with Ann Carlin, a girl from a wealthy New York City family. A few months later, he follows her to Cornell, and in this excerpt he meets her friends.

Collegetown [is] a sweet little slum of rooming houses on the other end of the campus. The Collegetown crowd—well, they're the bohemians. They dress *á la* Greenwich

SCANDAL

The young couple on the deserted beach thought they were alone. But they had been seen.

The next day the girl, Ann Carlin, was sent back to New York in disgrace; the boy, Dave Pope, was beaten up, and his family decided to move out of town.

But Dave and Ann met again in the fall at Cornell. Together they were drawn into the world of the college bohemians, where they began a frantic, desperate search for "kicks."

It was wild and thrilling... until the party went out of control and the horror started closing in.

Back cover of the paperback edition of Charles Thompson's novel.

Village and they're actors and writers and musicians and that sort of thing. I always thought they were a pretty ratty bunch, not my idea of good society. I'd never wanted to have anything to do with them.

The people who crowded around us this day were the most extreme slice of Collegetown life. I recognized a couple from having had classes with them: one was a tall soulful guy who acted in the university theater. His name was Arthur Mann and he wore the dirtiest khakis I have ever seen, rope-soled shoes, and a camel's-hair jacket held together at the navel by a piece of string. Then there was one Jim Troy, a great fat laugh of a guy whose clothes were good but he was too big to wear them. There were a couple of girls I recognized, beautiful girls. That was one thing about this mob. The guys were ratty, but the girls were great looking. Real dreams.

"Where are Bill and Jane?" they were saying. "Where's Hugh?" They kept up a steady stream of talk, much of it very witty, a lot of it in good up-to-date bop jargon. They were very bright people. I knew that from class; they often said the most intelligent things, the most perceptive things, but they almost never got good marks. They never studied. "Where's Hugh?" they said; then Hugh arrived, and I recognized him.

Hugh Masters is one of those legends. Even I had heard a lot about him. He was twenty-eight; he'd run through a fortune before he was eighteen; he'd knocked up the daughter of a California sheriff, and had left town in a stolen car; he'd spent three years in Paris after the war, pimping for a Montparnasse whore; he'd won two thousand dollars in a poker game with

Johnny Hodges.

(a) the mayor of Ithaca, (b) the sheriff, (c) the district attorney and (d) the Alpha Phi housemother; he'd spent two months in an Army stockade in California, and had scars to prove it; he'd deflowered the daughter of the dean of the School of Home Economics; he'd written two novels that any publishing house in the world would publish, but he wasn't satisfied with them and let them sit in his closet; he knew every dope peddler, gambler, bootlegger, and musician in Tompkins County; his father was a millionaire who'd disowned him; he'd been dishonorably discharged not once but twice from the Army; he could sing any song Rodgers and Hart ever wrote.

Even now that I've known Hugh well for a number of years, I'm hard put to separate the truth

from the fiction. For instance, Hugh did have scars from having been beaten up, and he was in a stockade, but I can't be sure the two go together. He did live three years in Paris and he knew a lot of whores, I'm sure, but that's all. He knocked up the sheriff's black-eyed daughter, because I've heard them talking on the phone, like old friends. Hugh's father paid for the operation; Hugh was only nineteen at the time. There were no novels, no poker game with the Alpha Phi housemother, and his knowledge of Rodgers and Hart was spotty. Still, the myth remains…

I sat there this day watching everyone and trying to figure all the angles. I felt slightly uncomfortable, as if I'd been cast into a nestful of Frenchmen. I wasn't sure I liked any of them—but, you see, they were coming on good recommendation. They were Ann's people now. If she liked them, there was something to say for them.

Nobody talked to me, but it wasn't because they were rude or didn't like me; they just had so much to get settled they hadn't any time for me. It was vital to decide how they'd get tickets for football games and whether they were going to the jam session Sunday and where Bill and Janey were (I never did find out) and who was going to help Jim Troy with his Greek and who was going to read Willie's new story and tell him if it was any good and whether Arthur was going to try out for *The Importance of Being Earnest*. It was all very serious, and without meaning to, I found myself getting interested.

I interrupted once, to ask about the jam session, and Ann said, "Oh, Dave—you've got to go down. Mel Fisher has this group, he'd love to have you sit in. They're real good, they make it all the way." I winced slightly at her language, but then Hugh said, "You cool, man?" and I said, "You know it. I'm Johnny Hodges[2] a second time." Then they all looked at me with some interest and Hugh said, "Come on up to my place tonight. Mel's going to fall by, and he'll listen to you blow."

"Crazy," I said. It was like coming home.

Robert Gutwillig '53

Tom Freeman, the narrator of Gutwillig's novel *After Long Silence* (1958), is a wealthy college student who lacks a sense of purpose. In this excerpt Freeman

---

[2] Johnny Hodges (1906–1970) was the lead alto saxophonist for the Duke Ellington Orchestra.

describes Cornell as it was when he met a fascinating character named Chris Hunt.

I was vaguely aware that things were changing that fall of 1950. I fretted that the school was getting too big—too many new buildings were going up all over the campus, and too many new freshmen were filling them. The buildings seemed coarser, and the freshmen younger. I worried about all the engineering schools and wished they were located somewhere else.

I thought [Cornell] was sallying forth into the Midwest, and I thought we should go back to the Ivy League where we belonged. I realized I was uneasy about the crumbling of standards, the passing of things that I had never experienced myself, but just believed in—that I supposed were mine by inheritance. But I didn't know what these things were. It just seemed too bad that they were changing.

AFTER LONG SILENCE

ROBERT GUTWILLIG

They Thought Love Was A Non-Stop Joyride

G330

35c

Things were going on that I didn't understand and didn't like. There was a war being fought in Korea, and I knew I should be intensely concerned, but I wasn't. No one was. All sorts of people had piles of money, and you couldn't find a place to park your car on campus. I suddenly discovered that I disliked most of my fraternity brothers. It looked as if most of the Class of 1951 was going into the service in June, and although none of us particularly cared for the idea, we really had nothing more urgent or concrete in mind.

The football team was winning the Ivy League title again; a boy drank a quart of martinis and fell down a flight of stairs and almost died, and drinking societies were banned; one night someone drained the pond in the middle of campus; a sorority girl had a baby in the third-floor john; some instructor of chemistry turned out to be a Communist. It was a very rainy fall, the leaves all turned and fell at once, the roads were slippery and the paths muddy. And then I met Chris.

Gerald Walker
(1928–2004)

Gerald Walker, a graduate of New York University, became a *New York Times* reporter and is the author of the murder mystery *Cruising* (1970). His article "The Man Who Inspired Three Novelists" is based on interviews with Cunningham's friends.

FROM *COSMOPOLITAN*, AUGUST 1959: The story involves one young man who, since his death in an auto crash in 1953, has so far found his way into three novels by three different authors… The inside story was hinted at when William Andrews, then book editor of the *Ithaca Journal*, reviewed ex-Cornellian Robert Gutwillig's *After Long Silence*.

Of Chris Hunt, the pivotal character in [Gutwillig's] novel, Mr. Andrews wrote, "[the reader] recognizes him as Hugh Masters from Charles Thompson's *Halfway Down the Stairs*. The original on whom Hugh Masters and Chris Hunt are based was the same Cornell student, a wild hellion but the hero of heroes in both of these books. In fact, Chris Hunt is also reminiscent of Joe MacFarlane in Clifford Irving's *On A Darkling Plain* (1956), also a novel about the Bohemian crowd at Cornell."

Behind these pseudonyms, however, is a real person. He was at Cornell between 1948 and 1953, and he either took the same courses, went to the same parties, had eyes for the same girls, or occasionally shared the same living quarters with Gutwillig, Thompson, and Irving. Each of these novelists saw [the man] from his own unique angle of vision… Both [Gutwillig and Thompson] show him as seven or eight years older and more worldly-wise than the students who flocked around him. Both allude to his discharge from the Army under questionable circumstances. Both mention his interest in writing, his Social Register background, the personal charm and sense of humor that accounted for his extreme attractiveness to women, his heavy drinking, and his enthusiasm for jazz, old cars, and hot rods… And in each of their novels, as the reviewer for the *Ithaca Journal* pointed out, the character "is symbolically sacrificed in a violent death" while the narrator mulls over the meaning of this in relation to his own life…

Robert Gutwillig '53

Larry Cunningham and I lived in an apartment with a couple of roommates in Collegetown. Charles "Torrie" Thompson and Clifford Irving were among our friends, and we were all writing novels. We all admired Larry greatly, because he was always eager to join us in the stupid stuff we liked to do. We had a blackjack game that ran for two or three years—sometimes we played all night, which kind of shot our attendance in class the next day. We were also crazy about old cars. Larry was older than we were, but in a sense he acted as if he were younger than we were.

Larry didn't observe social norms or say that he had a philosophy of life. He wasn't anti-establishment—he was totally apolitical. He felt that society was a crock and that he just wanted to "live." He came from a prominent family. His father was a big lawyer in Boston, and his mother was from an old-money family in Cooperstown. But he felt that his parents were constipated and he wasn't going to follow the prescribed path. I never talked to him about what he did in World War II, but I knew something bad had happened. Even at the funeral, his parents blamed everything on what had happened to him in the Army.

Sex wasn't easy to find for me, but Larry was a hit with the ladies and very experienced. He cut a broad swath until he fixed on one woman, Ann Stickley. She was more or less putting up with him, but still she went to bed with him all the time, morning and night. I think Larry might have been making up for lost time.

From my junior year on, I was being encouraged by Mike Abrams and Arthur Mizener[3] to go to grad school, but my drinking interfered with that. It wasn't until I got out of Cornell and the Army that I acknowledged that I had a drinking problem and that I had to deal with it. I was a problem drinker for the last two years I was at Cornell, and a lot of my friends were, too. I thought that drinking made me charming, and so on. Actually it was the opposite.

Robert Gutwillig is the son of Bernard Henry Gutwillig '15 (1895-1948), a successful businessman in New York City. Robert received a bachelor's degree and then served in the Korean War. He had a long career in book and magazine publishing.

Nicholas Cunningham

Nick Cunningham is Larry's younger brother. He received a bachelor's degree from Harvard in 1950 and an MD from Johns Hopkins in 1955. He is Professor Emeritus and Lecturer of Pediatrics at the Columbia University College of Physicians and Surgeons.

Larry loved jazz. He collected Bluebird 78 RPM records of Louis Armstrong and others, especially Art Tatum. My room was next to his when we were growing up. My sister and brother would be downstairs playing cantatas, and Larry would be upstairs in his room listening to jazz. I came to love it, too.

When the war came, he really wanted to be a pilot but his eyes weren't good enough. No matter how hard he tried, he could never pass the exam. So he ended up in

---

[3] Arthur Mizener was hired by the Cornell English department in 1951, just after publishing *The Far Side of Paradise,* the first major biography of F. Scott Fitzgerald.

the Army Air Forces on the ground crew, as a mechanic. He had taken a course in high school, and he loved tinkering with all mechanical things.

The war certainly changed Larry. His experience reminds me of Magio, the character Frank Sinatra played in the film of *From Here To Eternity*. Magio is kind of small, and he is also a mouthy guy. He insults the sergeant who runs the stockade. His downfall comes when he goes too far and is sent to the stockade, where the sergeant beats him to death. I don't know what happened to Larry, but it must have been a horrific experience.

I was in high school in California when Larry was sent to the Turlock prison camp in California. I was told that he was put there because he slept with the Colonel's wife, which would have done it.[4] But whatever he was going through, he made sure I never knew about it. He kept sending me cheerful postcards the whole time.

---

[4] According to Pierre Tonachel (see below), Cunningham did time in the stockade because he stole jet fuel, intending to use it in one of his cars. He received a dishonorable discharge, but his father used political connections to change it to a medical discharge.

Charles Thompson

FROM *HALFWAY DOWN THE STAIRS* (1957): Hugh's apartment that year was a long dark floor-through on Dryden Road, with high-ceiling rooms and fixtures out of the Age of Reason. He lived alone in it and didn't rattle, because so many people were always there. Hugh couldn't stand to be alone—he'd go out and pull people off the street. His bedroom, where the most interesting of his labors took place, was spectacular. It was painted Chinese red, with electric blue drapes; the bed was very large, plenty of room for two or three, and he had one of his friends'

Larry Cunningham served as a mechanic in the Army Air Corps during World War II.

more mystifying paintings mounted on the headboard so he had something to look at while he was lying on his stomach. The ceiling was covered with those gray pasteboard dividers used for packing eggs, the ones with the ovary-shaped depressions in them. The whole deal was something out of Vivian Connell.[5]

The night I went there with my sax, I found half a dozen strangers in the living room. One was Mel Fisher, a very small man about thirty, a musician. He was an itinerant alto sax man, a complete alcoholic, whom Hugh had persuaded to stay in Ithaca for a year. He had organized a group. Mel knew his music, even if he was a drunk. I saw his room a couple of times—a musty place over Gallagher's Restaurant—and it teemed with records and sheet music: Bartok and Ravel and Stravinsky's "L'Histoire du Soldat" and the real difficult moderns. He thought Johnny Hodges was the greatest man that ever blew, and since I agreed with him, we got along fine.

Hugh introduced us, and Mel sat down at the piano, which he played pretty well too, and said, "How about 'Take the A Train'? We'll take a twelve bar intro and two choruses, say thirty-six, OK?" and then we were into it.

I'll just say I did all right. The thing I liked was looking down from the corner of the ceiling I watched while I blew, and seeing the rest of the group watching me. Hugh and Ann sat together on one of the sofas; Hugh had his eyes closed and could tell he was

following it pretty well. Ann didn't know her music, but she knew I was good, and her eyes shone. The rest of them—a quiet, well-dressed pair I didn't know, and a slim, beautifully built girl with a plain face whom I didn't know either—sat pretty rapt, taking it all in.

When we finished "A Train" we tried "Thou Swell"—at my suggestion. It was one of the numbers I'd played down on the Cape; it brought back the summer with Ann, and the nice things about Philip and the life I'd had there. I guess I felt pretty strongly about it, because when the number was over, people clapped. That's a pretty big thing for just five or six people to do. It usually takes a crowd to clap, less than that and they're too embarrassed. I felt good about it.

After the number was over, Mel closed the piano and said, "I got to cut out, man. I got a date." He turned to me and said, "Man, you make it down to the Chanticleer Sunday, you hear? You're going to be great. But stop thinking you're Getz. You got your own style, and I really dig it." I just sort of nodded at him, because it embarrassed me to get praised in front of those people.

"This boy pays his dues," Hugh said. "I dig him all the way."

Mel looked at him affectionately. "Like I say. Make him practice." He walked very slowly out the door; all his movements were slow.

His departure left me standing in the middle of the room, stupidly holding my sax. I put it away as unostentatiously as I could, and then turned to the other people. The quiet couple were Janey Trem and Bill Abrams, who got to be good friends; the interesting-looking chick with the body was Kathleen White. They were the important

people, they and Hugh. They made my life go around that year. I loved them all. They were my world.

Whitney Balliett '51

[FROM 2001]: I first wrote about jazz at Exeter, and was probably influenced by Barry Ulanov at *Metronome,* a music magazine. I continued at Cornell, doing pieces for the *Widow* and the *Cornell Daily Sun,* where I printed my first timely review—of a concert given on December 10, 1948 by Duke Ellington, and run the next day. The head was simply "MUSIC" and beneath that "By Balliet" (sic). Here it is, a frazzled mixture of nerves, haste, and budding taste:

"Edward Kennedy 'Duke' Ellington presented his second Cornell concert in Bailey Hall last night under the auspices of the worthy Rhythm Club. His music was little short of impeccable. Twenty years' leadership in the field of jazz has not jaded the Duke, nor his great love of jazz.

Due to limited space, unfortunately, the hunt and peck method will have to be employed. The first half of the concert was notable for 'Reminiscing in Tempo,' a piece written in 1935, that will be suitable in 1955. It is a study in moods that is delightful in its warmth and humor. The Duke's new bass player, Wendell Marshall, showed fine technique and imagination in the cute 'She Wouldn't Be Moved.' Billy Strayhorn, the Duke's erstwhile arranger, presented Harry Carney's baritone in 'Paradise'; one can do no less than marvel at this man's command of his instrument. A two-part satiric rendition, 'Symphomaniac,' lampooned the 'King of Jazz,' Paul Whiteman, in

---

[5] Vivian Connell's novel, *The Chinese Room* (1942), is an overwrought effort about a woman's social and sexual awakening through her intimate relationship with a psychotherapist.

Larry Cunningham.

the next 44 years, with many more unsigned. He is remembered today mostly for his reviews and profiles of jazz musicians.

"Mr. Balliett did not use a tape recorder," according to his obituary in *The New York Times.* "Instead, he took notes furiously over several days of conversations and played them back as long, extravagant solos. This new emphasis on long-form quotations forced him to concentrate musical descriptions into highly poetic, cumulative glimpses of a musician's sound."

Balliett served as an ambassador for jazz, explaining and celebrating the music for audiences that were often unfamiliar with it. Another was Willis Conover (1920–1996), a producer and disc jockey whose jazz show on The Voice of America brought the music to eager audiences behind the Iron Curtain. "Jazz tells more about America than any American can realize," Conover told *Time Magazine* in 1966. "It bespeaks vitality, strength, social mobility; it's a free music with its own discipline, but not an imposed, inhibiting discipline."

Pierre Tonachel '52

My older brother and I were crazy about jazz and big bands. We lived in Staten Island, so we'd ride the ferry and then take the subway all the way up to Harlem to go to the Apollo Theater. We'd see Charlie Barnet, Benny Goodman, Lionel Hampton, and they would play on and on. The audience there was just wild. My older brother was 12, and I was 9. We were these two little white faces in a sea of black faces, and we just kind of fell into it. Nobody seemed to be concerned that we were there. In those days, people didn't pay much attention to what you were doing.

his heydays of 1929, closing with sharp consideration of the music of Dizzy Gillespie; Dizzy would have smiled grimly..." And on for two more game paragraphs...

[FROM 1956]: One of the smaller but more durable mysteries of the past twenty years has been the almost total lack of success that novelists and short-story writers have had in dealing with jazz. Jazz is notably unsentimental, as are, in the main, the people who play it. Yet countless bleary novels and stories have appeared in which jazz musicians, postured in various awkward attitudes, produce a cathartic, semi-divine music. At the same time, jazz seems to provide a safety valve for these writers, who invariably let loose a thick spray of metaphor and simile that form a distracting counterpoint to the subject matter...

Whitney Balliett was hired by *The New Yorker* in 1957 and went on to publish more than 550 signed articles there over

I got to Cornell in 1948. I quickly became involved with the student radio station, WVBR, and also with the Cornell Rhythm Club, which booked jazz artists. In November of that year, Dizzy Gillespie came to play at Bailey Hall. I heard that the band was staying at a place called Watermargin, so I went there after the show.

Two things struck me immediately when I got there. One was the diversity. I think half the black students at Cornell belonged to Watermargin. The other was that this was not an ordinary frat house party where you got as drunk as you could. Everyone was talking, and the students were talking to the musicians about the music. These were my people. We were all interested in the music. The band was staying there because that was the only place in town they felt comfortable.

Larry Cunningham didn't belong to Watermargin, but he was part of that community, and we became friends. He was a fascinating figure. Larry's father was a well-connected lawyer from Boston, and they lived in a house that was simple but very elegant. After dinner, the family would take out their instruments and play chamber music. This was where Larry came from, and I think he rebelled against it.

He was not a wild man. He was older than we were because he had been in the army. He was also quite attractive and intelligent. He had a great appetite for the things he liked. He liked women, and he liked cars, so he drove the women and the cars as hard as he could. But Larry wasn't focused on getting a degree, not at all. If you don't go to class, whether or not you're hung over or you're shacked up with a

On August 1, 1953, Cunningham died while driving an MG TC.

girl, it doesn't really matter—you're not going to pass. I think Larry may have understood that there was enough family money that he didn't need a career.

Anyway, we were just fascinated by him, because he was like a character out of Fitzgerald. These old cars that we drove—we drove them because they reminded us of *The Great Gatsby*.

Pierre Tonachel received a bachelor's degree. He is an artist in New York City.

Gerald Walker

With younger fellows, [Larry Cunningham] was the voice of experience as he talked of founding a new religion in which people would wear miniature gold electric chairs on chains around their necks, spreading the dogma, "what's right is what you like." One member of the baffled but fascinated coterie says, "there we were, a bunch of honest-to-goodness bourgeois kids, all eager to become something. But [Larry] didn't want to be anything except himself, which meant being free of all restraint. You might call him our acter-out, our walking id."

[In the summer of 1953, Larry returned to Cornell] to make up enough credits to get his degree, and show his family that he *could* finish something. Actually, he was growing concerned that his college friends were marrying and drifting away, that he was a failure and was getting older…

[Ann Stickley] was to be married on August 1. On July 31, [Larry] went to two Saturday night parties in Ithaca, got thoroughly drunk, and announced his intention of driving to New York City to attend the wedding the next day. Refusing to be dissuaded, at 5 a.m. he headed his MG convertible for Manhattan. He was drunk and had been up all night…an hour or so out of Ithaca, the MG's wheels went onto the shoulder and, in pulling the car back, [Cunningham] overcompensated and veered off the road on the other side. The car rolled over three times, going down a 15-foot embankment. He never regained consciousness.

Nick Cunningham

People wanted to know if it was suicide. I don't know. When you stay up all night drinking and then get in a car to drive a long distance, are you killing yourself? Especially when you're going to the wedding of the woman you really loved and should have proposed to, but never did? Clearly it was risky, foolish behavior. But Larry took risks all his life.

My mother admired courage, and she loved Larry for that. Larry always gave the impression of having no fear. We would go to Mount Washington in the winter, where

there is a famously steep run called Tuckerman's Ravine. Larry would ski straight down it with no hesitation. He drove fast, he skied fast, he did everything fast.

Halfway Down The Stairs and *After Long Silence* created big stirs at Cornell when they were published in March 1957 and May 1958. Reviewing Thompson's book in the *Cornell Daily Sun,* Kirkpatrick Sale '58 wrote, "one can hardly resist the comparison of this strange group of people with the modern Cornell. Certainly it can be said that there is no group now corresponding at all closely with the one which Hugh Masters led, and it is not likely that there will ever be. But also missing now is a general frivolous, intense, carefree, neurotic atmosphere that seemed to be present in some way in almost all of the people in Mr. Thompson's Cornell."

Sale, who was editor in chief of the *Sun* in 1957–58, might have known Thompson, who lived near campus in the late 1950s. Both of them were vocal opponents of a long-standing university policy toward undergraduates known as *in loco parentis* (in the place of a parent). Sale was one of

the chief organizers of a massive protest in May 1958 that put thousands of Cornell students in the streets, demanding an end to women's curfews and also objecting to the strict moralism of President Deane Malott. The protests became a barely-contained riot (see page 73). Sale went on to a long career as a radical journalist.

Another chief organizer of the 1958 protest was Richard Farina, who dropped out shortly before graduating in 1959. Farina's novel, *Been Down So Long It Looks Like Up To Me* (1966), is yet another impressionistic vision of bohemian life in Collegetown; the book's climax is a thinly veiled account of the riot Farina helped to incite. The novel quickly joined the anti-canon of 1960s hippie literature, even though Farina died in a motorcycle accident just as his book was being published. Like Larry Cunningham, Farina was 29.

Charles "Torrie" Thompson earned a master of arts degree from the English department in 1952. He then enlisted in the Navy and became a jet pilot. He went on to work as a writer and editor in Mexico, New York City, and Ithaca.

NOW WE ARE GROWN

By Charles Thompson

FROM THE LITERARY MAGAZINE *EPOCH*, SPRING 1955

Come, leave behind, now we are grown
this preening of wits, this bibliography.
Know that our motives have turned, and own
the lovely liberal girls and elms are gone.

Bank your garret fire and descend the stair.
There you find a useful weary day
resting in its flowered easy chair
with gin and tonic coming on a tray—

all thirsts are one. Come out in evening
where the boat is moored, and feel
the pleasant sin of peace without repining:
let your periphrastic ulcer heal.

The salesman's smoker is a real romance
when the naked lady flips upon the screen—
the barefoot princess never learned to dance,
but her breasts are bouncy as an angry dean.

We were scholars once, years in our head
while voices spoke of Age of Reason grace:
one unimportant yearning chilled and dead,
Academy a twilit ghostly place.

Charles Thompson

Notes on Sources

Citations from *The Cornell Daily Sun*, *Cornellian*, *Cornell Widow*, *Cornell Alumni News*, and *Ithaca Journal* are in the text.

General Histories

Glenn Altschuler and Isaac Kramnick, *Cornell: A History, 1940–2015* (Cornell University Press, 2014)

Morris Bishop, *A History of Cornell* (Cornell University Press, 1962)

Bob Kane, *Good Sports: A History of Cornell Athletics* (Cornell Alumni Magazine, 1992)

Prologue

For more on the GI Bill, see Glenn Altschuler and Stuart Blumin, *The GI Bill: A New Deal For Veterans* (Oxford University Press, 2009) and Suzanne Mettler, *Soldiers to Citizens: The GI Bill and the Making of the Greatest Generation* (Oxford University Press, 2007).

"Fourteen Future Nobel prize winners…" from Edward Humes, *Over Here: How the GI Bill Transformed the American Dream* (Harcourt, 2006), p. 6.

"In reality, the rate of premarital pregnancies…" from Alan Petigny, *The Permissive Society: America, 1941–1965* (Cambridge University Press, 2009), p. 114.

Chapter One

Kurt Vonnegut: Excerpted from speech to the Centennial Banquet of *The Cornell Daily Sun*, in *A Century at Cornell: Published to Commemorate the Hundredth Anniversary of the Cornell Daily Sun*, edited by Daniel Margulis (Cornell Daily Sun, 1980).

John Craig quote from hospice: Billy Cox, "Love, Johnny," *Sarasota Herald Tribune*, November 10, 2013, p. 8A.

Chapter Two

Elizabeth Warner: Excerpted from Carol Kammen, *First-Person Cornell* (Cornell University Library, 2006).

Don Christiansen: Don recorded the recollections of his *San Jacinto* shipmates at post-war reunions and produced a book, *The Saga of the San Jac: The Aircraft Carrier U.S.S. San Jacinto, CVL 30, in World War II* (privately published, 2005).

Chapter Three

Von Oppenfeld, "Max, Have a Cigarette!": Lynn Ermann, "Learning Freedom In Captivity," *The Washington Post Magazine*, January 18, 2004, p. 16.

Chapter Four

Vladimir Nabokov: From *Lectures on Literature* (Harcourt Brace Jovanovich, 1980), p. 381.

Stacy Schiff: From *Véra: Mrs. Vladimir Nabokov* (Modern Library, 2000), p. 175.

M. H. Abrams: Adapted from "A Conversation with M. H. Abrams, Part Two," posted at http://www.cornell.edu/video, retrieved on July 28, 2015.

Bruce Ames: Excerpted from Ames, Bruce N., "An Enthusiasm for Metabolism," *Journal of Biological Chemistry*, Vol. 278, No. 7 (2003), pp. 4369–4380.

Don Christiansen: Wilson Greatbach's early designs for pacemakers had many problems. His solutions are described in his memoir, *The Making of the Pacemaker* (Prometheus Books, 2000).

Robert Cushman: Excerpted from "The Founders and What They Stood For," published in *A Century At Cornell*.

Richard Feynman: All citations are from an interview by Charles Weiner, Altadena, California, March 4, 1966, at the American Institute of Physics; posted at https://www.aip.org/history-programs/niels-bohr-library/oral-histories and retrieved on July 28, 2015.

Gerhard Lowenberg: Excerpt from *Moved By Politics: 12 Episodes in an Academic Life* (Gray Pearl Press, 2012).

Mario Einaudi: From *The Roosevelt Revolution* (1959), p. 349–350.

Chapter Five

Gracious Living: Statistics from "Report of the Counselors of Students" in Cornell University, *Report of the President*, 1946–1947, p. 159.

Chapter Seven

Introduction, "About half of undergraduate men belonged to fraternities in 1950": Altschuler and Kramnick, *Cornell: A History, 1940–2015*, p. 54; "There was no written quota for Jews": Surveys by Cornell United Religious Work (CURW), 1947 and 1948.

David Kogan: All citations are from *The Diary of David S. Kogan* (New York: Beechhurst Press, 1955).

Jacob Sheinkman: From *The ILR School at Fifty: Voices of the Faculty, Alumni and Friends* (1995), retrieved July 28, 2015, http://digitalcommons.ilr.cornell.edu.

Sackman, Kushell, Wolcott, Sumner: Adapted from articles posted at http://www.watermargin.org/a/stories, retrieved July 28, 2015.

Marcham on crusades in the *Sun*: Excerpted from *A Century At Cornell* (1980), pp. 168–170.

Chapter Eight

Introduction, Frederick Marcham photo: p. 38 in Marcham, John, *The Photographs of Frederick G. Marcham* (Ithaca, NY: DeWitt Historical Society, 2000).

Introduction, Day quote: From Proceedings of the Board of Trustees, Oct. 6, 1945.

Harvey Sampson and Robert Kane quotes: From Kane, Robert, *Good Sports: A History of Cornell Athletics* (Cornell Alumni Magazine, 1992).

Chapter Nine

H.W. Long: Text of *Sane Sex Life and Sane Sex Living* is available online through Project Gutenberg (www.gutenberg.org) and other sources.

Sam Johnson: From *Carnauba: A Son's Memoir* (2001), a film by Alex Albanese and Landon Parvin.

Rose Goldsen: All citations are from Rose K. Goldsen, with the assistance of Jessie L. Cohen, *Report on the Cornell student body: based on a survey of 2,758 students representing a cross-section of undergraduate men and women in seven colleges of Cornell University* (Ithaca, NY: Social Science Research Center, Cornell University, 1951), p. 21.

Chapter Eleven

Robert Fogel: Excerpted from Susan Kelley, "The Great Quantifier," *Cornell Alumni Magazine*, March/April 2008.

Chapter Twelve

Gerald Walker: "The Man Who Inspired Three Novelists," *Cosmopolitan*, August 1959, p. 42.

Whitney Balliett: From *Collected Works: A Journal of Jazz 1954–2001*, St. Martin's Griffin (2002). Recording of Duke Ellington concert: *The Great Concerts: Duke Ellington, Cornell University 1948* (Nimbus Records, 2010).

Index of Names

CPSIA information can be obtained
at www.ICGtesting.com
Printed in the USA
BVHW05s0847011018
528938BV00021B/752/P

9 781495 169205